The German Workers
and the Nazis

The German Workers
and the Nazis

F. L. CARSTEN

SCOLAR PRESS

Published by
SCOLAR PRESS
Gower House
Croft Road
Aldershot
Hants GU11 3HR
England

Ashgate Publishing Company
Old Post Road
Brookfield
Vermont 05036
USA

British Library Cataloguing-in-Publication Data
Carsten, F. L.
  German Workers and the Nazis
  I. Title
  943.08608623

  ISBN 0–85967–998–5

Library of Congress Cataloging-in-Publication Data
Carsten, F. L. (Francis Ludwig)
    The German Workers and the Nazis / F.L. Carsten.
      p.   cm.
    Includes bibliographical references and index.
    ISBN 0–85967–998–5 : $59.95 (approx.)
    1. Working class—Germany—History—20th century.   2. National socialism—Germany—History.   3. Labor policy—Germany—History—20th century.   4. Germany—Social conditions—1933–1945.
  I. Title.
  HD8450.C34   1995
  943.088—dc20   94–19955
                                                                      CIP

ISBN 0 85967 998 5

Phototypeset in Sabon by Intype, London
and printed in Great Britain at the University Press, Cambridge.

Contents

Abbreviations and glossary

DAF	Deutsche Arbeitsfront (German Labour Front, compulsory organization for employees *and* employers)
Gauleiter	Nazi district leader in charge of a Gau
HJ	Hitlerjugend (Hitler Youth)
ISK	Internationaler Sozialistischer Kampfbund (International Socialist Fighting League)
ITF	International Transportworkers Federation (a trade union international, seat Amsterdam)
KdF	Kraft durch Freude (Strength through Joy, entertainment and travel section of the DAF)
KJVD	Kommunistischer Jugendverband Deutschlands (Young Communist League)
KPD	Kommunistische Partei Deutschlands (German Communist Party)
Landrat	Official in charge of a rural district
NSBO	Nationalsozialistische Betriebszellenorganisation (Factory Cells of the Nazi Party)
NSDAP	Nationalsozialistische Deutsche Arbeiterpartei (National Socialist German Workers Party)
Reichsbanner	Reichsbanner Schwarz-Rot-Gold (Republican Defence Organization, mainly Social-Democrat)
RGO	Revolutionäre Gewerkschafts Opposition (Communist-dominated trade union)
SA	Sturm-Abteilung (Brown Shirts of the Nazi Party)
SAJ	Sozialistische Arbeiterjugend (Socialist youth organization)
SAP	Sozialistische Arbeiterpartei (Socialist Workers Party, leftwing breakaway from SPD)
SD	Sicherheitsdienst der SS (SS Security Service)
Skat	German card game
SPD	Sozialdemokratische Partei Deutschlands (German Social-Democratic Party)
SS	Schutzstaffel (Hitler's blackshirted Protection Squads)
Treuhänder	Treuhänder der Arbeit (Trustee of Labour, Nazi official to deal with labour issues)

Preface

This book tries to combine an account of the German working-class opposition to Hitler and the Nazis with a description of the workers' daily problems and mood during the 12 years of the 'Third Reich'. There is of course a vast literature on German working-class resistance in individual towns as well as whole areas such as the Ruhr or Bavaria, as a glance at the bibliography will show. But to the best of my knowledge these two topics have never been discussed together, nor is there a study of working-class opposition as such – as distinct from that of the Communists or Social Democrats. My own contribution could not have been written without the earlier works of Tim Mason or Detlev Peuckert (who both died very young), to mention just two historians, nor without the voluminous source material which has seen the light of day in recent years. In the nature of the subject this material comes partly from internal Nazi sources, such as the Gestapo or the SD of the SS, or from Social-Democratic and Communist sources. In my opinion the two supplement each other and can be used by the historian in spite of their inbuilt bias.

The story told on the following pages is also part of my own life and I have used personal memories wherever this seemed appropriate. I joined the socialist youth movement when I was a schoolboy in Berlin, and the catastrophe of 1933 marked a deep fissure in my life. Through my political activities I got to know many of the men mentioned and I was close to a few of them over many years. To mention some names: Friedrich Adler, Werner Blumenberg, Fritz Erler, Edo Fimmen, Hans Gottfurcht, Robert Havemann, Paul Hertz, Hans Jahn, Waldemar von Knoeringen, Walter Löwenheim, Richard Löwenthal, Erwin Schöttle, Franz Vogt. I hope that my personal knowledge has not unduly influenced my judgement and that the account has gained from my recollections.

My thanks, as always, are due to the German Historical Institute, London, for its help in obtaining books and journals, and above all to my wife for her advice and help. She died when this volume was almost finished. It is dedicated to her memory.

F.L.C.
London, March 1994

CHAPTER ONE

National Socialists and workers before 1933

The National Socialist German Workers Party (NSDAP) was founded a few weeks after the end of the First World War in Munich by workers from the local railway shops with the name German Workers Party. The words 'National Socialist' were added after Hitler had joined the small party later in 1919. The party always prided itself on being a true workers' party, but its core was formed by lower middle-class people and white-collar workers, and comparatively few industrial workers joined it in the early years. Its 'socialism' always remained vague, limited to slogans such as 'breaking the shackles of interest', 'common weal before private interest', 'abolition of income not earned by effort and work', prohibition of speculation in land, participation in the profits of large enterprises. The preponderant red in the party's flag was to attract the workers, many of whom were bitterly disappointed by the results of the revolution of 1918–1919 and the failure of the Social-Democratic government. Some of them turned to the new German Communist Party (KPD), but all its efforts to foment a revolution on the Soviet model ended in defeat. In Bavaria in particular, after the collapse of the so-called Munich Soviet Republic in May 1919, a sharp turn to the right occurred. A reactionary government strongly opposed the so called 'Marxist' government in Berlin and there was bitter conflict between Munich and Berlin; this rightwing trend considerably benefited the National Socialists, especially in Munich. Hatred of the 'Marxists' along with that of the Jews provided throughout one of the strongest motive forces of the Nazis.

Yet workers did join the party, even before 1923. An analysis of party members for the years 1919–1923, based on the available data, shows that 19.4 per cent of the members belonged to the working class (most of them semiskilled or unskilled) compared with 25.2 per cent of white-collar workers and 21.7 per cent of artisans. The last two categories were strongly over-represented, and the workers equally strongly under-represented: in Germany – excluding agricultural labourers – they comprised over 37 per cent, and in Bavaria (where the membership was then concentrated) over 32 per cent.[1] Even outside Bavaria the NSDAP attracted working-class support. In 1922 29 per cent of the small branch in Mannheim came from the lower classes, and in 1923 some National Socialist factory councillors were elected in an important electrical factory at Oberschöneweide near Berlin.[2]

In the same year the chairman of one of the largest German unions, the metal workers, warned of the danger of the growth of the Nazi movement, 'although we need not compare ourselves with the proletariat of Italy', where the Fascists seized power in 1922. When the German trade union federation in April 1923 enquired about the strength of working-class support for the Nazis, its Munich committee replied that in their estimation about 2000 workers followed the party, without actually being members. The East Prussian committee replied to the same question that uprooted elements of the lower middle classes and workmen in trades where the old patriarchal relations still existed – such as bakers, butchers, chimneysweeps – supported the extreme right in the province.[3] In 1923, the year of the French occupation of the Ruhr and outbreaks of fervent German nationalism, the trade unions were clearly worried about working-class support for the Nazis. In November 1923, the month of Hitler's unsuccessful Munich Putsch, workers made up 18 per cent of the party's membership and artisans another 20 per cent.[4]

The failure of the Putsch and Hitler's very lenient months of imprisonment led to a temporary decline of the Nazi party, but it revived strongly after Hitler's release and resumption of the leadership. Above all, it spread from Bavaria to important industrial areas of North Germany. In the western Ruhr, in 1925–26 almost 50 per cent of the members came from the working class, and more in some towns such as Hamborn and Mülheim. This was an area with a particularly strong working-class population which was by no means immune to the nationalist current. In Hamburg, on the other hand, in 1926 most members came from the lower middle classes. Artisans, small traders and white-collar workers were very prominent, while 'real' workers were rather rare, as the former *Gauleiter* of Hamburg remembered.[5]

Nor did these characteristics change much in later years. Great efforts were made to attract workers to the party, but it was above all the middle and lower middle classes which flocked to it. In January 1927 the *Völkischer Beobachter* boasted that workers in large numbers came to hear Hitler when he spoke in Cologne, but this of course did not mean that they supported the party or joined it. In North Germany Nazi speakers from the working class were in great demand, but there were few of them. Workers were hardly ever found in leading party posts, not even in the large industrial cities.[6] Many of those who joined the party in the later 1920s came from the many *völkisch* and racist groups and parties which were then absorbed by the NSDAP, and their membership was almost exclusively middle-class. They also provided many of the local leaders. The same applied to the men of the Free Corps and other paramilitary organizations.

Yet there were also many workers, even before the great economic crisis broke in Germany. In the Ruhr again, in 1930 over 32 per cent of the members were workers in *Gau* Westphalia-North, over 33 per cent in *Gau* Essen and over 35 per cent in *Gau* Westphalia-South. A 'secret' report of the Westphalian *Gauleiter* Josef Wagner of 1930 even claimed that 57 per cent of the members were workers, among them 26 per cent miners. In Württemberg in the south, the lower class formed the absolute majority in half the branches for which figures are available, in areas where most people were working in industry and trade. Police reports from the Ruhr, on the other hand, time and again recorded the presence of middle-class people in the party meetings, and in 1930 estimated that only one third of the members came from the working class.[7] The picture was by no means uniform and within Germany varied a good deal from area to area. But it is also clear that many workers joined the party – according to its own internal statistics 34,000 before the great election victory of September 1930, or 28 per cent of the total membership, while in Germany as a whole 45 per cent of the population were workers.[8]

With the onset of the great economic and political crisis of the early 1930s and the steeply rising figures of unemployment, the masses turned towards the NSDAP as Germany's 'saviour' – and to a lesser extent to the Communists – and the working classes were no exception. Between the elections of September 1930 and the appointment of Hitler as chancellor in January 1933 233,000 workers joined the party according to its own internal statistics, or 34.8 per cent of the total: a significant increase from the earlier figures. Among them were no doubt many unemployed, the true victims of the crisis. In *Gau* Hessen-Nassau South the percentage was higher still, 38.7, in Württemberg as high as 42.5, while in the Western Ruhr it varied between 37.6 and 43.8 per cent.[9] It is true that workers were still under-represented in the country as a whole. This applied in particular to miners and textile workers, but other categories, especially the traditional artisan occupations – locksmiths, mechanics, fitters, metal workers – were overrepresented. It has long been believed that the Nazis only succeeded in recruiting marginal working-class groups: those employed in the public services (trams, public utilities), agricultural labourers, those who had moved into town recently, the unskilled and unemployed, as Carlo Mierendorff, a prominent young Social Democrat, wrote as early as 1930. But this was not the case. As has been stated by a researcher recently, the Nazi worker was neither 'atypical' nor a 'marginal type', but he belonged to the 'core of the German working class'. Strongly over-represented through-out were the white-collar workers; many of them adhered to a national-ist ideology and were members of a rightwing union, the *Deutschnationale Handlungsgehilfenverband*.[10]

Considerably more proletarian in composition than the party were its stormtroopers, the SA – not surprisingly so because during the crisis the young unemployed members were offered free quarters and sustenance in so-called 'SA barracks' in the large cities. Indeed, without a solid working-class component the Nazis would never have won the innumerable street and meeting hall battles against their enemies of the left. Among the Nazis (above all SA men) arrested by the police for political violence in the years 1930–32, workers were represented in 'massive' numbers. Of the new SA members of 1931 62 per cent were workers, of those of 1932 56 per cent. In Breslau 60 per cent of the SA men had been unemployed for years. In 1932 2600 of 4500 SA members in Hamburg were unemployed, or about 58 per cent, and only 700 of them received any unemployment benefit. In February 1931 the East German SA leader Captain Stennes stated in a letter to the SA chief Ernst Röhm that in some districts of Berlin 67 per cent of his men were unemployed. Some sources mention figures of up to 80 per cent unemployed, but more precise data are lacking.[11]

In predominantly rural areas, however, the figures were very different. There many peasants and their sons joined the SA, as well as agricul-tural labourers. In Silesia in 1930, industrial and agricultural workers together only formed 17 per cent of the SA membership, in the district of Königsberg in East Prussia in 1930–31 only 11.7 per cent.[12] It has to be remembered that in East Prussia and elsewhere agricultural workers under pressure from the estate owners would have joined the rightwing paramilitary association of the *Stahlhelm* rather than the SA and thus would have taken part in the illegal frontier defence units of the army: this the SA refused to do under the hated 'system' of the Weimar Republic.

The National Socialists naturally boasted of winning over Social Democrats and Communists to their side, but there is no statistical evidence. Both leftwing parties were worried about the drift of workers to the Nazis. As early as July 1930 a socialist newspaper editorial stated it was essential to win back these workers by a programme of 'rationally based socialist enlightenment'. In the same year Mierendorff wrote that the German Social-Democratic Party (SPD) emphasized too little 'the emotional components of forming the political will', which the Nazis overemphasized.[13] Mierendorff was deeply concerned about the suc-cesses of the Nazis which the SPD, preoccupied with the fight against the KPD, was unable to stem. The KPD too, at least internally, admitted in 1932 that the Nazis had succeeded 'in achieving a rather broad gain on the front of the unemployed'. And the organ of the Communist trade-union opposition (RGO) confessed at the beginning of that year: 'We believed that we possessed a monopoly of organizing the unemployed movement and therefore have not made any particular effort. Suddenly it appears that our monopoly has little substance.' In Württemberg unemployed workers simply declared: 'The SPD has betrayed us, you Communists are doing nothing, so we'll try voting for Hitler. Perhaps things will get worse, then we'll smash up everything and Bolshevism can take over.'[14]

The KPD also suffered from the fact that its uniformed paramilitary organization, the 'Red Front Fighters', had been prohibited in 1929 so that it could no longer compete effectively with the uniformed SA. But in an isolated working-class settlement, such as the miners' village of Hochlarmark in the Ruhr, the few SA men were treated as 'outcasts' and were 'considered half-baked'. In small towns and the rural areas, on the other hand, the Nazis were particularly successful in winning over Social-Democratic workers; there the pressure was greater.[15]

In general, the German workers were severely demoralized by the crisis. Their trade unions were rendered powerless and forced to concede large losses of wages. Unemployment benefits were only paid on a descending scale for 12 months. After that men and women depended on meagre 'welfare' handouts which did not cover the minimum living requirements. The employers used the crisis to cut wages and to curtail the unions' influence.[16] The power of the SPD was broken, its Prussian bastion destroyed by Papen in July 1932. Both leftwing parties were occupied fighting each other, as voters and members drifted from the SPD to the KPD. The latter declared in 1929 and later that the Social Democrats were 'Social Fascists': they must be driven out of the factories and unions, they were the principal enemy. The gulf separating the two parties widened, and the SPD retaliated in kind. If the KPD maligned Social Democrats as 'Sozis', the latter spoke of Communists as 'Kozis'.

In spite of the crisis, however, the two leftwing parties preserved the loyalty of the large majority of their members, and defections from their ranks to the Nazis were comparatively rare. It was rather different with their paramilitary organizations, especially their younger members who had never seen a factory from inside. I still remember the shock I experienced when I saw former members of the 'Antifascist Young Guards' shaking the collection boxes for the SA in their brown uniforms near the Kurfürstendamm. But that was in 1933. What the left parties worried about were the masses of their voters and sympathizers who might more easily transfer their allegiance. Yet the KPD vote increased to almost six million in 1932. That of the SPD slowly decreased but throughout remained above the seven million mark.

It has recently been claimed that 'a sizeable number of former SPD and KPD voters switched to the NSDAP at each election during the early 1930s',[17] but this is not borne out by the figures unless we assume that the opposite switch also took place, which seems rather unlikely. The combined vote of SPD and KPD increased from 12,440,000 in 1928 to 13,182,000 in 1930. It came to 13,243,000 in July 1932 and decreased very slightly to 13,228,000 in the November election of that year. A real decline only occurred in March 1933 under the Hitler government: to 12,030,000. But that was not a free election – the Nazi terror was already in full swing. With much more justification Tim Mason stated that in 1932 several millions of workers and their families must have voted for the NSDAP, perhaps 3.5 million or more. Among them were unemployed youngsters (the voting age was 20), workers of the railways, the post office, public utilities, municipal transport enterprises – 'uniformed workers' – and in certain areas industrial workers who were not unionized and had not voted for one of the leftwing parties. Other historians have mentioned unskilled workers, those working at home or in small enterprises, artisans, workers with a rural background.[18] It is equally important to remember that large numbers had never voted at all or had not voted for one of the 'Marxist' parties. We know that the Nazis were very successful in mobilizing the non-voters who came from all sections of the population. It would not be justified to classify all the various categories mentioned as 'atypical' workers, as has been done, so that in the end only union members and adherents of a leftwing party would be 'typical' workers. There is no doubt that the NSDAP with its radical propaganda was able to mobilize members of all social classes.[19] That was the secret of its success.

What has been said so far is confirmed by the fact that in industrial towns with a large working-class population the NSDAP in 1932 gained far fewer votes than the two leftwing parties together. For example, in Duisburg in July 1932 it got 63,868 as against 94,114; and in November 54,655 as against 91,598 votes, with the KPD alone surpassing it by a wide margin. In Dortmund, in November 1932, the NSDAP polled only 17.7 per cent of the vote, the two left parties together 51.5. In Bremen, the NSDAP in July 1932 polled 30.8 per cent of the total, the two left parties 48.1; in November it dropped to 21.2 per cent, while the left achieved 49.2. In Hanover a stronghold of the SPD, the NSDAP polled 39.9 per cent in July 1932, compared with 45.8 for the left; and in November 34.7 per cent as against 46.4 for the left. In Mannheim in the south the NSDAP gained 45,352 votes in July 1932, the left 71,110; in November the figures were 38,686 for the NSDAP and 70,236 for the left. The latter gained 46.6 per cent of the total, the Nazis only 25.6.[20]

The question how many workers voted for the NSDAP and to what groups they belonged cannot be answered more precisely. One thing, however, is clear: the Nazis did not achieve a significant breakthrough among the leftwing electorate until they were in power. In the Free City of Danzig, which was nominally independent and where all non-Nazi workers' organizations were destroyed in the 1930s, the party organizers made special efforts to recruit workers, but with very limited success. They were more successful with the municipal and railway workers, among whom Nazi influence became comparatively strong.[21]

Following the example of the KPD, which always tried to shift its weight from the street cells to its factory cells, the National Socialists also established factory cells, some as early as 1923. In Berlin, Nazi cells existed already in 1927 at Siemens and at the Knorr-Bremse. When a Siemens factory meeting decided to ask for better wages, the demand was put to the management by a Nazi and a Communist. In the following year a committee reported to an assembly of the Berlin party members that there were several such cells; they were summoned to help in the struggle against the trade unions. A few weeks later the cells were combined in the newly created Nazi Factory Organization, the NSBO, with Reinhard Muchow as leader. By 1929 the movement spread to Hamburg, Hanover and Bavaria. In March the Berlin party daily, *Angriff*, urged the members to participate in the election of factory councils: 'be conscious of your duty as revolutionary workers'. In Hamburg Nazi factory cells existed at the municipal railway, the slaughterhouse, the principal shipping line and in some banks, the last two consisting of office workers, but the movement could not make any headway in the docks or the factories. White-collar workers remained the group among which NSBO influence was particularly strong.[22]

From May 1930, the *Angriff* had a page largely devoted to NSBO propaganda, most of it written by Muchow, with topics such as 'extension of working time' and 'preservation of the eight-hour day'. In 1931 the NSBO acquired its own organ, *Arbeitertum*, sold for the small sum of ten pfennigs or given away. At the end of the year it had about 39,000 members, a rather modest figure. In factory council elections at Siemens in 1930 it obtained about 10 per cent of the workers' vote and 20 per cent among the white-collar workers, and at the municipal tramways of Frankfurt as much as 19.5 per cent. During the following years of severe crisis the NSBO grew quickly. In May 1932 it had 106,000 members, in August 170,000, and in January 1933 as many as 294,000. By then it had established, again following the KPD example, special sections for the unemployed.[23]

Yet in the annual elections of factory councils the NSBO did less well. In Berlin in 1931 the unions published the results of 2540 enterprises. There the Free unions gained 6583 mandates or 81.5 per cent, the Communists 733 mandates or 9 per cent, the NSBO, together with the *Stahlhelm*, a mere 36, a derisory result. Among the Ruhr miners it obtained 7728 votes, about 3.5 per cent of the total, in the Ruhr metal and steel industry 6300 votes, about 5 per cent, at Krupp in Essen 670 votes or 4.6 per cent, but among the office workers 1142 votes, nearly one third of the total. In 1931 the NSBO had only 2600 members in the three party *Gaue* of the Ruhr, with their huge working-class population.[24]

In Berlin, according to the *Angriff*, the NSBO early in 1931 had almost 60 factory cells, 16 of them in electrical and metal works and 10 in the transport company and utilities. In the same year the Berlin police reported that the leading metal workers' union, the DMV, was considerably weakened by the foundation of a 'red' Communist union which had 18,000 members, but many others resigned from the DMV. The danger was that these would fall 'for the lively propaganda of the National Socialists in the factories', whose cells grew 'in a manner not known so far'. They put up their own lists for the factory council elections, even where nothing had been known of them in the previous year. The splitting tactics of the KPD and its fight against 'social fascism' benefited the Nazis, the unions lost many members, but the new 'red' unions remained very weak. In the summer of 1931 the 'red' building workers' union noted that the Nazis were very active in the trade, that one building site of Siemens was entirely dominated by their followers. In many enterprises 'yellow' or 'national' workers' groups had existed for a long time. They were supported by the employers and refused to participate in strikes. They provided a basis on which the NSBO could build. But *Arbeitertum* distanced itself sharply from the 'yellow' union which it labelled 'parasites of the working class'. The NSBO wanted to be recognized as a true union and participate in negotiations about wages and working hours; it even organized actions against proposed measures of rationalization and attempts to cut wages.[25]

Above all, in contrast with the 'yellow' unions, the NSBO participated in strikes. Already in 1927, the Munich *Völkischer Beobachter* supported a coal miners' strike in Thuringia and denounced lockouts. In the big strike of the Berlin metal workers of 1927–28, the *Angriff* attacked enforced arbitration and the Berlin *Gauleiter* Joseph Goebbels emphasized that only Nazis and Communists wanted to continue the strike after a compulsory arbitration award. According to its own pronouncements, in 1930 the NSBO led or supported strikes in the Mansfeld copper mines, in the metal industries of Berlin, Hanover and

Saxony. In Hanover the NSDAP declared its solidarity with the strikers, threatened blacklegs with expulsion and agreed to give strikepay, food and clothes to those in need. In general strikes would be supported if they were economically motivated, but only with the approval of the NSBO leaders, and strikepay be given to those who had been members for at least three months. In 1931 the NSBO supported strikes in Berlin, Bremen and Backnang. *Arbeitertum* warned that any blacklegs would be expelled.[26]

In 1932 strike activity was intensified and a national strike fund was established at party headquarters. The best known example of this radical activity was the strike of the Berlin transport workers against a wage cut in November 1932. In the strike ballot of the tram, bus and underground workers, the three-quarters majority prescribed by the bylaws was not reached although a large majority voted for strike action. The unions then refused to sanction it, but the Communists called out the workers who followed suit. They were soon joined by the Nazis, and for a few days those who usually fought each other in the streets joined hands and brought the entire transport system to a halt. There was chaos. Drivers willing to work and the policemen protecting them were attacked, cement was poured into tramway points, high-tension cables were pulled down and sabotage committed on a large scale. Four NSBO members were elected to the central strike committee. On 4 November Joseph Goebbels noted in his diary: 'Our name among the workers has gloriously improved within a few days ... A positive fact of immeasurable importance.' In his opinion a 'revolutionary mood' existed in Berlin. Communists and Nazis organized street collections to support the strikers, but this was insufficient to maintain the strike. After five days it collapsed and a wage cut was accepted. At that time the NSBO had as many as 1300 members among the Berlin transport workers and it gained more from its radical stance.[27] In the subsequent general election the Nazis lost two million votes, but they were still by far the largest party. Three months later Hitler was the chancellor.

In general, the NSBO, like the NSDAP itself, was most successful among office workers and 'uniformed' workers, such as railwaymen or postmen, who often considered themselves a cut above 'ordinary' workers, and among the unemployed. But before January 1933 it penetrated the core of the industrial proletariat to a very limited extent, less so than the NSDAP. It seems doubtful whether it won over many Communists: rather those who left the unions on account of indifference or Communist splitting tactics, or because the unions proved unable to defend the workers' interests during the crisis.[28] Like the RGO, it organized many strikes, often against wage cuts, but they were hardly ever successful. Above all, the NSBO was *not* a trade union and did not possess the long-tested apparatus of the Free unions, with experienced factory councillors and local representatives who enjoyed the confidence of many workers. If the NSBO aimed at penetrating and conquering the unions,[29] this was certainly not achieved. The unions were much weakened in the early 1930s, but less so by the tactics of Communists and Nazis than by the severity of the crisis and the hesitant policy of their leaders. They were not responsible for the crisis and they became its victims. The crisis destroyed the fundaments of German society and of the republican order and vastly benefited the National Socialist movement.

In the middle of the Second World War, in April 1942, Hitler solemnly informed his lunch-time audience that 'the whole of the first few years of the "time of struggle" had been devoted to win the worker for the NSDAP'. To achieve this he used the most striking red for political posters and lorries covered completely by red posters and flags, instructed all his followers to appear in party meetings without tie and collar, so as to win the confidence of working people and to scare away 'the bourgeois elements'. With methods such as these he claimed to have won over 'many good elements of the working population'.[30] Perhaps his claim was less far-fetched than it sounded.

The facts mentioned in this chapter have been discussed by numerous historians and political scientists, at the time and in recent years. Their interpretations have differed widely, and many points are still controversial. The interpretations have varied from classifying the NSDAP as a lower middle-class party to a party which largely consisted of workers; and, indeed, if white-collar workers are included this seems to have been the case. As far as the blue-collar workers are concerned, it can be shown that they joined the Nazi movement in large numbers but were always under-represented compared with their strength in German society. The white-collar workers were over-represented, as were other social groups, for example artisans and students. The NSDAP succeeded in mobilizing all social groups but not to the same extent, and that was also true in the years after 1933. The NSBO came into being rather late in the history of the Weimar Republic. It only enjoyed lukewarm support by the party, presumably because of its radical stance, and it did not prosper much. The same applied to the Communist factory cells, for the bulk of the Communist workers were or became unemployed. Among the latter, Communist influence was stronger than that of the Nazis. But the SA succeeded in mobilizing large numbers of the unemployed who were desperate for change, any change that would terminate their intolerable conditions. At the end of 1932 5,800,000 unemployed were registered with the labour exchanges and many more did not do so. With their families they formed one third of the German population. But the misery spread among all social groups and affected the middle as well as the working classes. It was this misery which led to the spectacular rise of the NSDAP.

Notes

1. Detailed figures in Paul Madden, 'Some Social Characteristics of Early Nazi Party Members 1919–1923', *Central European History*, xv 1982, p. 43, who has evaluated all available early membership lists, mainly from Bavaria.
2. Detlef Mühlberger, 'Germany', in idem (ed.), *The Social Basis of European Fascist Movements*, London, 1987, p. 60; Michael Ruck, *Bollwerk gegen Hitler? Arbeiterschaft, Arbeiterbewegung und die Anfänge des National-sozialismus*, Cologne, 1988, p. 65.
3. Ibid., pp. 198, 203.
4. D. Mühlberger, 'The Sociology of the NSDAP: The Question of Working-Class Membership', *Journal of Contemporary History*, xv 1980, p. 496.
5. D. Mühlberger, *Hitler's Followers*, London, 1991, pp. 38ff.; Wilfried Böhnke, *Die NSDAP im Ruhrgebiet 1920–1933*, Bonn, 1974, p. 54; William Sheridan Allen, *The Infancy of Nazism*, New York, 1976, p. 40.
6. Max H. Kele, *Nazis and Workers. National Socialist Appeals to German Labor*, Chapel Hill, 1972, p. 121; Timothy W. Mason, *Sozialpolitik im Dritten Reich*, Opladen, 1978, pp. 52f.
7. Mühlberger, 'Sociology of NSDAP', pp. 499f.; idem, *Hitler's Followers*, p. 64; Böhnke, *NSDAP im Ruhrgebiet*, pp. 199f., 207.
8. Martin Broszat, *Der Staat Hitlers*, Munich, 1971, pp. 51f. Mühlberger, 'Sociology of NSDAP', gives 26.3 per cent for the working-class member-ship before the election of September 1930.
9. Broszat, *Staat Hitlers*, pp. 51f.; Peter Manstein, *Die Mitglieder und Wähler der NSDAP 1919–1933*, Frankfurt, 1989, pp. 138, 160; Mühlberger, *Hitler's Followers*, pp. 77, 115, 139; idem, 'Germany', p. 89.
10. Carl Mierendorff, 'Gesicht und Charakter der nationalsozialistischen Bewegung', *Die Gesellschaft*, 1930 i, pp. 497f. The opposite view held by Mühlberger, 'A "Workers' Party" or a "Party without Workers"?' Ms. to be published in 1994, pp. 39f., 44. I am very grateful to Dr Mühlberger for lending me his Ms. before publication. Hans Speier, *Die Angestellten vor dem Nationalsozialismus*, Göttingen, 1977, pp. 115–19.
11. Mason, *Sozialpolitik*, pp. 74f.; Mühlberger, *Hitler's Followers*, pp. 177, 180; idem, 'Germany', pp. 114, 123; Heinrich Benecke, *Hitler und die SA*, Munich, 1962, p. 207; Peter Longerich, *Die braunen Bataillone*, Munich, 1989, pp. 82–85.
12. Richard Bessel, *Political Violence and the Rise of Nazism. The Storm Troopers in Eastern Germany 1925–1934*, New Haven, 1984, pp. 36f.
13. Mühlberger, 'Sociology of NSDAP', pp. 501, 508 n. 37; Mierendorff, 'Gesicht und Charakter', p. 500.
14. Gunter Mai, 'Die nationalsozialistische Betriebszellenorganisation', *Viert-eljahrshefte für Zeitgeschichte*, xxxi 1983, pp. 600, 604; Conan Fischer, *The German Communists and the Rise of Nazism*, Basingstoke, 1991, pp. 138, 147.

15. Michael Zimmermann, 'Ein schwer zu bearbeitendes Pflaster', in Detlev Peukert and Jürgen Reudecke (eds), *Die Reihen fast geschlossen*, Wuppertal, 1981, p. 72; Michael Kater, *The Nazi Party. A Social Profile of Members and Leaders*, Oxford, 1983, p. 54.

16. Ulrich Herbert, 'Arbeiterschaft im Dritten Reich', *Geschichte und Gesellschaft*, xv, 1989, p. 323; Martin Rüther, 'Lage und Abstimmungsverhalten der Arbeiterschaft', *Vierteljahrshefte für Zeitgeschichte*, xxxix 1991, p. 249.

17. Fischer, *German Communists*, p. 119.

18. Mason, *Sozialpolitik*, pp. 62f., 67f.; Thomas Childers, *The Nazi Voter*, Chapel Hill, 1983, pp. 256f.; Heinrich August Winkler, 'Mittelstandsbewegung oder Volkspartei?', in Wolfgang Schieder (ed.), *Faschismus als soziale Bewegung*, Hamburg, 1976, p. 98; Jürgen W. Falter and Dirk Hänisch, 'Die Anfälligkeit der Arbeiter gegenüber der NSDAP', *Archiv für Sozialgeschichte*, xxvi, 1986, p. 215. Their claim on p. 211 that in 1932 22 per cent of SPD voters switched to the Nazis seems very doubtful because the SPD lost only 15 per cent from September 1930 to November 1932 and lost many votes to the KPD.

19. Ibid., pp. 215f.; Childers, *Nazi Voter*, pp. 265f.

20. Kuno Bludau, *Gestapo – Geheim*, Bonn 1973, p. 83; Kurt Klotzbach, *Gegen den Nationalsozialismus. Widerstand und Verfolgung in Dortmund*, Hanover, 1969, p. 79; Inge Marssolek and René Ott, *Bremen im Dritten Reich*, Bremen, 1986, pp. 77f.; Gerda Zorn, *Widerstand in Hannover*, Frankfurt, 1977, p. 39; Erich Matthias and Hermann Weber, *Widerstand gegen den Nationalsozialismus in Mannheim*, Mannheim 1984, p. 57, all with detailed figures.

21. Herbert S. Levine, *Hitler's Free City*, Chicago, 1973, pp. 122f.

22. Volker Kratzenberg, *Arbeiter auf dem Weg zu Hitler?* Frankfurt, 1989, p. 81; Allen, *Infancy of Nazism*, p. 86; Kele, *Nazis and Workers*, pp. 149f.

23. Ibid., pp. 154, 169ff.; Kater, *Nazi Party*, p. 55; Mai, 'Nationalsozialistische Betriebszellenorganisation', pp. 597ff.; Mason, *Sozialpolitik*, pp. 71f.; Peter D. Stachura, *Gregor Strasser and the Rise of Nazism*, London, 1983, p. 87. Kater's figure of 400,000 members for January 1933 seems an overstatement.

24. Kratzenberg, *Arbeiter auf dem Weg*, p. 205; Böhnke, *NSDAP im Ruhrgebiet*, pp. 173f.; Detlef Mühlberger, *The Rise of National Socialism in Westphalia 1920–1933*, London PhD thesis 1975, p. 358, with detailed figures.

25. Kratzenberg, *Arbeiter auf dem Weg*, pp. 227, 265f., 273; Kele, *Nazis and Workers*, p. 201; Matthias Frese, *Betriebspolitik im 'Dritten Reich'*, Paderborn, 1991, pp. 46f.

26. Kele, *Nazis and Workers*, pp. 122f., 201; Mai, 'Nationalsozialistische Betriebszellenorganisation', p. 585; Jeremy Noakes, *The Nazi Party in Lower Saxony 1921–1933*, Oxford, 1971, pp. 175ff.

27. Evelyn Anderson, *Hammer or Anvil. The Story of the German Workingclass Movement*, London, 1945, pp. 147f.; F.L. Carsten, *The Rise of Fascism*, London, 1982, p. 149; Mai, 'Nationalsozialistische Betriebszellenorganisation', p. 599; Kele, *Nazis and Workers*, p. 200; Heinrich August Winkler, *Weimar 1918–1933*, Munich, 1993, pp. 533f.; Elke Fröhlich (ed.), *Die Tagebücher von Joseph Goebbels*, Munich, 1987, ii, p. 270.

28. Similarly   Mai,   'Nationalsozialistische   Betriebszellenorganisation', pp. 604f.; Kratzenberg, *Arbeiter auf dem Weg*, pp. 271f.
29. Noakes, *Nazi Party in Lower Saxony*, p. 177.
30. Percy Ernst Schramm (ed.), *Hitlers Tischgespräche im Führerhauptquartier 1941–1942*, Stuttgart, 1963, pp. 261f.

CHAPTER TWO

The 'Seizure of Power' and the opposition

On 30 January 1933 Adolf Hitler was appointed chancellor by the ancient and mentally feeble President von Hindenburg, and on 5 March the last semi-free elections of the Reichstag were held. By that time the Nazi terror machine was in full swing, countless Communists and Social Democrats were arrested and subjected to barbaric methods of torture and imprisonment. The first 'wild' concentration camps were established, run by the SA and SS. The Gestapo (Secret State Police) was established by Göring as Prime Minister of Prussia. The KPD was driven underground. But even under these conditions the NSDAP failed to obtain an absolute majority of the votes. It made considerable gains and reached 43.9 per cent of the total, but a bare majority only with its German Nationalist allies. On 24 March the Reichstag, against only the votes of the SPD (the KPD being banned), granted full discretionary powers to the Hitler government. It could promulgate laws without consulting parliament and these could disregard the provisions of the constitution. This enabling law was to expire in 1937 and was then extended for further periods.[1] It was the end of the Weimar Republic, and the new government was not slow to use its powers to the full. There was no resistance.

When the Hitler government was appointed in January the KPD issued a call for a general strike which was a complete failure. Later, lower party units made some preparations for sabotage but they were cancelled on orders from above. Mass arrests soon broke up the cohesion of the party structure, and it took considerable time before a functioning underground organization was established; vital preparations had been neglected because the party 'could not be forbidden'. Nor were they any better on the Social-Democratic side. The leaders of the Berlin SAJ (the party youth) were expressly forbidden to prepare their organization for underground work. The result was open conflict between the SAJ and the SPD leaders. When some energetic young activists tried to get duplicating machines and typewriters from SPD offices to prevent their confiscation, they were coldshouldered and unable to obtain them: they had to steal them and find safe places for them.[2]

In some towns, however, preparations had been made since the autumn of 1932. In Leipzig, which had a strong antifascist tradition, small groups of five were formed with special links to the local leaders. In 1933 these groups simply continued to operate, at least until 1934. In Hanover, a similar organization was created from the most active members of the SPD, the *Reichsbanner* (the paramilitary association) the workers' sports and hiking clubs, with the approval of the SPD leaders, in case the party should be forbidden. The organization was centralized, its leaders known only to a few; special liaison members were to maintain contacts between the leaders and the sections with their group leaders.[3] But these were exceptions rather than the rule. In many other towns the activists of the *Reichsbanner* and the party youth groups early in 1933 waited for the signal from Berlin to take action – but the signal never came. In any case, resistance against the combined forces of police, army, SA and SS would have been quite hopeless and any stores of weapons were totally inadequate. The bitter strife between SPD and KPD prevented any concerted action.

In the midst of the turmoil the elections to the factory councils were held in March–April 1933 and brought significant gains to the NSBO. In the Ruhr mines it gained 30.9 per cent of the vote, very slightly more than the Free unions and three times as much as the Communists. At Krupp in Essen it obtained 26.9 per cent, considerably less than the Free and the Christian unions, at Mannesmann in Duisburg 31.7, at the Gute-Hoffnungshütte in Oberhausen and at Klöckner in Hagen as much as 42, at the August-Thyssenhütte in Dinslaken 55, and at the Cologne municipal trams even 66 per cent of the vote. The works in the Ruhr were among Germany's most important steel plants, the core of heavy industry. In March 1933 the NSBO had over 371,000 members, in May 727,000. It had become a strong and powerful organization, not afraid to challenge the managers. When the freely elected works councils were removed by decree there was no resistance.[4]

Nor was there when the trade union offices were occupied by the Nazis on 2 May and their properties confiscated. It was in vain that the union leaders urged the German workers to participate in the official MayDay celebrations organized by the Nazis who declared the 1st of May a national holiday. What had been slowly built up over decades vanished overnight, to the advantage of a new Nazi organization, the German Labour Front (DAF). The DAF was not a trade union, and the NSBO was refused recognition as a union by the authorities. Under the new regime both had to maintain 'work peace' and to cooperate with the employers, who received the title of 'factory leader'.

It has often been discussed why the German workers accepted so passively the destruction of their organizations and of their basic rights.

They were no doubt demoralized by the severity of the crisis and surprised by the suddenness and completeness of the Nazi takeover, the effectiveness of the terror machine. The labour movement was paralysed by a deep split. The KPD still pursued its old discredited line of the 'united front from below', which meant winning over Social Democrats to the Communist line, and the bitter attacks on the 'social fascist' SPD leaders. It blamed the treason and capitulation of the SPD and union leaders for Hitler's easy victory. It was convinced that the Nazi dictatorship would not last long and would open the path for the victory of the 'proletarian revolution'. In March the leaders of the Leipzig KPD proclaimed: 'March with us under the red banners of freedom of the coming Soviet Germany.' In the summer of 1933 the KPD Central Committee declared that the dictatorship would not last, it would fail because of its 'inner contradictions' and be replaced by a 'Bolshevist Germany'.[5] But among the Social Democrats similar illusions were rife. Had not the party successfully withstood persecution under Bismarck's Law against the Socialists and time and again defeated all efforts of the Prussian police? Had it not drawn strength from persecution? Even leftwing intellectuals thought, as Germany had had three different chancellors in 1932, the new one would not last all that long.

After the dissolution of the unions the SPD leaders realized that their party would soon follow suit. On 4 May, after a 'dramatic debate', they decided to send six of their number abroad although it was argued that, whatever might happen, the leaders ought to stay with the masses of the members. The meeting passed in 'full harmony'. Before the Reichstag met later that month the party deputies decided by a large majority after massive Nazi threats to participate without making a statement of their own and to vote in favour of Hitler's declaration on foreign policy. Even before this decision two of the leaders secretly crossed the Czech frontier. At a meeting in the Saar district (still administered by the League of Nations) it was decided on 21 May to transfer the seat of the party to Prague. But this met with much opposition inside Germany, and soon there was open conflict between the leaders staying in Berlin and those in Prague. The latter decided to publish, with the help of the Sudeten German Social Democrats, pamphlets and papers sharply attacking the Hitler regime and to establish 'frontier secretariats' to channel the material into Germany and to receive reports from underground party groups. Six secretariats were formed in Czechoslovakia, two each in Poland, Switzerland, France and Belgium, one in Denmark and in Luxemburg, all close to the German frontiers. The situation of the party in Germany became 'desperate'.[6]

One of the first publications of the exiled leaders was a revolutionary manifest 'Revolution against Hitler! The historical task of German

Social Democracy', which announced a radical break with the party's past. 'Against despotism there is no parliamentary or constitutional opposition, but only the way of revolution'; a party with the aims of Social Democracy 'can therefore only exist as a revolutionary party'. Between National Socialism and socialism no compromise was possible, 'only a fight to the death'. The pamphlet at the same time drew a clear dividing line to the Communists. 'The existence of the Communist Party, its unteachable adherence to a false doctrine, makes the task of fighting Hitler's despotism more difficult . . . It cannot be the aim of the great freedom struggle against the fascist state to replace the facist workers' penitentiary by a Bolshevist one.'[7] The SPD remained faithful to its old libertarian and democratic ideas and would have no truck with the proponents of a dictatorship. It could hardly give a different answer to the protagonists of the 'social fascism' thesis and of the 'united front from below'. In Germany meanwhile a conference called in June by Paul Löbe elected new party leaders and publicly repudiated those in Prague, claiming that they alone represented the party. It was of no avail, for a few days later the SPD was prohibited and its parliamentary mandates were declared null and void. Clearly, there could be no accommodation with the Hitler regime.[8]

After the conference called by Löbe, two emissaries of the Prague leaders met secretly party secretaries and other participants whom they considered 'relatively safe' in a villa in Charlottenburg, 'to hear their opinion about underground work'. They pointedly asked whether the others were willing to take part and to distribute the 'papers and pamphlets coming from Prague'. The party secretary from Magdeburg expressed his pleasure 'about the meeting with the Praguers, they at least want to do something'; they had to learn from the Nazis who worked underground for ten years. In his area he had created 'a net of young and younger people willing to work'. But he warned not to send too much material, that would result in a breakdown. Most of those present expressed their agreement, some only hesitantly. The warning was only too well justified. At the outset the frontier secretaries organized the transport of illegal literature 'with incredible carelessness', used the post to send it to well-known SPD local officials, posted parcels from post offices near the German frontier, without any discretion, with the result that they could be seized easily.[9] What had been easy under Bismarck's Law against the Socialists when the *Sozialdemokrat* was smuggled into Germany in very large quantities, was no longer possible in 1933.

Some frontier secretaries, however, soon established good working contacts inside Germany. Hans Dill, the former party secretary from Nuremberg, used a young waiter working on a dining car from Czechoslovakia to Munich to carry and hand over his material and created a network of agents in Lower Bavaria. In Upper Bavaria another frontier secretary, the young and idealist Waldemar von Knoeringen, built a number of support groups in Augsburg, Munich and other towns; but he found it difficult to establish contacts in the factories for the workers were frightened and their solidarity weak. In December he criticized the careless distribution of material which the party leaders practised and pleaded for theoretical literature to train the members: 'the first task is the ideological strengthening of our comrades and the education of leaders.' The distribution of large quantities of underground literature was less important. Another frontier secretary, the solid and sturdy Swabian Erwin Schöttle, who worked from Switzerland, had several hundred supporters in Stuttgart; there and and in other Swabian towns his 'Political Circulars' were distributed in fair numbers.[10]

The principal vehicle of clandestine socialist propaganda was the monthly *Sozialistische Aktion*, printed in Prague in small size on very thin paper, around which underground groups were formed in Germany where it found avid readers. Its editor was Paul Hertz, one of the emigrated leaders, a highly intelligent and flexible politician. The journal for years provided a link between the isolated and badly shaken party groups and kept up their spirit.

This spirit varied from place to place and often from generation to generation. In many places the activists came from the *Reichsbanner* and the SAJ, while the older party members were disheartened by the defeat and retired into passivity. From Brunswick it was reported that the ordinary members were against any 'action' and only met in small groups to exchange information. But the former *Reichsbanner* leader Erich Gniffke established a sales network for coal ovens with outlets in many towns, which employed many Social Democrats and supplied the emigration with news. In Neu-Isenburg near Frankfurt too, there was no active opposition. The Social Democrats only met to play cards or drink a glass of beer. In Frankfurt itself an active SPD group distributed material such as *Sozialistische Aktion* and sent it by motorcycle to nearby towns, to Darmstadt, Mainz, Hanau, Offenbach and Wiesbaden. The recipients only knew their own small group and not the others. According to a Gestapo report of 1935 (after mass arrests) in the Rhine–Main area the SPD was organized in regular districts, four of them in Frankfurt and more in neighbouring towns. But many Social Democrats from the outset spurned any underground activity and only met in sports or bowling clubs or in certain cafés: one of them belonged to a former SPD Reichstag deputy. In Frankfurt a separate group of old members of the Free white-collar union had prepared themselves carefully for underground work, such as conduct after arrest, avoiding police observation, distribution of leaflets. On MayDay 1933 they held their own celebration in the woods after escaping from the official do.[11]

In Mannheim there existed a large group of about 150–200 SPD activists, surrounded by passive readers of *Sozialistische Aktion*. As in Frankfurt, 10 pfennigs were paid for a copy, and 5 pfennigs by the unemployed; about 1500 copies were distributed in Mannheim and its district. Very carelessly membership cards were issued and contributions receipted, at least at the beginning. The leader had occupied leading posts in the SAJ and the *Reichsbanner*. The basis consisted of socialists of long standing who knew each other well. In Stuttgart too, contributions were collected and leaflets distributed, for example calling for a 'No' vote in the Nazi plebiscite of November 1933. In Dortmund two different ideas were current among the SAJ: to participate in activities of the SPD and to continue on their own. The latter group had contacts to similar groups in other Ruhr towns and to Holland from where it received its material. In most groups the emphasis was on discussions which took place on excursions or in circles of friends. Such opportunities were also provided by a gardening club and a ladies' singing club, 'Red Earth', until it was dissolved by the Gestapo. The outstanding example of activity was a bread factory with the very suitable name of 'Germania' in Duisburg; it was bought by August Kordass and distributed its wares over a wide area of the Lower Rhine, mainly to old SPD members. Most of the drivers were old party members who brought the loaves together with *Sozialistische Aktion* and other material smuggled by sailors or couriers across the nearby frontiers. Kordass gradually got rid of the few loyal Nazis among his workers on grounds of 'insufficient performance'. When he finally gave notice to the DAF factory trustee at the end of 1934 the Gestapo pounced and mass arrests followed.[12] Rather surprisingly, it took that long to act against a firm which was so blatantly anti-Nazi in its composition.

Another centre of underground activity was Hamburg with its long and proud socialist tradition. There, too, young members of the SAJ provided one of the driving forces of underground work, in small groups named after the old party leaders Ignaz Auer and Paul Singer, and also Jack London. Many others joined the Hamburg Hiking Club formed by former members of the *Naturfreunde*, the socialist hiking association which had been dissolved. Another disbanded organization was the workers' sports club 'Fichte'; its members were invited to join the Hamburg Teachers' Gymnastic club. This, in the words of the later prosecution, meant 'a hidden building of contacts among people with identical views to facilitate meetings'. They read underground material, discussed its contents and collected money to support the families of political prisoners. Members of other workers' sports clubs joined *en masse* the so-called 'bourgeois' clubs such as Helius or the Watersports association and so preserved contact over many years. In the autumn of 1933 an attempt was made to create an SPD organization for the whole city, including neighbouring towns. Couriers delivered underground literature at regular intervals to groups of ten or twenty, contributions were collected and receipted by signed postcards. The members were mainly skilled workmen who had grown up in the movement, many of them dismissed in the spring from posts in the unions, the coop or social insurance. The largest groups were in the workers' settlements with their strong socialist milieu. Later a weekly, *Rote Blätter*, was produced with 3–4000 copies and also dispatched to other towns. In Uetersen, a small town in Holstein, a former *Reichsbanner* leader organized small groups of SPD, *Reichsbanner* and union members. He had close contact with the local KPD and took part in meetings of its leaders, but this was exceptional. There leaflets and papers were produced in cooperation by members of both leftwing parties.[13]

In Bremen an underground *Reichsbanner* group was organized by young activist members. It waited for the coming crisis of the Nazi system which would be used to enforce a democratic-socialist course. The group comprised a large proportion of former members and their expectations were running high, as they did elsewhere. For the SPD, Anna Stiegler, leader of the Social-Democratic women, took the initiative in April 1933 and mobilized the women to support political prisoners. She found that the women were eager to be summoned, organized large excursions and birthday celebrations with discussions and informative lectures. Committees were chosen, the larger one with representatives of every town quarter. A separately organized SAJ group distributed material smuggled from abroad to several hundred friends and had good contacts in every district. For the anniversary of the so-called Bremen Soviet Republic of 1919, which had been defeated by troops of the Berlin government, the SPD issued a call to visit the graves of the fallen and about 3000 people obeyed the summons, apparently not hindered by the police. In Halle the organization was looser. A laundry served as the channel for collecting information about opposition groups. Its owner, an old union official, travelled over a wide area of the province and of Thuringia: nearly all his customers came from the SPD and the unions. He was arrested several times but nothing could be proved against him.[14]

In Augsburg, the People's Choir 'Lassallia' (named in honour of Ferdinand Lassalle) changed its name to 'Richard Wagner Choir' and was able to preserve some continuity. But in October a new chairman was appointed who declared the Hitler salute to be obligatory. The Free rowing club of Düsseldorf changed the name of its boating house to 'Young Siegfried' to escape dissolution. Other clubs accepted new leaders from the political right and some kind of *Gleichschaltung* (streamlining). In Bremen the *Naturfreunde* located a former SPD member who had early changed over to the Nazis to prevent the seizure of their house.[15] But many other associations were less successful and were dissolved.

Perhaps the best organized and most efficient Social-Democratic organization was the 'Socialist Front' of Hanover, the origins of which went back to 1932. Its leader was Werner Blumenberg, a party journalist. The section leaders and others were trained in methods of police observation and interrogation, using the teaching manuals of the criminal police. The town was divided into eight districts, below which small groups of five were formed. Contacts only existed, according to Blumenberg's scheme, between the leaders and those directly below them, and from these to the group leaders. In addition to local groups there were about ten factory cells and groups recruited from the workers' sports clubs, the gardening association, the people's choir. In the workers' settlement the socialist milieu was so firm that practically all SPD members cooperated. There were perhaps 6–700 members. Every few weeks the *Sozialistische Blätter* were issued and sold for 20 pfennigs, about 300 copies in Hanover itself and several hundred more in other towns. The organization understood itself as the realization of a socialist united front and avoided negotiations with other groups; the limitation to the old SPD milieu was part of its success while it lasted. Towards the exiled Prague leaders it adopted a critical attitude on account of their past failures.[16]

Social-Democratic activity was to a large extent limited to the preservation of contacts between well-known and proven party comrades and did not attempt any 'mass' propaganda as the Communists did. This made it more difficult for police spies to penetrate the groups. The old milieu with its many ramifications continued to exist, be it only in the form of hiking and excursions, of bowling, beer and Skat clubs, of a *Stammtisch* in a well-known party pub, of private celebrations and reading circles. The milieu was particularly strong in the workers' settlements which had been built in Berlin, Hamburg, Hanover and other towns with their strong human contacts.[17] It also showed itself in the eagerness with which the *Sozialistische Aktion* and other material were received and read. One of those engaged in smuggling it from Czechoslovakia later wrote that 'only reliable people' received it, for it was not intended to start a popular movement but to strengthen the backbone of those who were loyal to the cause. The enthusiasm of many youngsters was also based on the belief that the regime would not last, that their sacrifices would soon be rewarded. In October 1933 the party leader

Otto Wels wrote to Karl Kautsky from Prague about 'the optimism with regard to the duration of the regime which animated the young workers' – an optimism which he shared on the basis of his own faith.[18]

Relatively close to the SPD were some smaller parties which had broken away from it in the early 1930s or earlier. The largest of them was the Socialist Workers Party (SAP), founded in October 1931 and then combined with a smaller group which had been expelled from the KPD for 'rightwing deviationism'. As early as March 1933 the SAP held an underground conference near Dresden which was attended by about 60 people from all parts of Germany; at that time it had about 15,000 members. The debate was dominated by the heavy defeat suffered by the German proletariat, and an illegal leadership was chosen. This warned all party groups to change their work from quantity to quality, to avoid all expansive activity, to form small groups of five, and not to meet in the flats of well-known SAP members. Couriers would provide all contacts between the leaders and the lower eschelons. But already in August four members of the new leadership were arrested when a Gestapo agent posed as a courier sent from Prague. The warning was not heeded. Young members distributed handbills in Dresden at the factory gates. In Breslau the local leader Ernst Eckstein was murdered by the Nazis, a large demonstration was held at the graveside, pamphlets were put into letter boxes, and many arrests followed.[19]

In Dortmund the SAP in 1933 had about 300 members and cooperated closely with the *Naturfreunde*, who met regularly. In Mannheim it had about 80–100 members plus small groups in Heidelberg and Ludwigshafen. There it issued a journal, *Das Fanal*, in a large edition. Two of the local leaders organized study meetings to read well-known Marxist texts and give short lectures; contributions were collected. In Bremen, there were about 70 members, most of them very young, organized in small cells. In Berlin the membership had shrunk to about 700 by 1934, and when Willy Brandt reached Berlin in 1936 disguised as a Norwegian student, to 300. 'The gap created by the Gestapo was frighteningly large, much larger than I had ever imagined', he wrote later. When one important SAP official was arrested in 1934 he even agreed to accompany an agent to Berlin and to arrange meetings with party activists. But he was rescued by them in a daring exploit and spirited abroad via clandestine channels.[20]

A much smaller, élitist organization was the ISK, the *Internationaler Sozialistischer Kampfbund* (International Socialist Fighting League). It had broken away from the SPD on account of its Marxist ideology. It was founded by the Göttingen philosopher Leonard Nelson, who recruited many ardent young pupils. The ISK members were strict vegetarians and the five vegetarian restaurants maintained by it served as useful meeting places for the small groups and brought in some money. In July 1933 a meeting of the local leaders held in Saarbrücken adopted guiding lines for underground work based on a long perspective and intensive training of the members. Groups of five were to be organized with the ISK as the core so that new members could be recruited. The principal stress was on trade union activities based on factory cells, and this was strongly supported by the ITF, the International Transportworkers Federation in Amsterdam. Its secretary Edo Fimmen, a well-known leader of the international union movement, in August 1933 concluded an agreement with the ISK; from October the *Neue Politische Briefe* were published abroad and smuggled into Germany with the help of ITF sailors and transport workers to be distributed by ISK members. For years they conducted effective underground propaganda, and in spite of all Gestapo efforts, spies were unable to penetrate the small groups.[21]

Equally small was the *Rote Stosstrupp* (Red Shocktroop) formed in 1933 in Berlin by activist young socialists and *Reichsbanner* members who were critical of the SPD leaders in Prague and the past policy of the party. It issued at regular intervals a journal with the same name as well as leaflets for the elections of November, urging voters not to vote for the NSDAP and to vote 'No'. Links existed to other German towns, from Stettin and Brelau to those in the Palatinate. But somewhat incautious activities soon led to mass arrests in Berlin and elsewhere. Their aim had been to create 'an illegal organization based on strictest discipline'. This had not been achieved, but they realized that strikes and demonstrations were out of the question as long as the masses were not disenchanted with the regime.[22]

Among the welter of small underground groups which sprang up in Berlin in 1933 one deserves mention because it made more of an impact and lasted considerably longer. It was founded by Walter Löwenheim who as a young man had been prominent in the Communist Youth International, had left the KPD in the later 1920s and joined its right-wing Opposition. In 1929 he began with the formation of a secret élitist organization which aimed at penetrating SPD and KPD and reuniting the split German working-class movement by occupying leading posts in both parties and fundamentally changing their policies. The members of the 'Org.' – as it was known among the members – were trained in long political courses and introduced to the 'conception' of Löwenheim, based on Marx and the history of the labour movement as seen by him. His guiding star was Lenin and especially 'What is to be done?'; like him he wanted to form a party of professional revolutionaries. Most of the members were very young and knew each other only under conspirative names. This had nothing to do with the fear

of a fascist takeover but sprang from the strict conspiratorial rules held
by Löwenheim and his 'Circle'. In 1931 the 'Org.' had its first success.
The leaders of the Berlin SAJ intended to join the new leftwing party,
the SAP, which had just split off from the SPD. But Löwenheim and
his friends persuaded them to stay in the large party and to work inside
for its reformation in a revolutionary sense. In consequence it was from
the SAJ that new members could be recruited, before the Nazi takeover
and after, and the 'Org.' began to grow. But the destruction of the two
leftwing parties in 1933 destroyed at the same time its old idea of
working inside them, and it was decided to withdraw the members
from the remnants of the old parties.[23]

Thus the 'Org.' became an independent underground organization
with a membership of 100–150 in Berlin. So far it was unknown to
the Gestapo and indeed to any wider circles of the left. In 1933 Löwenheim outlined some of his principal ideas for a wider public. The
manuscript was smuggled out of Germany and given to Friedrich Adler,
the secretary of the Socialist International. He was strongly impressed
and recommended its publication to the exiled SPD leaders. It appeared
late in 1933 with the title 'Neu beginnen! Fascism or Socialism', as a
basis for discussion for German socialists, and in this way the 'Org.'
acquired a name. Löwenheim attributed the defeat of the labour movement to the 'bourgeois ideologies' which penetrated both parties: in
contrast with them, his own group possessed true Marxist understanding. He pleaded for complete rejuvenation of the movement which must
be led by socialists inside Germany (meaning his own group), not by
the discredited old leaders. He correctly stressed a very long view
and the necessity of alliances with democratic non-socialist groups. Yet
the final aim was not a bourgeois democracy but the 'sole rule of the
socialist party'.[24] The pamphlet – one of the first voices from the socialist
underground – made a strong impression inside and outside Germany.
The group was able to spread to Saxony and Thuringia, to Mannheim
and Württemberg, and later to Bavaria. It above all attracted younger,
critical socialists who were dissatisfied with the old course and the old
leaders, who wanted valid methods of conspiracy and were opposed to
any 'mass action'. As two members of the small group in Mannheim
wrote later, what mattered most was 'training to be able to survive
under fascism', to form 'survival cells of the old labour movement',
capable of taking action if the opportunity arose.[25] But many members
were dissatisfied with a course of passivity. As there was no outside
activity they escaped persecution for the time being. Reports on conditions in Germany were collected and sent abroad.

The party suffering terribly from persecution was of course the KPD,
with its open tactics and old propaganda methods. Red flags were

hoisted on factory chimneys, slogans painted on walls, leaflets distributed as if nothing had changed. After several death sentences against
young Communists in Hamburg in the spring of 1933 (because of their
participation in shooting affrays with the Nazis), the KJVD (the KPD
youth) staged street demonstrations to save them. On MayDay 1934
such demonstrations were organized in several Berlin districts. They
resulted, as a leading party official remembered, in 'severe blows to the
party', or the comrades 'very reasonably' refused to obey orders. In
the Berlin Siemens works, comrades sold pictures of the arrested KPD
leader Ernst Thälmann and special Thälmann stamps. In Hof in Bavaria
newspapers smuggled from Czechoslovakia were sold. As one participant remembered: 'That was not underground work but almost public'
and could not go well for long.[26] Such methods were almost universal,
for the masses must be mobilized.

In May 1933 the Central Committee adopted a resolution stating
that the KPD was forced to 'a temporary retreat'; only opportunists
could conclude that the working class had 'suffered a defeat' or 'lost a
battle'. In October the district leaders of the Ruhr called for mass
mobilization: 'slogans must appear on all walls' and were to be shouted
in the evenings at street corners. Underground trade unions with a mass
membership were to be founded, but even in the Ruhr the Communist
miners' union could not do much work and remained very weak. Early
in 1934 the leaders of the Lower Rhine district adopted the slogan
'Fight for Soviet Power!' In June the Central Committee issued an even
more illusory proclamation: 'A broad revolutionary upswing occurs in
the country. The hatred of the fascist tyrants is growing from day to
day . . . You stand on the eve of the German proletarian revolution . . .
Go on to the streets with our demonstrations, organize with us the
political mass strike, the general strike for the overthrow of the fascist
dictatorship!' After the war a leading Communist remembered: the
fiction of the coming people's rising dominated the thinking of the leading officials, they worked according to the old schemes, the old activity
continued. They felt they were the exponents of a movement of millions,
of the entire working people, and did not realize the isolation of the
activists increasing from day to day, the ever growing solid consolidation of the Nazi party among the working masses.[27]

What also remained was the old party structure, with a political, an
organizational and an agitprop leader on each level. This greatly facilitated the work of the Gestapo which only had to put the names to the
office in question to find whom they were looking for. In many cases
they were able to obtain 'confessions' under severe torture, to turn
round comrades under pressure to become police agents. Many of them
had been infiltrated into the party before 1933, some of them occupied

leading posts and were responsible for many arrests. In June 1933 the police found on a chicken farm belonging to the secretary of the regional adviser for West Germany three suitcases containing an 'archive', copies of letters and minutes of meetings. Later the remainder of the 'archive' was seized in the lodging of the district secretary, including a report on the party's work in the whole area of the Lower Rhine. If the Gestapo discovered a party treasurer, it only had to follow him to find the members of his area, and many treasurers kept lists of addresses. In Bremen in August 1933 the Gestapo arrested numerous party officials, some of them at a meeting of the local committee which was shadowed by it. In Düsseldorf the former leader of the local committee introduced a Gestapo agent as 'an instructor from Berlin' who then proceeded to distribute contribution stamps printed by the Gestapo, collected the dues for the benefit of its chest and established links to higher party eschelons. In Augsburg the re-formation of the KJVD was supervised by a spy who time and again spurred the others to more activity and proposed the most radical plans. In Herne the Gestapo found in the autumn of 1933 a complete membership file consisting of cigarette cards with the abbreviated names of members and the amount of their payments. In Allenstein in East Prussia a Gestapo agent was for years 'a KPD official and belonged to the circle of the initiated', so that the Gestapo could wait quietly until the arrests were 'worth while'. In Bremen the Gestapo discovered in the course of the year ten cases of underground literature transported by sea. In July the Kassel Gestapo reported that they had arrested 16 officials, the third leadership group for Hessen-Waldeck, so that there the party lacked personnel and material to renew its activity.[28]

From Kassel the party instructor wrote to Frankfurt in December 1933 that there had been so many arrests that nothing remained of the leading group, the whole organization was badly shaken and links to the local groups had been broken. With great difficulty he succeeded in forming a new leading group of four and to re-establish some links; there were still 180 members. In Munich and Nuremberg in the summer of 1933 officials of auxiliary organizations had to be used to fill the 'central leadership' posts. The party leaders believed that much was achieved when couriers and instructors were able to report the appointment of new leaders on the levels of district, subdistrict and urban quarter, but the reservoir of experienced officials was soon exhausted. In Berlin in the autumn of 1933 the whole district leadership was arrested, including an archivist in charge of the KPD archives and the files of innumerable officials. Until October there existed in Berlin a leading group for the whole of Germany, while the remainder of the Central Committee – later the whole – moved to Paris. The 'internal' group led the party districts by written instructions, weekly couriers, monthly personal reports by the *Oberberater*, who was responsible for a group of three to five districts, and personal discussion with district officials. The larger districts had to send part of the party dues collected to Berlin, while the smaller ones received small subsidies. It was a rigid bureaucratic structure, upheld against heavy odds and with terrible sacrifices.[29]

On the local level too, the behaviour was very often careless. At Whitsun 1933 members of the KJVD from all the Ruhr towns assembled in a tent camp on a local heath, with only the most elementary precautions. In Cologne, as an activist remembered, all organizations including 'Red Help' continued to work in a broad fashion, and members 'still met in large groups' – one knew too much about each other. In Kassel membership dues were collected by using lists with the imprint 'Society for Law and Justice'; in Hanover by using white stamps of 10, 20 and 50 pfennigs for the 'battle fund'; in May cigarette cards of the make *Trommler* were used as identification. In the area of Mainz slogans were painted: 'We young workers of Germany do not want war. We fight against the militarization of youth. We defend the Soviet Union!', or 'Soon the day of freedom will dawn, then we will be the judges!' In the Ruhr an alleged opposition group of SA and SS claimed that their members were politically persecuted and called for a class war. Another leaflet urged the payment of higher wages, against rising prices, reduction of all taxes and cancellation of arrears, a surtax on millionaires and profiteers, allegedly in the name of a middle-class opposition.[30] Unfortunately we do not know what echo among the workers this and countless other leaflets aroused, but we do know that the majority became apathetic and disillusioned. The Communist milieu which had undoubtedly existed in many towns was no longer firm and many members were unwilling to risk too much.

The KPD also continued its old fight against any 'deviatonists' among its own ranks. In Hanover there existed a group of 'Conciliators' – which meant they were critical of the party's ultra-left tactics, for example towards the SPD – and in August they circulated a paper sharply criticizing the orthodox party line. They formed a 'Committee for Proletarian Unity' with about 100 members and issued their own paper, 'Class Struggle'. The official KPD went so far as to publish in its own journal, 'Lenin's Way', the names of four leading members of the 'Conciliators' who were expelled. But the Gestapo waited until the autumn of 1934 before carrying out arrests, probably observing the members meanwhile.[31] Long careful periods of observation so as to destroy whole networks were one of its standard practices.

One young KPD instructor, Bertha Karg, was sent to Düsseldorf in

October 1933 and found all Communist links wiped out so that she had to spend the nights hungry and freezing in the parks. In her desperation she approached the diocese praeses Dr Joseph Rossaint in front of his vicarage and asked for help. In discussions she succeeded in winning his confidence – he was an active pacifist – and established a link to a leader of the Catholic youth, the *Sturmschar*. When its leaders from all parts of Germany met on All Saints Day, Karg was able to address a carefully selected audience. She was introduced as a former trade union official and stressed the necessity of common resistance. 'Today it is the Communists, Social Democrats and unionists – tomorrow it will be you who will be persecuted if you do not rise in time and fight!' She was successful, addresses were exchanged, some Catholic groups received Communist material, and in some places common leaflets were issued. A proclamation to the youth of Germany was drafted. But at the end of January 1934 Karg was arrested and later sentenced to 15 years in a penitentiary. In 1937 Rossaint, too, received a sentence of 11 years for treason and three other Catholics lesser ones.[32] It was a rare example of cooperation of Catholics and Communists.

The Communists steadfastly believed that the proletarian revolution was just round the corner, that it was essential to preserve a 'mass party' under a centralized leadership. This partly explains their enormous activity in the early years of the Third Reich. Although their efforts met with little success their faith was not shaken. Those who were prepared to join an underground group were a small minority of the working class. The 'revolutionary masses' were a figment of KPD imagination. Many workers were willing to make their peace with the regime, even before it reaped any spectacular success, and many hoped that it would give them work.

Many expressed their dissent by a negative vote in the plebiscites arranged by the Nazis. In Bremen, for example, the percentage of 'No' votes was highest in the working-class quarters, in November 1933 as well as August 1934; in the second case it reached 25.2, 26.5 and 29.2 per cent of the total in three working-class districts. The majority of the Bremen shipwrights adopted a negative attitude to the regime, especially at the 'Weser AG' with its old socialist tradition and highly skilled workmen who were protected by the management. As no sabotage occurred the Gestapo could not intervene and even recommended to former political prisoners to seek work at the Weser AG. But this was an exceptional case. In 1934 the Gestapo had to admit that in the plebiscite of August 25 per cent of the voters 'or more' had voted 'No' in Catholic and working-class areas.[33]

Many others expressed their criticism or disagreement without belonging to a specific party. In 1933 more than half the people sentenced by the Special Court of Munich for *Heimtücke* (a vague term covering any anti-Nazi atttitude, malicious remarks, not rendering the Hitler salute, etc.) did not belong to any party. There were 425 such cases; 40 per cent of them were Communists, 55 per cent had no party affiliation. The remainder belonged to the SPD, SAP, or the Bavarian monarchists. In 1934 80 per cent of the cases had no political link. No figures seem to be available for other parts of Germany. There was no broad opposition movement but numerous more or less isolated cases of opposition.[34] But it is very remarkable how quickly the remnants of the German working-class movement recovered from a crushing defeat and took up the cudgels against an all-powerful regime which enjoyed mass support.

Notes

1. Ernst Rudolf Huber (ed.), *Dokumente zur deutschen Verfassungsgeschichte*, iii, Stuttgart, 1966, p. 604 and n. 2.
2. Personal recollections; Rudolf Küstermeier, *Der Rote Stosstrupp*, Berlin, 1970, p. 6.
3. Erich Matthias, 'Die Sozialdemokratische Partei Deutschlands', in idem and Rudolf Morsey (eds), *Das Ende der Parteien*, Düsseldorf, 1960, p. 189; idem, 'Der Untergang der Sozialdemokratie 1933', *Vierteljahrshefte für Zeitgeschichte*, iv 1956, p. 218: Ms. by Werner Blumenberg of 1936.
4. Frese, *Betriebspolitik*, pp. 51, 55, 456; Klaus Wisotzky, *Der Ruhrbergbau im Dritten Reich*, Düsseldorf, 1983, pp. 31ff.; Wilfried Viehbahn and Walter Kuchta 'Widerstand gegen die Nazidiktatur in Köln', in Reinhold Billstein (ed.), *Das andere Köln*, Cologne, 1979, p. 299.
5. Carola Stern, *In den Netzen der Erinnerung*, Reinbek nr. Hamburg, 1986, pp. 86f.; Siegfried Bahne, 'Die Kommunistische Partei Deutschlands', in '*Das Ende der Parteien*, p. 696.
6. Matthias, 'Sozialdemokratische Partei', pp. 182ff.; Friedrich Stampfer, 'Die dritte Emigration', in Matthias (ed.), *Mit dem Gesicht nach Deutschland*, Düsseldorf, 1968, pp. 73–76 (an edition of the Stampfer papers).
7. *Revolution gegen Hitler! Die historische Aufgabe der deutschen Sozialdemokratie*, Karlsbad, s.d. (1933), pp. 2, 15.
8. Matthias, 'Sozialdemokratische Partei', pp. 185ff.; idem, *Sozialdemokratie und Nation*, Stuttgart, 1952, p. 18.
9. Stampfer, 'Die dritte Emigration', pp. 182ff.; Hartmut Mehringer, 'Die bayerische Sozialdemokratie bis zum Ende des NS-Regimes', in Martin Broszat, etc. (eds), *Bayern in der NS-Zeit*, v, Munich, 1983, p. 354.
10. Jonathan F. Wagner, 'The Hard Lessons of a Political Life', *Internationale Wissenschaftliche Korrespondenz zur Geschichte der deutschen Arbeiterbewegung* (quoted as 'Internationale Korrespondenz'), xxix 1993, p. 196; Hartmut Mehringer, *Waldemar von Knoeringen*, Munich, 1989, p. 98; idem, 'Die bayerische Sozialdemokratie', p. 393; Roland Müller, *Stuttgart zur Zeit des Nationalsozialismus*, Stuttgart, 1988, p. 167.

11. Reinhard Bein, *Widerstand im Nationalsozialismus*, Brunswick, 1985, pp. 77, 83; Dieter Rebentisch and Angelica Raab, *Neu-Isenburg zwischen Anpassung und Widerstand*, Neu-Isenburg, 1978, p. 200; Lothar Bembenek and Fritz Schumacher, *Nicht alle sind tot, die begraben sind*, Frankfurt, 1980, pp. 52f.; Susanna Keval, *Widerstand und Selbstbehauptung in Frankfurt*, Frankfurt, 1983, pp. 193–97; Wolfgang Wippermann, *Das Leben in Frankfurt zur NS-Zeit*, iv, Frankfurt, 1986, p. 41; Thomas Klein (ed.), *Die Lageberichte der Geheimen Staatspolizei über die Provinz Hessen-Nassau 1933–1936*, Cologne, 1986, pp. 481, 509.

12. Matthias and Weber, *Widerstand*, pp. 143ff.; Müller, *Stuttgart*, p. 167; Günther Högl and Udo Steinmetz, *Widerstand und Verfolgung in Dortmund*, Dortmund, 1981, p. 130; Kurt Klotzbach, *Gegen den Nationalsozialismus. Widerstand und Verfolgung in Dortmund*, Hanover, 1969, pp. 129, 140ff.; Kuno Bludau, *Gestapo-Geheim! Widerstand und Verfolgung in Duisburg*, Bonn, 1973, pp. 26f., 36f.; Aurel Billstein, *Der eine fällt, die andern rücken nach*, Frankfurt, 1973, p. 107.

13. Frank Bajohr, 'In doppelter Isolation', in Wilfried Breyvogel (ed.), *Piraten, Swings und Junge Garde*, Bonn, 1991, p. 20; Ursel Hochmuth and Gertrud Meyer, *Streiflichter aus dem Hamburger Widerstand*, Frankfurt, 1980, pp. 46ff.; 313f.; Matthias von Hellfeld and Arno Klönne, *Die betrogene Generation*, Cologne, 1985, pp. 75f.; Karl Ditt, *Sozialdemokraten im Widerstand*, Hamburg, 1984, pp. 75ff., 81; Fritz Bringmann and Herbert Diercks, *Die Freiheit lebt!* Frankfurt, 1983, pp. 60f.

14. Marssolke and Ott, *Bremen im Dritten Reich*, pp. 209, 212f., 217–20; Detlev Peukert, *Volksgenossen und Gemeinschaftsfremde*, Cologne, 1982, p. 145.

15. Gerhard Hetzer, *Die Industriestadt Augsburg*, Munich, 1981, p. 185; Reinhard Mann, *Protest und Kontrolle im Dritten Reich*, Frankfurt, 1987, p. 203; Marssolek and Ott, *Bremen*, p. 155. There are many similar examples from other towns.

16. Matthias, 'Untergang der Sozialdemokratie', p. 218; Gerda Zorn, *Widerstand in Hannover*, Frankfurt, 1977, pp. 107, 115ff.; Hans-Dieter Schmid, 'Sozialdemokratischer Widerstand', in *Widerstand im Abseits*, Hanover, 1992, pp. 22, 24, 27f.

17. Mehringer, 'Bayerische Sozialdemokratie', p. 371; Klaus-Peter Schulz, *Proletarier, Klassenkämpfer, Staatsbürger*, Munich, 1963, p. 157; Ludwig Eiber, *Arbeiter unter der NS-Herrschaft*, Munich, 1979, p. 134.

18. Letter of 23 October 1933: Matthias, 'Sozialdemokratische Partei', p. 266.

19. Jörg Bremer, *Die Sozialistische Arbeiterpartei Deutschlands*, Frankfurt, 1978, pp. 62–65, 72f., 76f., 80f., 83; Jan Foitzik, *Zwischen den Fronten*, Bonn, 1986, pp. 48ff.

20. Högl and Steinmetz, *Widerstand und Verfolgung*, p. 159; Matthias and Weber, *Widerstand*, pp. 214, 223f.; Marssolek and Ott, *Bremen*, p. 230; Willy Brandt, *Erinnerungen*, Berlin 1990, p. 111.

21. Foitzik, *Zwischen den Fronten*, pp. 85ff.; Viehbahn and Kuchta, 'Widerstand in Köln', p. 320; Bein, *Widerstand*, p. 123.

22. Küstermeier, *Roter Stosstrupp*, pp. 12ff., 22, 25, with quotations from the journal.

23. Personal recollections of the author who became an active member early in 1932. See also Gerhard Bry, *Resistance, Recollections of the Nazi Years*, West Orange, N.J., 1979, recollections of another member.

24. *Neu beginnen! Faschismus oder Sozialismus*, Karlsbad, s.d. (1933), especially pp. 38–42, 58f.
25. Matthias and Weber, *Widerstand*, pp. 240–43; Schadt, *Verfolgung und Widerstand*, p. 105; personal recollections.
26. Hochmuth and Meyer, *Streiflichter*, p. 35; Anton Ackermann, 'Ich kam aus der illegalen Arbeit in Berlin', *Beiträge zur Geschichte der deutschen Arbeiterbewegung*, vii 1965, p. 829; Anon., *Dokumente des Widerstandes. Eine Artikelserie der 'Hamburger Volkszeitung'*, 1947, p. 49; Eiber, *Arbeiter*, p. 147.
27. Klotzbach, *Gegen den Nationalsozialismus*, pp. 170, 173; Bahne, 'Kommunistische Partei', pp. 714, 734; Mann, *Protest und Kontrolle*, pp. 200f.; Allan Merson, *Communist Resistance in Nazi Germany*, London, 1985, p. 120.
28. Ibid., pp. 91, 127; Wippermann, *Leben in Frankfurt*, iv p. 37; Marssolek and Ott, *Bremen*, pp. 248, 251; Mann, *Protest und Kontrolle*, p. 201; Barbara Dorn and Michael Zimmermann, *Bewährungsprobe. Herne und Wanne-Eickel 1933–1945*, Bochum, 1987, pp. 155, 158; Klein, *Lageberichte*, p. 57; Christian Tilitzki, *Alltag in Ostpreussen 1940–1945*, Leer, 1991, p. 29; Mehringer, 'Die KPD in Bayern 1919–1945', *Bayern in der NS-Zeit*, v, p. 192.
29. Christine Fischer-Defoy, *Arbeiterwiderstand in der Provinz*, Berlin, 1982, p. 109; Dorn and Zimmermann, *Bewährungsprobe*, p. 158; Mehringer, 'KPD in Bayern', p. 88; Horst Duhnke, *Die KPD von 1933 bis 1945*, Cologne, 1972, p. 112; Detlev Peukert, *Die KPD im Widerstand*, Wuppertal, 1980, p. 134.
30. Ibid., p. 105; idem, *Widerstand und Exil der deutschen Arbeiterbewegung*, Bonn, 1982, pp. 272f.; Fischer-Defoy, *Arbeiterwiderstand*, p. 82; Franz Josef Heyen, *Nationalsozialismus im Alltag*, Boppard, 1967, p. 101; Peter Dohms (ed.), *Flugschriften in Gestapo-Akten*, Siegburg, 1977, pp. 448, 455; Klaus Mlynek (ed.), *Gestapo Hannover meldet*, Hildesheim, 1986, pp. 45f.
31. Mlynek, *Gestapo Hannover*, p. 34; Petra Schepers, 'Das Komitee für proletarische Einheit', *Widerstand in Hannover*, Hanover, 1992, pp. 47, 50.
32. Berta Carola Karg, 'Mein Kampf gegen die braune Diktatur', in Richard Löwenthal and Patrik von zur Mühlen (eds), *Widestand und Verweigerung in Deutschland 1933 bis 1945*, Berlin, 1984, pp. 106–09.
33. Marssolek and Ott, *Bremen*, pp. 146, 152; Hans-Josef Steinberg, 'Die Haltung der Arbeiterschaft zum NS-Regime', in Jürgen Schmädeke and Peter Steinbach (eds), *Der Widerstand gegen den Nationalsozialismus*, Munich, 1985, pp. 871f.; Peukert, *Volksgenossen*, p. 57.
34. Peter Hüttenberger, 'Heimtückefälle vor dem Sondergericht München 1933–1939'; *Bayern in der NS-Zeit*, iv, p. 446; Martin Broszat, 'Resistenz und Widerstand', ibid., pp. 691–708, especially p. 708.

CHAPTER THREE

Years of difficulty 1934–1935

The years 1934–35 were years of great difficulty for the Hitler regime. There was still very severe unemployment, and the many workers employed on *Notstandsarbeiten* (works to relieve distress) received only a pittance and no proper wages. Food and other prices were steadily rising, while wages remained stationary. Hitler's renunciation of the Treaty of Versailles was a popular step, approved by a large majority, but no successes in the field of foreign policy could compensate for the domestic difficulties. The murder of Ernst Röhm, the SA leaders and many other alleged enemies of the regime in June 1934 led to a severe political crisis, and almost open political discussions took place for a short time; there seemed to be a very brief return to semi-democratic conditions. The crisis also brought greater influence to the army which had prevailed against its enemies of the SA and imposed its will on Hitler, who was forced to turn against his old comrades-in-arms. That two Reichswehr generals could be killed in cold blood like so many others, and the murderers go scotfree, revealed to many the true character of the regime.

Yet Nazi propaganda was on the whole very successful. Early in 1935 the SPD frontier secretary Hans Dill wrote to the party leaders in Prague that his friends in Germany were saddened by 'a progressive increase in stupidity on account of the indescribable Nazi propaganda' which affected the grumblers too: 'Everybody grumbles about mistaken government measures, but Hitler is totally innocent; for he could not know everything, he could not be everywhere, but when he got the right information he intervened immediately and did what was in the people's interest.' From Berlin it was reported early in 1934 that large sections of the working class were won over by the regime, 'especially the faith in Hitler is surprisingly strong'. While the circles of old SPD members were not influenced by Nazi ideology and were 'to a large extent unshaken', it was different with the members of the sympathizing organizations – the workers' sports clubs, the Free-thinkers, etc. – many of whom were 'more or less *gleichgeschaltet*'. From southern Bavaria it was reported that the majority of the working class were indifferent towards the Third Reich; a considerable part of those who were not *gleichgeschaltet* were disheartened and accepted their fate. From Saxony a reporter wrote it was 'frightening' how the workers accepted everything that was demanded of them as a matter of course. There was not even silent opposition to the compulsory rendering of the Hitler salute which was accepted 'as a matter without any importance'.[1]

Nazi propaganda among the workers effectively used antibourgeois sentiments. The strong emphasis on *Volksgemeinschaft* (people's community) could easily be understood as the abolition of bourgeois privileges and separateness: if the people were to form one community all these must disappear. The propaganda of the German Labour Front (DAF) to some extent also encouraged populist impulses in the factories where it tried to exercise influence.[2] One thing however the DAF could not do: intervene in wage conflicts or achieve any increase in wages. In 1934 one of its spokesmen informed the employers that the National Socialists despised any 'Marxist' wage policy, for the DAF wage questions were something very different from cheap 'Marxist market cries'. Therefore it left regulation of wages to the employers and would only intervene if they neglected their duties as 'factory leaders'. Wages were not to rise and in 1935 a DAF circular instructed all its subordinate organs to see to it 'that the legal wage levels were not to be transgressed', and these were the depressed levels of the crisis years. No wonder that many workers looked at the DAF with a good deal of scepsis, even if it tried to curtail too blatant forms of exploitation and at times acted as a kind of cushion between employers and employees.[3] All matters of wages and working hours were to be controlled by the so-called *Treuhänder der Arbeit* (trustees of labour) appointed in 1933, not by the DAF. The state assumed functions previously left to the employers' associations and the unions.

In addition, the propaganda methods of the DAF speakers often were rather crude. Early in 1935 even the Gestapo of Hanover informed Berlin that its 'tone' was not able to win the workers who 'kept aloof' from the movement and the state; time and again DAF speakers told former Marxists that, 'like their old leaders, they had been pigs and knaves, but now a golden time had dawned which made them decent human beings'. This tone alienated the workers, and attendance at DAF meetings declined considerably. So it did at other meetings, for example those of the Nazi Welfare Organization (NSV): another Gestapo report, this time from Aachen, found the attendance so poor that it was reminiscent 'of the worst battle years of the movement'. This was also due, they wrote, to 'a certain distrust of the orderly administration of the Winterhelp scheme' caused by known cases of embezzlement and malversation of its officials. These influenced the population which – in a strongly Catholic area – very much preferred to give to collections of the church rather than to those of the Nazi movement. Another popular criticism of the Winterhelp scheme was that many millions were collected but the poor only received small quantities of groats and other cheap food, while the better food and the money 'disappeared', causing much distrust and discontent.[4]

In contrast with the DAF, the NSBO often pursued a more radical course, as it had done before 1933. In some factories its representatives enforced higher wages, called on the workers to refuse lower rates for piecework, achieved the cancellation of dismissals and closures. When the manager of one Ruhr mine wanted to dismiss certain workers, the NSBO in April 1933 demanded revocation; when this was refused the manager was arrested. Finally a compromise was reached according to which some Communists and older workers were given notice. At another mine a list of active Marxists was compiled to which the NSBO did not object, and they were duly dismissed. The 'old fighters' of the NSDAP demanded to be given priority in getting jobs, but the employers often found the new workers ill-disciplined and unsuitable, and did not want to create unrest, thus many 'old fighters' remained unemployed. In March 1934 a special appointee of the *Treuhänder* for Westphalia wrote that in many negotiations with the NSBO he found its representatives animated by the 'pure spirit of the class struggle'. He had to side with the employers to prevent the economy from being stifled by the 'pervasion of the class struggle' and quite often had to threaten the NSBO side with the Gestapo. In his opinion every worker had 'to look at himself as a soldier of the economy'.[5] No wonder that many NSBO men objected to such an attitude. The employers insisted on their rights as 'enterprise leaders' and were determined to remain masters in the factories and mines.

Strong rivalries existed between the NSBO and other Nazi organizations. Early in 1934 the Gestapo reported that the NSBO wanted to represent the interests of working members of the SA and SS and insisted that they must join the NSBO; their speakers clashed in public and issued orders against each other. In short, the dissatisfaction of the other organizations with the NSBO had assumed forms which were quite 'intolerable'. In the opinion of the Gestapo, agreement could not be reached because quite often senior NSBO posts were filled by men 'who occupied them before as Marxists'. At the same time an article in the NSBO paper *Arbeitertum* proclaimed: 'As ruthlessly as we act against employees who disturb the work peace we will proceed against employers who believe that their time has come, that they can reduce the German workers to the state which they occupied decades ago. That time has passed for ever.' A director who infringed the discipline of his works would have to go to a concentration camp 'like the simple Communist'. A few months later the author of the article was moved to the lowly position of a DAF official in a small district near Berlin. In Münster NSBO members were observed by an SA leader when they installed listening devices under the tables of a local singing club, and the police strongly objected to the assumption of its functions by both organizations. In any case, many NSBO officials had become too ambitious and, as far as the preservation of factory peace was concerned, too radical and independent. The NSBO did not put the smooth working of the 'system' above its own interests, and so it lost its power and its principal leaders. The spirit of the class struggle must be eradicated root and branch.[6] But with the employers' attitude hardening, how could social harmony be created on the shop floor?

Many workers heartily disliked the continuous collections for the Winterhelp and many other purposes. At Blohm & Voss in Hamburg the management in 1935 announced monthly deductions from the wages varying from 23 pfennigs to one mark: if the workers agreed they were to sign a form and hand it in, and about 60 per cent complied. At a large steel works in Bochum the workers were to give a fixed percentage of their taxes and a minimum of one mark a month and to declare their willingness in writing. When this method did not meet with sufficient response it was announced in 1936 that in future the amount would be deducted from the wages unless the worker declared in writing that he was unable to contribute for financial reasons. In an Augsburg factory dissatisfaction arose because the workers were to give the equivalent of half an hour's overtime, and later one hour of overtime was deducted from the wages. So were quite generally the compulsory contributions to the DAF. In April 1935 the Cologne Gestapo stated that the contributions to the many organizations, societies, collections and other requests 'for a long time have had no proper relation to the means of existence'. In June the Gestapo of Münster concurred. In that month eight different collections took place there: for the HJ, the air force, the navy, the artisans' day, two for youth hostels, the Red Cross, mother and child, in the streets as well as from house to house. The people reacted by 'visible passivity with regard to the activities of the movement' and the earlier enthusiasm declined.[7] No wonder people asked what happened to all the money, especially in Münster where many local DAF and NSBO officials were arrested in 1934 for corruption and embezzlement.[8]

Yet there was one aspect of DAF work which found almost general approval. That was *Kraft durch Freude* (KdF: Strength through Joy), a gigantic organization in the service of the Nazi cause and of increasing production. It organized concerts and visits to exhibitions, the theatre and opera, excursions to other towns and the mountains, holidays by the seaside, in the Bavarian Alps and by ship to more distant places, above all sports from gymnastics to swimming, skiing 'for everybody' and numerous other activities. All these were made available to the masses at reasonable prices. In 1934 2,300,000 people took part in holiday tours; by 1938 the number rose to 10,300,000. It was claimed that nearly 50 per cent of the participants were workmen. In Saxony a KdF trip to Munich including food was offered for 30 marks to textile workers who expressed approval on account of the cheap price. In 1935 Hans Dill reported that one of his contacts had returned very impressed from a sea voyage. Other workers lacked the money even for shorter excursions. They criticized that the whole 'show' was arranged to impress them, that the presence of strangers prevented them from talking freely, that they were never 'among themselves'. If they uttered an incautious remark that would be duly noted; but they also remarked that the Social Democrats had never done anything like it.[9]

The great show pieces were voyages to Norway or Madeira on special KdF boats. These the workers could not afford and they were called voyages for the *Bonzen* (bigwigs). One irate Bavarian worker did not consider KdF a mark of merit for those in power but a 'lump of meat thrown to the workers so that they would not see what happened to the millions collected by the DAF'. But there were many opposite voices. From Saxony a Social Democrat wrote about a swimming course in which more than fifty women participated. Most of them came from the lower classes, hardly a 'Heil Hitler' was to be heard. Those who had belonged to a workers' sports club 'felt as if they were at home'. Many former comrades of the *Naturfreunde* association now travelled with KdF – 'there simply is no other possibility'. Other sports activities organized by KdF were equally popular.[10]

Far less popular were the monster parades on MayDay, participation in which was made obligatory for the workers. Of several thousand Krupp workers in Magdeburg only a few hundred arrived in 1935 on the arranged square. Some alleged that they had to go for a pee, and with the large numbers involved there was no real check. The Ruhr miners knew they would not be paid for the day unless they came and registered, and then many quietly disappeared: whereupon the Nazis used SA men to note their names and pay was cancelled. At other mines the march was accompanied by works' police to prevent anyone from straying. One miner later recorded that in spite of all precautions already on the march from Hochlarmark to Recklinghausen, almost half the complement used to vanish.[11] The workers simply disliked being marshalled about and having to listen to boring speeches, and so they went to do something more useful or to have a holiday.

The old factory councils of the Weimar Republic were replaced by so-called *Vertrauensräte* (councillors of confidence) who were supposed to look after the workers' interests. Often these were the old NSBO cell leaders who did not possess the necessary experience. In 1934 and 1935 there were elections, but the lists of the candidates were compiled by the employer and the DAF factory trustee. The election results differed widely and are only known in certain cases. At a Krupp steel factory 88 and 93 per cent of the workforce participated in 1934 and 1935; 71 and 69 per cent of them accepted the whole list and over 19 per cent rejected it, while 9 and 11 per cent respectively only crossed out some names. At the Ruhr mines too, participation was very high, but in some cases 40 per cent abstained and in others, where the miners were on short work, the lists were rejected. At an earthenware factory where the local NSDAP leader was a candidate he was rejected by 64 per cent of the voters, while a Communist and a Social Democrat did much better. In the district of Cologne in 1934 only 51 per cent of the voters accepted the lists in their entirety, and 55 per cent did so in 1935. There, too, participation was very high, amounting to 88 and 91 per cent. In 1934 7 per cent rejected the list entirely, and in 1935 8.7 per cent. In one factory a candidate was rejected because he had put himself out for the Winterhelp collection.[12]

In 1934 many workers openly criticized that the candidates were selected by the employers, while the old law gave this right to the workers. Many found that the candidates stood for the employers' interests, not those of the employees, so they would not vote for them: the new law did not mean progress but retrogression. But in 1935 the Aachen Gestapo stated that among the workers 'the number who stand for the *Führer* and his idea is steadily growing, . . . that the German worker more and more begins to feel not as belonging to the class of the proletariat but as a fully valued member of the people's community'. It was an optimistic interpretation, perhaps based on wishful thinking. According to a Gestapo report from Stuttgart of the same year, many workers criticized that those elected by them did not always possess their confidence and did not show sufficient energy towards the management, especially with regard to social measures to be taken in the enterprise. As the workers no longer had any influence on the selection of candidates, distrust was the natural consequence.[13] In any case, the experiment of election was not repeated after 1935.

Many *Vertrauensräte* tended to side with the employers and to reject the workers' demands as contrary to work peace. But they often mentioned the demands in their meetings with the employers and sometimes achieved an improvement. Complaints, opposition to dismissals, questions of leave, wages and working hours figured prominently in the meetings at the Krupp steel factory. The management used the meetings to notify the workforce of internal matters, to announce orders and measures to be taken. At other factories the *Vertrauensräte* tried to discuss hirings and dismissals, the levying of factory fines, matters of internal organization and, later, the problems caused by labour shortages. But the management opposed any cooperation in questions of working hours, wages and personnel. They wanted to use the *Vertrauensrat* as a 'handy instrument' to run their works, not as a negotiating partner.[14]

It is not surprising that many workers looked at the *Vertrauensrat* as a tool of the employer and often turned with their complaints to members of the old factory council who had been removed from office. The workers equally disliked that their DAF membership dues (and others) were deducted from their wages: a method upon which the DAF insisted. There were strong protests in the Ruhr and elsewhere, for many considered the dues too high and disapproved of the high salaries of the DAF *Bonzen*. A Berlin factory owner even spoke in 1936 of 'enormous embitterment' caused by the wage deductions. In Bavaria in the same year a DAF report stated that in some enterprises the workers refused to pay the DAF dues. Talk about the *Bonzen*, their cars and luxurious way of life seems to have been common, as even the Gestapo found; and naturally comparisons were made with the alleged *Bonzen* of the Weimar years.[15] In short there was much criticism – of certain measures of the regime and some of the leaders – but this criticism did not touch the person of Hitler. As the Dortmund Gestapo put it in July 1935: 'The recognition of the *Führer's* great successes in the field of foreign policy ... goes parallel with discontent of wide sections about economic events which cannot be overlooked.' Their colleagues from Kassel even claimed in 1934: 'Confidence in the *Führer* is unlimited and criticism of many subordinate authorities is as strong as ever.' A German woman returning from abroad was horrified by the amount of dissatisfaction and wrote: 'The unity of the people existed only on one single point, the person of the *Führer*.' Another report even found that Hitler's energetic action against the SA leaders on 30 June 1934 aroused 'special sympathies and strong confidence, precisely in that part of the working class which hitherto stood in opposition to the National Socialist movement and was even willing to take part in the fight against the National Socialist state'. In the same year Hans Dill reported that in Upper Franconia 'the mass basis of the Hitlers' was shrinking but that there was no abuse of Hitler, 'the great hope'.[16]

Early in 1936 the reports of the exiled SPD leaders noticed a widespread opinion 'that Hitler himself has good intentions, only his subleaders don't carry out his will correctly. But this view is no longer as prevalent as it was six months ago. Now Hitler is made responsible for certain things'. With regard to the violent anti-Semitic propaganda of Julius Streicher, people said: if Hitler told him that he could not do this he would have to stop. On the other hand, the same reports stated only a few months later that in a well known electrical firm in Berlin, Hitler's anti-Semitic diatribes found a positive echo among the workers: there were indications 'that anti-Semitism influenced the workers more strongly than at the beginning of Nazi rule'. On another point there was general agreement. When the German army reoccupied the Rhineland in March 1936, workers in Chemnitz remarked that after all the Rhineland belonged to Germany, and Germany must be able to do there what it wanted. Hitler showed that the method of the *fait accompli* was the only way to achieve anything. His audacious step gained in a few hours what negotiations had failed to achieve in many years. From a strongly Catholic area the Gestapo reported that the occupation of the Rhineland further increased Hitler's authority; those who still had reservations about his person or his foreign policy had shrunk to an insignificant group.[17] In spite of all criticism there was a basic consensus, especially on foreign policy.

We do not know how the official anti-Semitic propaganda was received by the workers or the population at large, and the incident of its approval in a Berlin factory may have been an exception. But we also know that there was strong anti-Semitism in Germany long before the advent of Hitler, due to the lost war and the inflation, the 'stab-in-the-back' legend, the economic misery of the postwar years, and vicious *völkisch* propaganda. It particularly affected the middle classes, but the working class was not immune. After 1933, two distinct strains have to be distinguished: the attitude to Jewish shops and the Nazi boycott, and that to Julius Streicher and his foul *Stürmer*, which specialized in sex attacks by Jews on German maidens. The reports we have of criticisms of Streicher and his paper come from Catholic areas and were partly due to the sex flavour of the *Stürmer* which was publicly displayed all over Germany.

From Aachen the Gestapo reported in 1935 that 'the *Stürmer* was repudiated very decisively by wide circles of the Catholic population' on account of its anti-Semitism which 'in this form is incomprehensible to the local people' and because the articles were considered unsuitable for the young. In Bavaria the *Stürmer* display cases installed by the NSDAP were often demolished and even National Socialist mayors were opposed to their resurrection so as not to disturb the local peace. In Düren in the Rhineland complaints were raised in 1934 when a Labour Service unit marched through the town singing 'When Jewish blood spurts from the knife then things will go much better'. The people of Münster were even more scandalized when another unit on Ascension Day marched past the church and sang 'To the gallows with the Jews, to the wall with the Blacks' (the Catholic clergy). The mayor and the local NSDAP leader expressed their disapproval, although the regime at that time was engaged in a vicious anti-Catholic propaganda drive.[18]

Reports about popular dislike of the Nazi boycott of Jewish shops also come from strongly Protestant areas. From Hanover the Ministry of the Interior was informed that just before Christmas 1934 tear gas was thrown into Jewish shops and Woolworth. But on the next day 'a specially strong human throng' went into these shops. In 1935 the *Gauleiter* of Pomerania had to admit 'to his regret' that not only the working people but also the better situated bought largely in Jewish shops. From Münster the local NSDAP reported before Christmas 1936 that they observed with 'shame' the large crowds entering the Hertz department store; to them it looked as if the entire anti-Jewish propaganda 'had not been heard'.[19] But this was an exceptional admission of failure. We cannot ascertain the social composition of the crowds rushing into Jewish shops; but it seems reasonable to assume that among them were many working men and women and that at least some were moved by pity with the persecuted minority. That indeed was what the *Landrat* of Kreuznach in the Rhineland reported in 1935: the boycott had not the intended effect, the turnover of the Jewish shops had not declined at all, for the circles which 'condemned such excesses in principle' often pitied the Jews.[20]

Many workers approved of Hitler's foreign policy – the occupation of the Rhineland and later that of Austria. German patriotism was a strong force, affecting all social groups. But there also was a nagging fear that his policy might lead to war. Already in December 1934 the Hanover Gestapo recorded that the whole population followed events in foreign policy with great interest and realized how threatening the situation was, as the possibility of war was discussed abroad there were hardly any illusions on that score. In 1935 the Gestapo of Kassel noticed a widespread fear that the armaments industry, which allegedly stood under Jewish influence, was driving to war. A report received by the exiled SPD leaders from north-west Germany stated that large sections of the working class hoped for deliverance from National Socialism by war; earlier on people had put their hope for deliverance in a military dictatorship or the restoration of the monarchy, 'and now it is war'. From Silesia it was reported in 1936 that the workers' attitude to war was negative, even among the young. The opponents reckoned on a German defeat because 'all' (other countries) would be against Germany, so that the war could not last long, and that would be the end of the Nazi 'system'.[21] That the war would not last long was another illusion, as was the hope that a military dictatorship would take over – expressed in the current jingle, 'In the Third Reich we march, in the fourth we govern'. Interestingly enough, these people expected a German defeat: the memory of 1918 was very much alive.

The real difficulties of the Hitler government in the years 1934–35, however, were not political but economic. Due to the rapid rearmament of Germany and the curtailment of all but the most essential imports, severe shortages of food developed that affected the lower classes in particular. In May 1934 the Kassel Gestapo reported that the cheaper varieties of margarine were in very short supply. In the district of Schmalkalden this caused strong resentment; there the large majority lived 'in the most meagre conditions' and had to rely on subsidized margarine as they could not afford butter or lard. A year later there was strong disquiet among the working population of Münster because margarine was bad and expensive, and the cheap 'peasant butter' unobtainable on account of new regulations issued by the Reich Food Estate. In the summer of 1935 there was a potato shortage in the Ruhr. Old potatoes were unobtainable and new ones too expensive for the poorer classes. There was severe disquiet, scenes which had not occurred since the worst years of the First World War. In eastern Westphalia margarine and pork were unobtainable, oil was too expensive, the price of a pound of pork and beef had risen by 20 pfennigs. In Hanover there were severe shortages of margarine, oil, potatoes; vegetables and fruit were very expensive and difficult to get. In Upper Silesia fat, meat and vegetables were in short supply and women protested in the markets, but the shortages were somewhat relieved by smuggle from Poland.[22]

From Cologne the Gestapo reported in September 1934 that in particular the workers were affected by 'a mood of economic catastrophe', and a year later that the shortages in particular hit the poor who could not get any bacon or lard. Potatoes were too expensive and of poor quality. From Hamburg shortages of meat and butter were reported in the autumn. Women clashed because one got a quarter of butter more than the other, and lively discussions about the food situation took place. In several Rhenish towns such as Düsseldorf and Elberfeld the butter shortage led to angry mass gatherings so that the police had to intervene. The women were not afraid to speak openly. In some cases angry shouts against the Nazis and the government could be heard.[23]

The food shortages caused considerable price rises, especially of basic foods essential for working-class households – at a time when wages were low and fixed. According to the Dortmund Gestapo, between 1933 and 1934 the price of meat rose by 20 to 23 per cent, that of potatoes by about 30, that of cheese by about 40, that of dried beans and peas by 40 to 110, that of fats by 52 to 104 per cent. Nor could the price rises be stopped. Between 1934 and 1935 the price of margarine rose by 66 per cent, that of potatoes and vegetable oil by 33, and there were steep rises in the price of meat, fats and butter. But in 1936 the situation became somewhat easier. If the statistical office of Essen declared that between January 1933 and January 1936 food prices rose by 15.5 per cent, that was a clear understatement. In October 1935 the Kassel Gestapo estimated 'cautiously' that in that year alone prices rose by 20 to 25 per cent. In September 1934 the Dortmund Gestapo reported that instead of 'Heil Hitler' workers lifted their right arm saying 'potatoes 3.75 marks' and got the answer 'dried peas 50 pfennigs'. In August and September 1935 the Reich Minister of Labour complained to the Minister of Food and Agriculture about the 'considerable and continuous decline' in the purchasing power of wages since the previous year and stressed the 'most unfortunate results' of price rises in the 'social and political' field.[24]

Wages were low, even for skilled metal workers, often lower than before 1933. In 1935 a skilled worker in a south-west German iron works earned for 50 hours of work 58.40 marks but received only 42.43 because of deductions for taxes, social insurance and DAF dues. A worker employed at the construction of a weir was paid 21.20 marks but received only 11.70 after deductions for food, sleeping accommodation, etc. While the wages of skilled metal workers were slowly rising, those of textile worker fell very considerably compared with the Weimar period. In March 1934 the Hanover Gestapo had to admit that the wages of simple workers often did not reach the level of unemployment benefit. Even if they surpassed it by a few marks, there were the many deductions and the employed worker had to spend more on clothes etc., so that many preferred the continuation of benefit to employment. A Dutch journalist commented that in Germany the creation of work meant that the workers received as wages what they used to get as benefit, sometimes less. An industrialist from Upper Silesia told him that the workers earned only 90 marks a month; they ate potatoes and bread, the price of which was kept low, but the quality declined on account of all kinds of admixtures. After work they could do nothing but sleep. The mood there was one of hopelessness.[25]

In a distressed area such as Upper Franconia the workers often earned less. In the town of Selb which depended on the porcelain industry and had catastrophic living conditions, many workers on short time earned only about 10 marks a week from which taxes and insurance were deducted as well as Winterhelp and DAF dues, but there was no protest. In the summer of 1935 a NSDAP local group reported that the textile workers earned only 15 to 18 marks a week and were unable to collect stores of fuel and potatoes for the winter. The frontier secretary for that part of Bavaria, Hans Dill, wrote: 'Wages depressed, no rights in the factories, shortage of all important foodstuffs, declining quality of essential items such as meat, in addition the continuous collections and rising Nazi terror', but no spirit of resistance. At most a building worker would grumble in a pub: 'I shit on the Third Reich, if I get only 57 pfennigs an hour, I prefer to be in Russia.' The workers on the Autobahn in Pomerania received only 51 pfennings an hour. In the Saar, after its return to Germany in 1935, the cost of living index rose by 20 to 25 per cent within a few weeks. A local mayor stated in 1936 that undeniably social distress existed among the miners who previously earned enough to get by; meat, eggs and fat were in short supply. A calculation of an expert in the Reich Chancery estimated the average wage at 25 marks a week, the deductions at 11 per cent. After paying for food, rent, heating and lighting there was virtually nothing left for clothes and better kinds of food such as eggs, cheese or vegetables.[26]

Naturally there was considerable dissatisfaction, which was duly noted by the authorities. In September 1934 the Cologne Gestapo recorded a distinct deterioration of the workers' mood, affecting not only former Marxists but even workers who stood for National Socialism. This was due to a continuous deterioration of working and living conditions and the never-ending price rises for food and articles of daily use. But the workers showed no interest in politics or hardly any. What moved them was the problem of daily bread. In the same month the Kassel Gestapo reported that, if the current price rises continued, broad sections of the people would show 'severe dissatisfaction'. Even now 'eruptions of unrest and discontent' could only be contained with difficulty; workers as well as artisans and small peasants discussed time and again the high salaries (that is, of the party bigwigs). In October the Aachen Gestapo stated that the general mood was badly affected by the price rises, especially of food, the difficulty of getting potatoes for the winter and their high price which the poor could not afford, and the feared rationing of food. In December Hanover wrote of 'severe depression' among the workers on account of the fixed minimum prices for agricultural produce, of growing hatred of the peasantry, and much dissatisfaction that the unemployed received their benefits plus help from the Winterhelp, so that they allegedly got more than employed workers. In the summer of 1935 unrest grew further because of new price rises of potatoes, vegetables, fruit, milk, eggs and butter.[27]

From Münster the Gestapo reported in April 1935 on much unrest among the workers on account of low wages, 'which to most workers on account of the food prices hardly guarantee a minimum of existence'. They considered the contributions to various organizations and the Winterhelp as being further deductions from their wages. The average weekly income of a textile worker came to only 20 marks, from which many still had to find the interest and amortization for their small houses acquired since the war. The governor of the Westphalian province wrote that many compared their meagre wages with the high salaries of leading officials and the allowances paid to the Nazi Reichstag deputies and others, and many talked again about the *Bonzen*. In June the Gestapo stated that the general mood made them fear 'the worst'; if no help came workers were murmuring about a hunger strike. The Kassel Gestapo found it 'intolerable' that mining and basalt workers working under most primitive conditions only received 'a starvation wage' of 12 to 13 marks a week. The wages paid to the Autobahn workers had no relation to the expenditure of strength, health and clothes and the additional food required.[28]

In August 1935 the Aachen Gestapo stated that many miners could not afford even the cheapest margarine and had to take bread, cabbage and potatoes as their nourishment into the mines. The low wages and the unsatisfactory living conditions made them lose confidence in the government, while certain categories of officials and party bosses need not cramp their style in any way. In Hanover it was found that 'only a very small part of the working class reached the minimum of existence'. The opinion was widespread that prices such as the present ones had never been asked previously. From Kassel it was reported early in 1936 that the men coming home from work were received by their women with complaints about high prices, for the women were 'plagued every hour by worry how to feed their men and children on the next day'.[29] Many similar reports exist from other parts of Germany. Yet there was no resistance to these intolerable conditions. Whatever strikes occurred were of short duration and were quickly settled. The old fighting spirit of the German workers was broken; terror and hunger kept them quiet. In 1935 even the Gestapo feared that the situation might become 'rather difficult in the winter',[30] but the fear did not materialize.

The passive mood of the workers was clearly reflected in the reports which the exiled SPD leaders received from inside Germany. Early in 1934 a comrade wrote from Berlin that, in his opinion, 'the depolitization and the absolute silence about the conditions was a result of the psychological pressure put upon the masses'. Considerable sections of the working class had been won over and the belief in Hitler was still surprisingly strong. A travel report said that not only was there no public opinion but no group opinion either; the individual was isolated, thinking and judging only for himself; there was a lack of political will and often a lack of character. In the summer of 1934 a report from Saxony said: 'The automatism with which the factory workers accept everything is frightening'; they only grumble when the dozens of collection lists and collectors appear. From the Ruhr it was written that the workers would not risk anything: 'whoever has work, however badly paid, wants to keep it on any account.' The indifferent workers – and that was the majority, especially in the Ruhr – largely believed in Hitler. The fact that through 'the creation of work' many unemployed obtained jobs, even if bad ones, impressed them a lot. In the autumn it was reported from Berlin that for workers who after long unemployment got work under more or less reasonable conditions, this overshadowed everything. They did not praise Hitler and still made critical remarks, 'but below this surface there is a passive, resigning acceptance of the political state of affairs'.[31]

At the beginning of 1935 the general mood was described as showing 'that the effects of the economic crisis on the worker's power of resistance were more devastating than was believed hitherto'. If someone after long unemployment got a job, 'he suddenly becomes timid . . . The National Socialists have not conquered the factories . . . But the National Socialists have destroyed the self-confidence of the working class, have buried the power of solidarity and paralysed the will of resistance'. From Bavaria it was reported that people had become accustomed to the state of affairs and, unless things got much worse, the writer did not believe that any danger threatened the regime from the workers. In some smaller works in the Chiemgau the workers' mood was not for Hitler nor positively for any other way: 'they let things take their course'.[32]

Early in 1936 a report from central Germany stated that even former members of the SPD or the *Reichsbanner* were saying: the Nazis have given us work. Although wages were low they need not sit passively at home and feel life was a burden: 'For me, it is all the same whether I make shells or build an Autobahn, I want to work. Why did you [meaning the socialists] not make a serious effort to create work?' From Bavaria it was said: people grumble about economic pressure and the enforced participation in parades and similar spectacles, on the other hand they recognize that Hitler has often done the right thing, for example abolished the small German states, taken action against the 'Blacks' (Catholic clergy) and energetic steps to create work; and even those who criticized quite vigorously approved of the regime's foreign policy. From the Palatinate it was reported in June that many workers had made their peace with Hitler and did not even bother to listen to foreign broadcasts. When an order was issued to hang out the flags they would quickly put out 'the rag'. Berlin workers, to justify their passive acceptance of the regime, would argue that there were also good sides to National Socialism and its leaders – even Hermann Göring, in spite of all his bad traits, had his advantages.[33]

In the summer of 1936 a report from Bavaria stated that the workers were much less interested in political developments than other social groups, and less critical towards them. 'Political indifference has reached frightening proportions in the proletariat. Even when one listens to political discussions among workers they usually show an incredible lack of knowledge of political events. The depolitization of the masses systematically fostered by the regime has made the greatest progress among the workers.' This was confirmed from south-west Germany: 'By far the larger part of the workers more and more lack any interest, what prevails is the politically indifferent who can always be used to a denunciation of his comrades.' They only agreed on one thing, that the wages were too low. Elsewhere, too, the workers were described as 'strongly depoliticized'. They 'work on their allotments, they collect stamps, but don't discuss anything, even in a familiar circle they spurn political discussions'. But when Robert Ley, the chief of the DAF, visited an Upper Silesian mine the miners did not respond to his 'Heil Hitler' whereupon he asked what the matter was. In reply, three workers declared that their work was heavy and their wages too low, all their approaches to the DAF having brought no result. A workers' delegation stated their complaints and Ley promised he would help them.[34]

This political indifference did not prevent individual workers from making unfavourable, spiteful remarks – a tendency which the Gestapo noted in 1935. But these remarks concerned economic matters which were discussed in factories, shops and pubs.[35] There was a lack of enthusiasm for the political offers of the regime and the features of Nazi propaganda. Anyhow, many workers were far too tired after long hours of work to go to meetings or take part in rallies. Their concerns were non-political: wages, food, prices and living conditions, which were bad enough. And they wanted to be left in peace.

There was much criticism, within the framework permitted by the Nazis, and many workers insisted on their 'rights' as equal members of the 'people's community'. When the management of an aerodrome under construction in Pomerania in the summer of 1935 gave a 'beach festival', the building workers were not invited and were strongly dissatisfied, especially because the fête took place under their very eyes. The well-known film of the Nuremberg party rally of the same year with its spectacular parades and searchlights, 'The Triumph of the Will', was criticized because it did not feature large work projects, such as labour on the Autobahn and in industry and agriculture. Therefore few workers went to see the film. It was criticized in general that unemployment was still too severe, that the 'emergency workers' employed on construction or melioration often received what a Pomeranian *Landrat* described as 'starvation wages', especially for men with a family. In another case from Pomerania the labour exchange sent men for work from a distance of ten miles and paid their fares, but the local people were unemployed.[36]

As the Cologne Gestapo put it in the spring of 1935: 'The worker carefully avoids criticizing publicly because he fears trouble of different kinds. But he proceeds in a clever way to criticize working methods, wages, etc. In working-class circles voices can often be heard declaring that capital has regained its power over the worker.' Indeed, the director of one of the largest German chemical firms, Glanzstoff, in his speech on MayDay 1935 praised the army as 'the best example existing in Germany' and spoke of 'non-commissioned officers of labour'.[37] What was needed in the works in his opinion was military discipline, orders to be carried out with military precision. The factory managers, promoted to 'enterprise leaders', were determined to keep the workers in their place.

In their disputes with the employers about piece rates, wages or working hours, the workers usually got no help from the NSBO and DAF representatives in the enterprise, either because they were too inexperienced or did not want to spoil their relations with the employer. From a textile factory in the Rhineland it was reported in 1936 that on such occasions workers with trade union experience tried to make the Nazi *Vertrauensrat* 'livid' and induced him to approach the employer. The latter showed the door to him and no help came from the DAF. Thus they could demonstrate how powerless the *Vertrauensrat* was, to the Nazis' disadvantage. In another textile factory the piece rates were reduced by 30 per cent, which meant 15 marks less in wages per week. The *Vertrauensrat* was bombarded with complaints and protested to the manager who chucked him out. Enfuriated he called a meeting which decided to take strike action. But then the manager negotiated with the old union factory councillors with the result that the former wages were restored: as the report said, it was a lesson given by the management and the union representatives.[38]

Characteristically, the workers frequently turned for advice and help to the Free union representatives in the factory. From the Munich railway shops it was reported in the summer of 1934 that socialists and unionists who had suffered victimization were respected and their advice was often asked. In a Berlin factory, on questions of wages and contracts the workers asked the old union councillor for information. He then sent them to the *Vertrauensrat* who was not well enough informed and in turn sent them back to the old unionist, even asking him to study recent changes in the contract. From north-west Germany it was recorded in 1935 that only the experienced union representatives were respected by their co-workers. To stress the difference between 'then' and 'now' they always gave information on labour law and social regulations and thus earned general respect. In Saxony, it was stated, the development of wages, leave, prices and workers' rights under Nazism taught the workers the importance of the work of the Free unions and what their loss meant. A Bremen shipwright remembered that the old unionists used to meet on the loo for discussions. Elsewhere the old factory councillors tried to continue their tasks and were considered their true representatives by their colleagues.[39] But of course local conditions varied a great deal.

The years 1934–1935 undoubtedly were a difficult period for the Nazi authorities in their relations with the workers. What helped them greatly was that there was not one single working class with its own organizations but that it was atomized. Even within a single factory, the different sections and compartments had very little knowledge of each other, and did not hear of militant action undertaken in a different compartment. When the workers met it was at what was significantly called a *Betriebsappell*, a semi-military rollcall, to receive instructions and to listen to appeals by one or the other Nazi bigwig. As we shall see, action was undertaken in one or the other enterprise, but it was hardly ever successful and usually on a very small scale. The workers had genuine grievances, but they were hamstrung by the ubiquitous terror, the fear of losing their jobs, and equally by lack of organization and the prevailing sense of apathy. The small underground groups were unable to take advantage of the situation and, had they tried to do so, would have been quickly liquidated. Working-class solidarity, insofar as it existed at all, was limited to small pockets in individual factory compartments or in small workers' settlements.

Notes

1. Eiber, *Arbeiter unter der NS-Herrschaft*, p. 110; *Deutschland-Berichte der Sozialdemokratischen Partei Deutschlands (Sopade)*, i 1934, pp. 29f., 208. These volumes contain the reports of the SPD frontier secretaries from 1934 to 1940, quoted henceforth as *Deutschland-Berichte*. There is a reprint of 1980.
2. Karl Otmar Freiherr von Aretin, *Nation, Staat und Demokratie in Deutschland*, Mainz, 1993, p. 225; Gunther Mai, 'Warum steht der deutsche Arbeiter zu Hitler?' *Geschichte und Gesellschaft*, xii 1986, p. 234.
3. Wolfgang E. Wicht, *Glanzstoff*, Neustadt/Aisch, 1992, pp. 202f.; Eiber, *Arbeiter*, p. 84; Mason, *Sozialpolitik*, pp. 245f.
4. Mlynek, *Gestapo Hannover*, p. 286; Bernhard Vollmer (ed.), *Volksopposition im Polizeistaat*, Stuttgart, 1957, pp. 95, 115: reports of October and November 1934 and January 1935.
5. Wisotzky, *Ruhrbergbau*, pp. 57ff., 63; Frese, *Betriebspolitik*, p. 80; Broszat, *Staat Hitlers*, p. 189.

6.   Klein, *Lageberichte*, p. 78; Joachim Kuropka, *Meldungen aus Münster 1924–1944*, Münster, 1992, pp. 259f.; Kratzenberg, *Arbeiter auf dem Weg*, pp. 141, 166; Mai, 'Nationalsozialistische Betriebszellenorganiation', p. 611.

7.   Gerhard Nitzsche, 'Deutsche Arbeiter im Kampf gegen faschistische Unterdrückung und Ausbeutung', *Beiträge Zur Geschichte der deutschen Arbeiterbewegung*, i 1959, p. 141; Gustav-Hermann Seebold, *Ein Stahlkonzern im Dritten Reich*, Wuppertal, 1981, p. 266; Hetzer, *Industriestadt Augsburg*, p. 116; Martin Rüther, 'Lage und Abstimmungsverhalten', p. 244; Kuropka, *Meldungen*, p. 162.

8.   Ibid., pp. 625ff.: Gestapo report for July 1934.

9.   Mason, *Sozialpolitik*, p. 185; Klaus-Michael Mallmann and Gerhard Paul, *Herrschaft und Alltag*, Bonn, 1991, pp. 141f.; Eiber, *Arbeiter*, p. 103; *Deutschland Berichte*, iii, 1936, no. 7, pp. 884f., iv, 1937, no. 10, p. 1700.

10.   Herbert, *Arbeiterschaft*, p. 337; *Deutschland-Berichte*, iv, 1937, no. 3, p. 316, iii, 1936, no. 7, p. 884.

11.   Ibid., ii, 1935, no. 4, p. 416; Michael Zimmermann, *Ausbruchshoffnungen*, in Lutz Niethammer (ed.), *'Die Jahre weiss man nicht, wo man die heute hinsetzen soll'*, Berlin–Bonn, 1983, p. 106; Dorn and Zimmermann, *Bewährungsprobe*, p. 113; Zimmermann, 'Ein schwer zu bearbeitendes Pflaster', p. 78.

12.   *Deutschland-Berichte*, ii 1935, no. 1, p. 37; Frese, *Betriebspolitik*, p. 178; Wolfgang Zollitsch, 'Die Vertrauensratswahlen von 1934 und 1935', *Geschichte und Gesellschaft*, xv 1989, pp. 371ff.; Klaus Mammach, *Widerstand 1933–1939*, Cologne, 1984, p. 89; Rüther, 'Lage und Abstimmungsverhalten', pp. 239, 245.

13.   Ibid., p. 236; Vollmer, *Volksopposition*, p. 198; Willi Bohn, *Stuttgart Geheim!* Frankfurt, 1978, p. 78.

14.   Frese, *Betriebspolitik*, pp. 202, 212–15, 217.

15.   Wisotzky, *Ruhrbergbau*, pp. 111f.; *Deutschland-Berichte*, iii, 1936, no. 1, p. 13, no. 12, p. 1591; *Bayern in der NS-Zeit*, i, p. 255; Martin Rüther, *Arbeiterschaft in Köln 1928–1945*, Cologne, 1990, pp. 254f.

16.   Peukert, *Volksgenossen*, pp. 70, 86; Klein, *Lageberichte*, p. 147; Vollmer, *Volksopposition*, p. 52; Eiber, *Arbeiter*, p. 110.

17.   *Deutschland-Berichte*, iii, 1936, no. 1, p. 16, no. 12, p. 1588, no. 4, p. 477; Vollmer, *Volksopposition*, p. 371.

18.   Ibid., p. 293; Ian Kershaw, 'Antisemitismus und Volksmeinung', *Bayern in der NS-Zeit*, ii, p. 291; Vollmer, *Volksopposition*, p. 69; Kuropka, *Meldungen*, p. 444.

19.   Mlynek, *Gestapo Hannover*, p. 315; Robert Thévoz, Hans Branig, Cécile Lowenthal-Hensel (eds), *Pommern 1934/35 im Spiegel von Gestapo-Lageberichten*, Cologne, 1974, p. 82; Kuropka, *Meldungen*, pp. 287f.

20.   Heyen, *Nationalsozialismus im Alltag*, p. 134: report for June 1935.

21.   Mlynek, *Gestapo Hannover*, pp. 261f.; Klein, *Lageberichte*, p. 242; *Deutschland-Berichte*, i, 1934, no. 6, p. 502, iii, 1936, no. 8, p. 966.

22.   Klein, *Lageberichte*, p. 99; Kuropka, *Meldungen*, p. 160; *Deutschland-Berichte*, ii, 1935, no. 8, pp. 953, 956ff.

23.   Rüther, *Arbeiterschaft in Köln*, p. 237; *Deutschland-Berichte*, ii, 1935, no. 11, p. 1271; Peukert, *KPD im Widerstand*, p. 214.

24.   Wisotzky, *Ruhrbergbau*, pp. 87f.; Peukert, *Volksgenossen*, p. 63; Peukert

and Frank Bajohr, *Spuren des Widerstands*, Munich, 1987, p. 164; Mason, *Sozialpolitik*, p. 150; Klein, *Lageberichte*, p. 322.

25. Ulrich Schüren, 'Rahmenbedingungen für den Widerstand', in *Widerstand und Exil der deutschen Arbeiterbewegung 1933–1945*, Bonn, 1982, pp. 201, 208; Rüther, 'Lage und Abstimmungsverhalten', p. 233; Mlynek, *Gestapo Hannover*, p. 117; Paul Stoop (ed.), *Geheimberichte aus dem Dritten Reich*, Berlin, 1990, p. 185.

26. Eiber, *Arbeiter*, pp. 88, 97f., 111, 122; Thévoz, Branig *et al.*, *Pommern*, p. 39; Mallmann and Paul, *Herrschaft und Alltag*, pp. 47f.; Mason, *Sozialpolitik*, p. 165.

27. Rüther, *Arbeiterschaft in Köln*, p. 235; Klein, *Lageberichte*, pp. 161f.; Vollmer, *Volksopposition*, pp. 94, 123; Mlynek, *Gestapo Hannover*, p. 273.

28. Kuropka, *Meldungen*, pp. 153, 156, 269; Wisotzky, *Ruhrbergbau*, p. 88; Klein, *Lageberichte*, pp. 274, 312.

29. Vollmer, *Volksopposition*, p. 256; Mlynek, *Gestapo Hannover*, pp. 415, 471; Klein, *Lageberichte*, p. 373.

30. Vollmer, *Volksopposition*, p. 256.

31. *Deutschland-Berichte*, i, 1934, no. 1, pp. 12, 29, no. 2, pp. 120, 208, no. 4, p. 429, no. 7, p. 666.

32. Ibid., ii, 1935, no. 1, p. 137, no. 9, p. 1076.

33. Ibid., iii, 1936, no. 2, pp. 156f., no. 3, p. 307, no. 6, p. 673, no. 4, p. 480.

34. Ibid., iii, 1936, no. 7, pp. 829, 838, no. 12, p. 1563, no. 9, p. 1166.

35. Peukert, *Volksgenossen*, pp. 56, 70, 132; Bohn, *Stuttgart Geheim*! p. 77.

36. Thévoz, Branig *et al.*, *Pommern*, pp. 63, 127, 171; Mason, *Sozialpolitik*, p. 127.

37. Rüther, *Arbeiterschaft in Köln*, p. 201; Wicht, *Glanzstoff*, p. 165.

38. *Deutschland-Berichte*, iii, 1936, no. 1, p. 86, no. 9, p. 1170.

39. Ibid., i, 1934, no. 5, pp. 432f.; ii, 1935, no. 1, p. 37, no. 11, p. 1311; Michael Voges, 'Klassenkampf in der "Betriebsgemeinschaft" ', *Archiv für Sozialgeschichte*, xxi 1981, p. 357; Marssolek and Ott, *Bremen*, p. 154; Frese, *Betriebspolitik*, p. 88.

CHAPTER FOUR

The hazards of opposition

There was not only apathy and indifference but also considerable opposition. Apart from the small underground groups which continued their activities, there was a good deal of spontaneous resistance and local strike activity. These were limited in time and size: one construction site, one factory compartment, one small enterprise. They lasted usually a few hours or at most a day or two, and many were unsuccessful and terminated by punitive measures.[1] But at a time when all strikes were declared illegal they showed that the old spirit of working-class militancy was still alive. What we know about them comes from police reports or those of the exiled SPD leaders, for nothing about them was published in the press.

Strikes occurred in particular among workers engaged on public works, the construction of roads, stretches of Autobahn or barrage dams. They were paid miserable wages, housed in barracks away from home and badly fed. In the autumn of 1934 unemployed men from Berlin were doing roadwork near Bremen. Their wives were to receive ten marks a week but in reality only got six. The workers themselves were paid at the weekend 3.70 marks after all deductions. When their protests met with no success they downed tools and were taken under escort to Berlin police headquarters. At the labour exchange they were treated as refusing work and all benefits were blocked. In November 30 workers on an Autobahn site in Franconia went on strike because they were not given travelling money. They were threatened with arrest and concentration camp but defiantly sang the 'Internationale', whereupon 20 of them were sent as 'work-shy' to the Dachau concentration camp. In October more than 200 men employed on a barrage site in the Rhineland refused work because their wages, after all deductions, amounted to less than their earlier benefits. When this was changed and the wages were increased to 2.50 marks above the benefits the refusal continued. The workers argued that even members of the NSDAP declined to work on that site. Those refusing to work lost their claim to benefit for an unstated time.[2]

In March 1934 two short strikes occurred at Ruhr mines because the management had taken measures against National Socialists. In one case a Nazi official employed at the mine attacked the 'profit greed' of the employers because they did not offer jobs to the unemployed and was sent on leave – whereupon the miners refused to go down the pit until he was reinstated. This the *Treuhänder* did but he also imposed a fine on the miners for the Winterhelp scheme. In the other case a foreman was moved for alleged faults in his work. To get this rescinded the *Vertrauensrat* prepared strike action. The speech of its chairman pleading for work peace was constantly interrupted by shouts demanding action; but the movement ended without success when a representative of the DAF hierarchy appeared and work was resumed. At a third mine a vote was prepared as to whether the miners were willing to continue work under the existing management; the meeting ended in uproar and the Gestapo intervened. Actions initiated by the *Vertrauensräte* were very exceptional as they usually cooperated closely with the employers.[3]

In 1935 there were more strikes. In the spring about 400 glass-grinders at a firm in Pirmasens in the Palatinate, who earned only 10 to 13 marks a week for 48 hours' work, struck for three days after fruitless negotiations. Nobody said 'strike' but everybody knew what it was. When the wages of the herring picklers in Emden were reduced from 42 to 38 pfennigs a ton, the women workers adopted a policy of passive resistance – they came but did not work. As the fish threatened to go bad the old wages were restored. In the summer the Gestapo reported small strikes of construction workers in East Prussia and Thuringia for higher wages as well as sabotage on an aerodrome near Potsdam. In the autumn there were eight similar reports from building sites all over Germany, again involving small numbers, in the largest case 60 'emergency workers'. In one instance three workers were arrested for collecting signatures against a decision of the *Treuhänder*, in others they refused to work ten hours or to do overtime. The workers of one Silesian firm declined to listen in the lunch hour to a Hitler speech, apparently without serious consequences.[4]

In June 'emergency workers' employed to build a Germanic memorial in Heidelberg declined to work at night and demanded 30 per cent more for overtime. As the memorial had to be ready by a certain date their demand was conceded. Less successful were the workers of a cut-glass factory in Bavaria where the skilled workers earned only 12 marks and the unskilled 6 to 7 marks a week. When the manager refused their demand for higher wages the workers, including 17 SA members, went on strike. The DAF spokesman threatened them with the Dachau concentration camp, but one worker replied among cheers that they would be given bread and water there, and that was exactly what they got at home. But the threats achieved that work was resumed after three days.[5] These few cases demonstrate that not all strikes in the Third Reich were unsuccessful, that if work was urgent the demands would be met against all the inclinations of the authorities. In some cases, but by no means all, the presence of Communists among the workers or the distribution of Communist leaflets were mentioned, but this was rather exceptional. It hardly needed Communist propaganda to mobilize the workers against intolerably low wages.

More and larger strikes occurred in 1936. Early in the year about 200 workers of a leather factory in Worms stopped work for four hours because their piece rates were to be cut. The DAF promised its help and asked for silence 'because such methods might set an example elsewhere'. In Chemnitz the electrowelders of the Auto-Union suspended work for three days because the firm did not keep its promise to improve their conditions, and they gained a bonus. A lowering of the piece rates caused a strike in a compartment of about 150 men in another Saxon firm producing aviation motors. The men refused to resume work when told that their action was directed against the state, and all were dismissed. Some were arrested but others soon found new jobs on account of the shortage of skilled workmen. In June a strike broke out in the Opel factory near Mainz affecting about 300 men whose piece rates were to be cut. The strikers were arrested and 260 of them given immediate notice. When the Gestapo discussed the case it was said that the strike had 'considerable political importance', had created 'a certain feeling of martyrdom' and furthered among the Opel workers 'a spirit of solidarity'. The authorities became frightened when Communist slogans were found written in the works toilets and Communist leaflets appeared a few days later. The Gestapo was convinced that the strike had long been prepared by Communist agitators and it decided to infiltrate its agents among the Opel workers. The dismissed workers complained to a labour court but it decided to reject the plea on the grounds that their action was directed against the people's community.[6]

Other strikes concerned not the relatively well-paid skilled workers but 'emergency workers' employed on construction sites. In July 350 of them went on strike on a military aerodrome in the Saar because they earned less than unemployment benefit and their leaders were arrested. In Hesse ten workers engaged on a melioration project struck because their wages were too low for the dirty and wet work. Near Nuremberg 15 men working on the Autobahn were arrested because they tried to enforce the rehiring of a worker dismissed for disobedience. In Augsburg a worker was arrested because he tried to urge his colleagues to strike against his dismissal. So was a former Communist because he provoked a strike in a brick-kiln on account of bad weather and whistled the 'Internationale'. Near Koblenz 13 'emergency workers', among them some SA men, struck for two days for better wages. On a construction site of the *Luftwaffe* near Königsberg 25 men missed work one day because they were soaked through by rain. On an Autobahn site near Stuttgart 38 men left work and simply went home. On other sites six workers declined to do a nightshift (presumably because they did not get extra pay); 11 workers near Kassel, and near Dessau 16 building workers refused work because of wage differences. Workmen sent from Silesia to East Prussia returned home because they had to leave their families behind and the wages were lower than in Silesia, where they later engaged in 'foul slander'.[7] All these and other small conflicts were carefully recorded.

Two hundred men at a textile factory in Saxony struck because the management wanted to impose a wage cut of 25 per cent. Mediation by the DAF achieved that the cut was limited to 10 per cent and work was resumed on the following day. In the summer of 1936 there were reports about strikes of agricultural workers in Saxony and in East Prussia. Twelve Upper Silesian men and women refused to work on a noble estate near Halle because of low wages. Ten of them restarted work after two days, the other two went home. In Neuss in the Rhineland three workers were arrested because they collected signatures against the DAF among their colleagues, made propaganda against a decision of the *Treuhänder* and so disturbed the 'work-peace' of the National Radiator Works.[8]

Altogether a total of 179 labour conflicts were recorded for 1936, with a peak in July and fewer during the winter months. But only ten involved between 51 and 100 men, and only nine more than 100; few lasted longer than one day. Most were on a small scale but they worried the authorities of the Third Reich and proved that not all was well on the labour side. When the Opel strike was discussed in the Reich Ministry of Economics the reporter stressed that 1936 had seen more strikes and labour conflicts than the previous years, and he criticized the DAF as well as the *Treuhänder* because they often misjudged the situation and did not take the 'correct' measures to 'unravel' the conflict.[9] He did not say whether the 'correct' measures meant simply calling in the Gestapo or whether he had other measures in mind.

There were very few cases of sabotage of production and, interestingly enough, the one definite case of 1936 occurred at the Opel works, a few weeks after the strike and the mass arrests. There at night a room used to deposit motors was inundated with hoses and cables were cut. About 200 motors made for the army were rendered useless. At fortification works in central Germany an attempt was made to add dissolvants to the cement mixture, but that could easily have been due to negligence. The explosion of an oil cauldron in an Augsburg factory on the day of the Rhineland occupation probably had nothing to do with that event, and no sabotage could be proved.[10] Sabotage was not a weapon the German workers were accustomed to and was very rare even during the war years.

Apart from strikes and sabotage small acts of defiance occurred, either by courageous individuals or by small groups, or what was construed as defiance by the ever watchful authorities. In Hamburg an elementary school teacher refused to render the Hitler salute when the Nazi flag was raised. Thereupon the headmaster told her that, if she repeated the refusal, an SA man would be posted behind her and would kick her with his boot until she 'saluted decently'. In 1935 an Autobahn worker in Bavaria complained to a co-worker that in the old Reich he had had work but when the Third Reich came he lost it, otherwise he would still have his job in a porcelain factory and need not slave on the Autobahn; military conscription was only introduced to prepare for the coming war. He was sent to prison for two months. From Kassel the Gestapo reported in 1934 that in the old town discussion groups or clubs could be observed as in the old days. There they argued time and again that the wages were hardly higher than unemployment benefit and that the National Socialists had not fulfilled their promise: 'No official (to earn) more than a thousand marks a month as long as one German is unemployed.' The Gestapo also observed that in the district of Schmalkalden the workers no longer gave anything to the collections and that little or nothing could be raised in the countryside: people insisted that first the church conflict must be ended.[11]

Not only the 'Internationale' but the singing of other 'Marxist fighting songs' figured in police reports. In May 1933 a policeman reported that near Bremen a unit of the Labour Service had sung 'When we march side by side and sing the old songs . . .'. At a finishing celebration of emergency works near Hanover in 1934 a worker played on his mouthorgan 'We are the working men, the proletariat' which some others sang with him. When arrested it turned out that the player had joined the *Stahlhelm* in 1933 and with it was transferred to the SA. In a small town near Nuremberg the workers of a wood factory in 1934 refused to march behind the flag to see a film about the Nazi hero Horst Wessel who was murdered by Communists; only four men appeared and the visit was abandoned. In another small town the unemployed congregated daily in front of the labour exchange to have discussions 'not exactly suitable for the ears of the Gestapo'. In a small town in Baden nine workers were arrested in 1935 because they induced their colleagues to demonstrate in front of the town hall and the mayor's house to demand payment for New Year's Day.[12]

More fortunate were the workers of a building site in the Ruhr who were ordered to do unpaid holiday work. They marched to the DAF office and demanded repayment of their contributions because, they declared, they had not joined to be shat upon and their dues were duly repaid. The miners of a mine on the lower Rhine were informed in 1935 that they would have to give 20 per cent of their wage tax for the Winterhelp; of 4000 men 370 refused to comply. They were sharply reprimanded by the manager and threatened with dismissal, whereupon the large majority caved in; two declined and were dismissed. In a Bavarian armaments factory the specialized workers of one compartment who had worked in the firm for many years declined to render the Hitler salute and opposed the many deductions for the DAF and the Winterhelp. Then the DAF in the autumn of 1935 announced the obligatory use of the Hitler salute but the men agreed to continue the old form of greeting. The manager asked them to obey but nothing changed. As the firm could not do without these workers they were left alone. At Siemens in Berlin it was announced that in future wages would be paid monthly instead of weekly, which meant a small loss because of larger deductions. Due to strong opposition the order was rescinded after a few weeks. On an Autobahn site in northern Bavaria the workers' mood became more and more critical. If a new worker gave the Hitler salute he would not be spoken to for days and no one would react to his greeting. On other sites open criticism of the regime could be heard daily. The opinion heard only too often was 'the bloody swindle must finish soon'. In the Junkers aviation works at Dessau 285 workmen were arrested in the years 1933–35, not on account of any illegal activity but because of criticism, spreading of rumours, etc. In the years 1934–36 the Munich Special Court tried 1127 cases of *Heimtücke*, the large majority of them not belonging to any political group.[13]

Occasionally the true mood of the workers emerged when they had to listen to a Hitler speech. Before the 'elections' of 1936 the workers of Blohm & Voss in Hamburg were told they would only receive their pay after listening to a radio transmission of his speech at Krupp's. There was much unrest because the workers who stopped work at 3 p.m. were not permitted to leave. First singly, then in unison they shouted 'We have hunger, we want our wages!' At 5.15 the wage windows were opened and there was no retribution. At the Bavarian Motor Works in Munich all employees had to go to a large hall to hear the same speech, and there was no applause. The men stood at the back of the hall and took no notice of what happened in front; the mood was 'icy', a participant reported. In the same factory later in 1936 the workers again had to listen to Hitler, and the gates were locked. During the speech the workers talked to each other, so that order had to be kept by SA men. When strong applause was heard through the radio the workers, assuming it was the end, demanded the gates to be opened and pushed through when the porters obliged, and even used the windows to get out. In a factory at Kiel the workers listened to a speech by a Nazi orator without showing any feeling, with their hands in their pockets. Even before he finished they turned to leave. As a retribution some were to be dismissed, but in an armaments factory all highly qualified men were needed – until finally one victim was found who was not so well qualified.[14]

In a compartment of the AEG in Berlin all workers refused to sign a form asking for a deduction of 10 per cent of their wage tax for the benefit of the Winterhelp. When a Nazi functionary asked one or the other man for his reason the reply was 'too little wage!' And the same happened apparently in other Berlin factories. In a large electrical firm groups of politically conscious men would act jointly without prior consultation. If one or two Nazis turned up in such a group their life was made as difficult as possible: the man is useless, his work is faulty, etc. This went on until the man in question either stopped work or was discharged. In another Berlin factory the men would look a Nazi over very carefully – if he did not conform he would be isolated. Even SA men would fit in and adopt this common attitude. But solidarity could not develop because of the spy-system maintained by the firm. Another large firm hired a metal-stamper sent by the DAF. Shortly after his arrival several men were interrogated by the police on account of critical remarks made by them. It was not long before the new man complained to the management that his colleagues annoyed him as much as they could and created constant difficulties for him. Three men were arrested but nothing could be proved. A week later a large piece of metal hit the head of the new worker and he was incapacitated for three weeks. It was also noted, however, that when defensive action was taken in a factory compartment the other workers had no idea that a strike had occurred elsewhere in the factory.[15] The compartments and the workers within them were isolated.

Yet, surprisingly, the Gestapo noted that what they termed a *Hetzvers* (hate verse) in 1936 turned up simultaneously in Berlin, Leipzig, and Karlsruhe in the south:

> Hitler without woman,
> Peasant without pig,
> Butcher without meat,
> That is the Third Reich.[16]

Against this kind of 'mouth propaganda' the Gestapo was powerless.

On the other hand it was reported from a Saxon factory that the women who were opposed to Hitler were spat upon by their co-workers who declared that whoever voted 'No' in a plebiscite should be put against a wall and shot.[17] That was certainly an exception, and so was the opposite. In some large enterprises the workers remained passively anti-Nazi. The MAN at Augsburg had a workforce of 4500 men who were 'not pro-Nazi. The workers are rather indifferent or, better put, they give way under pressure'. On the Friday before the plebiscite of 19 August 1934 they were ordered to listen to Hitler, and the porters not to let anyone leave; all the gates were closed excepts for a side gate, but the workers themselves succeeded in opening the gates and soon the yards were almost empty. The motor works of the 'Hanomag' at Hanover, according to the Gestapo, had a workforce consisting largely of Social Democrats and Communists who held most of the posts of master and foreman. If someone offered the Hitler salute the answer was *Guten Tag*. Nazi workers were treated badly. In December 1934 cyclists distributed hundreds of Communist leaflets at the factory gates which were picked up by the workers. But when the police checked soon after, only ten copies could be found; none were surrendered voluntarily and the police search met opposition.[18]

Stronger still was opposition on some of the Bremen wharfs. In 1935 a local Nazi official reported to his party on the 'Weser AG': if a worker dared to use the Hitler salute it met with 'icelike rejection by at least 90 per cent', the man in question would experience 'the greatest difficulties' and suffer victimization. 'I have so far not seen anyone who dares to come to work in the brown SA trousers', the report added. When the cruiser *Scharnhorst* was launched in 1934 in the pressence of Hitler, the large majority did not join in the singing of the 'Horst-Wessel Song'. On another wharf with a complement of 2500 men, only 250 attended a meeting convened for the *Vertrauensrat* elections of 1935; when a second meeting was held the figure shrank to 200. These were enterprises with old socialist and union traditions and very highly qualified workers. But how quickly opposition could disintegrate was shown by the example of another Bremen wharf. When the DAF started a campaign for a Reich Enterprise Competition the old trade unionists decided that it had nothing to do with them, and no one would participate. This was repeated in the following year. But then an old unionist and former factory councillor did take part – and was promoted. 'That meant of course the end in the compartment . . . They all changed sides, and one could only talk with two or three men', as one former shipwright remembered.[19] It was difficult to withstand the blandishments of the regime: there were too many opportunists.

The outbreak of the Spanish civil war in 1936 gave new encouragement to the opposition. Many German Communists and others went to Spain to join the International Brigades, and the events were discussed in many factories. The workers' sympathies were with the

Republic, while the Nazis sided openly with Franco. From Munich it was reported that people realized: 'in Spain a decisive battle is waged, of great importance to us Germans', that the workers again took courage, that some who for years had not taken part in political discussions now participated, that foreign radio stations were eagerly listened to. But it was feared at the same time that Hitler and Mussolini by their deceptions would 'prevent the Western powers, in particular France, from supporting the legitimate government effectively, while they would always find ways and means to provide the Nationalist side with troops and material'. When guns and shells for Franco were loaded at Hamburg, small hand-bills were distributed: 'No arms for Franco!' and 'Long live the freedom struggle of the Spanish people!' In a Bremen armaments factory the workers siding with the Republic were betrayed, as were the women in the Berlin Osram works who collected money for the Republican side. In Hamburg a conductor of the Mitropa company was caught with a large sum given by railwaymen from Hamburg and Altona. In the Waldenburg mining area and in central Germany more money was collected, as it was in Berlin by men who even went from door to door. When a DAF speaker in December 1936 addressed a meeting on the events in Spain in a small Bavarian town he was interrupted by shouts 'Don't lie, keep to the truth' and similar remarks. Even some *Vertrauensräte* kept quiet when workers expressed their sympathies with the Spanish government.[20] The disappointment was all the greater when the Republic lost its battle and Franco slowly triumphed.

The years 1934–35 saw the largest extension of the underground network of the SPD, usually formed around readers of the *Sozialistische Aktion*. According to one estimate, perhaps 2–300,000 men and women read it and discussed its contents. A recipient in Berlin suggested that each reader should make a little pinhole in his copy; when it came back to him it had 216 holes. The exiled leaders estimated that the party early in 1934 had 300 groups in Germany with about 20,000 members. This did not mean a tight organization such as the Communists time and again tried to build, but rather loose circles of friends and colleagues, small clubs and readers of the paper. But then mass arrests set in and destroyed the large majority of the networks. What remained were the innumerable little clubs and circles, the *Stammtische* of old friends who met to play Skat and drink beer, who sang or played instruments, or who found suitable cover in a 'bourgeois' sports club.[21] As the Stuttgart Gestapo stated in August 1935, they 'form only small and smallest groups and circles, which have no links above and below ... What has generally taken place is getting together in clubs, on outings, in bathing places and in the country, in small groups to

exchange news, the cultivation of old connections through personal
visits and meetings in factories'.[22]

While in 1933 many Social Democrats believed that the Hitler regime
could not possibly last long, later a more realistic attitude began to
prevail. From Saxony the exiled leaders were informed in 1935 that
they did not believe in a counter-movement due to the suppression of
free opinion. If things continued 'normally' they would have to reckon
with a longer duration, that is, several years; unless something unexpected occurred one would have to adopt a 'long perspective'.[23] This
point was vital for the underground organization. If a long perspective
prevailed, it was essential to form small cadres, to train them properly
and to avoid any 'mass' activity. In south-west Germany this issue
caused strong political differences and a virtual split. Emil Henk and
Otto Calvi formed a strong network covering several towns and rejected
the course advocated by the Prague leaders, pleading for small, well-
trained groups linked by couriers, an élite to lead the masses if the
regime was destabilized. They found the apparatus directed from Prague
too slow and cumbersome and technically backward, and they strongly
criticized the policy advocated by their frontier secretary. There were
heated discussions and, after a conference held in September 1934 in
St Gallen, it came to a split. The Henk–Calvi group broke with the
leaders in Prague and began to cooperate in Mannheim with the SAP
while remaining separate. In the autumn, however, a courier had an
accident in the Palatinate, the police found leaflets and other material,
and Henk and many others were arrested.[24]

In Bavaria the same development occurred. At Whitsun 1934 two
young emissaries from Augsburg, Bebo Wager and Eugen Nerdinger,
went to see the frontier secretary, von Knoeringen, in Bohemia and in
their discussions informed him and the other frontier secretary, Hans
Dill, that at first a small organization must be formed which could
analyse the situation in Germany and 'use the experience in a socialist
sense'. There were sharp controversies. Dill favoured a mass organization and wide methods of agitation but did not succeed in overcoming
the Bavarians' opposition 'to the old form of Social Democracy'. Knoeringen, on the other hand, who had meanwhile established contact to
the *Neu Beginnen* group, strongly sided with the visitors and encouraged them to organize a small group in Augsburg. But there the new
ideas were opposed by activists of the *Reichsbanner* who wanted a
broad organization and distrusted the ideas put forward by former SAJ
leaders. For the plebiscite of August 1934 stickers to vote 'No' were
distributed in Augsburg, but the leaders of the smaller group insisted
they should be given only to reliable Social Democrats. The police
found only seven of the stickers. Criticism of the Prague leaders and

their 'open' methods was fairly common. At a meeting of group leaders from Düsseldorf and Cologne in the north to Stuttgart in the south, held in March 1935, the delegate of the Hanover 'Socialist Front' rejected what came from Prague and repudiated all contacts with it, while others present were less radical in their attitude.[25] Many were convinced that the old methods simply would not work.

Distrust also existed of the Communists and their ever repeated efforts to create a 'united front' which were redoubled after the Seventh World Congress of Comintern in 1935. In the spring the SPD received a report from Westphalia that it was out of the question to negotiate with Communist organizations with the aim of common underground work in Germany. Whoever did so outside the country 'must know he has no mandate to do so from any existing underground socialist group'. They would not let themselves be misused 'as objects of Russian foreign policy and as an advertisement of Russian party policy'. They rejected any cooperation with hard-line Communists but desired a united front under their own leadership of Communists of good will as well as Christian workers who were 'longing for the end of servitude'; the Communists who joined them were fed up with the KPD and Comintern. A few months later it was reported that the underground Social Democrats rejected the Communist slogan to join the Nazi mass organizations (such as DAF) and to disrupt them from within. They say whoever has to participate in this all the time 'is no longer with us', but 'whoever is with us simply cannot stand it, it must sicken him too much'.[26]

In November 1935 two SPD leaders met two of the KPD in Prague but the discussion brought no result. Cooperation with the KPD, the SPD leaders found, would weaken their position because the Nazis could claim that the SPD had gone over to Bolshevism; this would drive those 'who were prepared to put their confidence in a Social Democracy clearly pledged to democracy once more to the right'. In January 1936 the exiled SPD leaders once more discussed the attempts of the KPD to reach agreement about common actions. Some days before they discovered in the SPD group in Prague a Communist cell which conducted its work 'according to all the rules of Communist disintegration'. The members of the cell were instructed in their work not to appear as Communists but always as 'leftwing Social Democrats' or as 'revolutionary Socialists'. The SPD leaders directed the frontier secretaries and other party representatives 'to refuse any organizational connection with Communists and in particular any agreements and arrangements with Communist spokesmen or organizations', and the same principle was to be observed in meetings with comrades from inside Germany.[27] In view of the well-known Communist tactics of using any cooperation to win recruits for their own party and to undermine the other, this negative attitude was easily understandable. There also was a fully justified fear that the KPD groups were often riddled with Gestapo spies or that arrested Communists had been 'turned round'.

Many Social Democrats tried to uphold the party's traditions, whether this was the celebration of MayDay (not in the Nazi form) or visits to the graves of dead leaders. On All Saints' Day 1934 thousands visited the graves of Wilhelm Liebknecht, Paul Singer and Hugo Haase in Berlin, walking silently along the gravesides, but 18 who deposited flowers were arrested. Twelve months after the murder of a *Reichsbanner* man in Bremen, a large demonstration took place at his grave and a wreath was deposited with the words 'Not all are dead who have died, for they can't kill the spirit'. On the next day arrests began. On Ascension Day 1934 thousands met in Hamburg at the grave of the murdered Reichstag deputy Adolph Biedermann. The *Reichsbanner* leader Karl Ruggaber from Württemberg had been sent to a concentration camp early in 1933; when he was released many months later he was close to death. At his funeral in January 1936 1500 of his comrades assembled and the speeches contained hidden threats to the regime. Later funerals also attracted large crowds of sympathizers.[28] It was difficult to prevent such silent demonstrations, but anyone making a speech or depositing flowers ran the risk of arrest. The closeness of the Social-Democratic milieu made large crowds assemble almost spontaneously, as long as this was not prevented by brute force.

In 1935 the underground SPD groups suffered waves of arrests which in many cases meant the end of their active work. Often the mass arrests were due to the distribution of the *Sozialistische Aktion* or of stickers and leaflets. The groups were also not immune to infiltration by the police. In Munich, the 'Red Rebels' – like many other groups – put up stickers for the plebiscite of August 1934. The Gestapo let them act so as to discover their whole net; the link to the emigration, a dining car waiter, was the brother of a police official. In April 1935 all were arrested. In Hamburg, mass arrests of SPD and SAJ members took place from the end of 1934 which continued into 1936 and later. In Frankfurt, a courier in 1935 lost from his motorbike folders with addressed numbers of the *Sozialistische Aktion* and most members of the group were arrested in October. In Stuttgart, one of the leaders was arrested in the same year but succeeded in escaping and sought help from a friend in Mannheim. A parked motorcycle led the Gestapo on the right track to a flat where they found the escaped man. On the same day another comrade was to be met at Ludwigshafen station with material ready for distribution. When no one came to meet him he simply went to the flat which was just being raided by the Gestapo. He had on him well over a thousand copies of *Sozialistische Aktion* and 3000 leaflets 'Down with Hitler!' More arrests virtually destroyed the whole SPD network in the area of Mannheim. In Upper Franconia Social Democrats were arrested in the summer of 1935 and the party's work came to an end.[29]

The most fateful action undertaken against the underground SPD was that against the bread factory 'Germania' in Duisburg, simply because it covered such a wide area and employed so many Social Democrats. Interrogations soon confirmed that the *Sozialistische Aktion* was delivered everywhere with the loaves. More than a thousand people were arrested, the first in April 1935, from Aachen to Cologne and throughout Westphalia, especially the drivers and their assistants. Several died under inhuman tortures. A chain of mass trials took place at the regional court in Hamm and heavy 'treason' sentences were imposed. The result was the almost complete destruction of the SPD organization on the Rhine and Ruhr from which it could not recover. In Hanover too, mass arrests virtually destroyed the organization of the 'Socialist Front'. A spy succeeded in penetrating to the top of the group, but the leader, Werner Blumenberg, became suspicious, followed him and then escaped just in time. Some of the arrested were deceived by fictitious interrogation protocols according to which Blumenberg too was arrested and would be confronted with them, and much was revealed.[30]

In November 1935 the Hanover Gestapo complained that many former SPD members had collected in clubs which outwardly were quite inoffensive, such as co-ops and a League of Families with many Children. In Hannoversch-Münden there had been a public mass protest against a houseowner who refused to let a flat to such a family: an event reminding them of 'past Marxist methods'. They also noted the activities of former working-class choirs which had restarted in their old composition and become centres of 'Marxist agitation and calumniation'. In April 1935 a concert of the *Berliner Singgemeinschaft* took place. 'One thought to know everybody and in fact recognized many comrades whom one had not seen in such numbers for many years', one of those present remembered:

> And those whom we did not know personally we recognized never-theless: we all came from the different corners of the labour movement . . . We simply knew that we were among ourselves, we still belonged together . . . I surely was not the only one who had tears of grief and fury in his eyes. At that moment we regained courage, not only to wait until the brown nightmare had passed but to do something against it . . . We left the concert differently from the way we had come, we had regained a little courage.[31]

If the Gestapo looked suspiciously at the workers' choirs, the suspicion was justified. With all major socialist groups destroyed and the members safely behind bars, it was in societies such as these that something of the old subculture and a feeling of solidarity survived.

In the autumn of 1936 a report from inside Germany described the situation:

> Many from time to time give something for the prisoners, i.e. for support of their families. Many gladly read the literature, but it is a different matter to help distributing it. Nearly all think that something ought to be done, but many believe it too dangerous for themselves for one reason or another.[32]

Given the enormous risk, that attitude was understandable, and what could the small underground groups achieve against the might of the Nazi regime?

Loosely linked to the SPD were the organizations of Free unions which were supported by the international trade union federations to which the German unions had belonged. The most important of them was the International Transportworkers Federation (ITF) which had its seat in Amsterdam and from the outset adopted a totally uncompromising attitude towards the Hitler regime. In the spring of 1933 its journal, *ITF*, wrote:

> In Germany, absolute, brutal, remorseless fascist dictatorship prevails today. With German thoroughness ... Meanwhile there can be but one line of action for the ITF with regard to the present regime in Germany: fight without quarter. As the ITF has fought and still fights the black plague in Italy, so it will have to make war with all the means at its disposal on the brown plague in Germany.

In September 1933 the manager of the ITF office, Jacobus Oldenbroek, went to Germany to meet Hans Jahn, a leading official of the railwaymen's union who told him of his 'desperate efforts ... to stir the German trade union movement to activity'. Jahn had even offered to abscond with some union funds but was overruled by other officials who wished 'that the Nazis should find everything in order when they came'. Jahn told Oldenbroek he was building a network throughout Germany with contacts in many stations, workshops and depots in Berlin and that he had secured the address material of his union. Oldenbroek continued his journey to Stettin to meet Wilhelm Voss, leader of the Pomeranian sections of the sailors' union who, like Jahn, had seized the addresses to prevent them from falling into NSBO hands. In Leipzig, Franz Poralla undertook to contact all important officials of the railwaymen's union in Saxony but found only 14 willing to cooperate. As one of them wrote later, many 'resigned or for opportunist reasons joined the ranks of the Nazis. Every walk through the town or an office became agony. Seldom that a colleague found courage to exchange a few free words in the street. The friend of yesterday became the enemy of today.'[33] Such were the difficulties facing people who refused to knuckle under.

Jahn and Voss became travelling salesmen so that they could travel 'on business' over a wide area. Soon they established links in many towns, mainly with former officials of the railwaymen's union. When Oldenbroek visited Germany again he stressed in his meetings with trade unionists, that the regime could not be overthrown from one day to the next and that a long view must be adopted. In 1934–35 Jahn met representatives of the illegal union in many towns, from Hamburg and Bremen in the north to Augsburg and Nuremberg in the south. In 1935 he spoke in Duisburg about the aims and tasks of the union. His work was strongly supported by Edo Fimmen, the ITF secretary, a robust and powerful Dutchman, who did more than anyone else in the international labour movement to support the German opposition. He did not want any complicated theoretical programmes but to link the efforts to the spontaneous trade unionist impulses of the ordinary workmen. The ITF material printed in Holland was smuggled into Germany in large quantities, in railway wagons or onboard ships sailing up the Rhine. Exactly as with the *Sozialistische Aktion* and the Communist material, the very quantities smuggled created a dangerous situation.[34]

This applied equally to an international transportworkers' conference organized by the ITF at Easter 1935 in Roskilde in Denmark. It was attended by 31 German unionists and union officials from Britain, France, Holland and Skandinavia. Fimmen spoke on the international situation and emphasized that the regime could not be quickly overthrown; the non-Germans were to be shown that some Germans stood for a free labour movement and had started to rebuild it. Jahn and Voss reported on their efforts, which were supplemented by many others present. Fimmen issued an emotional call to work for the ideas and ideals of socialism and warned them not to establish links to other underground groups for reasons of security, but Jahn was in favour. In the summer of 1935 the first arrests took place as the Gestapo got to know about the conference (which could hardly be kept a secret). Jahn was among those arrested but was soon released and managed to escape abroad, together with his family. Large parts of his network were discovered and harsh sentences were passed in 1936–37. From April 1936 an employee of the German embassy in Paris had access to a postal box used by the principal union leaders outside Germany, so that the Gestapo was well informed about the activities and methods of the organization.[35]

In 1935 the ITF published what it called 'an immediate trade union programme' with a long catalogue of demands (which of course could not be realized then): wages to be raised to the level of 1932, lower taxes, restoration of the social insurance level to that of May 1932, removal of the employers and tradesmen from the ranks of the DAF, free election of factory councillors, restoration of collective bargaining and of protection against dismissal, of the right of strike and a free press, three weeks of paid leave, extension of the public economy. The demands no doubt found an echo among the workers who had lost their basic rights, but how many were willing to risk everything to achieve them? In and near Berlin another former official of the railwaymen's union in 1934 collected reports and distributed a proclamation to the German people as well as *Sozialistische Aktion*. His group too suffered many arrests, as did a group of former officials of the metalworkers' union which had contacts outside Berlin. According to a report of 1935, this union saw as its main task to restore self-confidence, to collect reports from the factories, to establish contact, to give legal advice and to represent members, if possible, at the labour courts in case of conflict.[36] It was a more modest programme and it was more realistic.

For the white-collar workers, Hans Gottfurcht undertook the reformation of their dissolved union. Officially employed by an insurance company he travelled widely and approached former union officials in Saxony and Silesia to renew contacts. He was briefly arrested in 1937 and soon after had to leave Germany. Another former union official in 1936 travelled to Copenhagen to meet representatives of the international union movement and colleagues who had left Germany. He continued to work from Berlin and hid his links so successfully under business affairs that they were not discovered by the Gestapo. The union of clothing workers had loose contacts in many parts of Germany, but a meeting arranged to take place in Berlin in June 1936 was betrayed and aborted. In 1934 22 members of a building workers' union were sentenced in Hamm because of underground union activities and meetings in a wood and a cemetery.[37] It seems that none of these efforts got as far as that of the railwaymen in establishing a fairly wide network.

Also linked to the SPD, at least after 1934, was the group *Neu Beginnen*, partly because it received financial assistance from the exiled SPD leaders, partly because it recruited new members among the frontier secretaries and other SPD members abroad, and of course from underground Social-Democratic groups in Germany. In 1935 its leader, Walter Löwenheim, became convinced that the Nazi regime could not be overthrown from inside Germany, that all opposition efforts were doomed to failure; therefore the underground groups should be liquidated and their members emigrate, leaving only a few 'listening posts' of perhaps 20 to 30 people inside the country. But inside the Berlin organization strong opposition to this 'liquidation course' developed, and in the summer of 1935 Löwenheim and his group of leaders were deposed by the large majority of the members. They believed that, as the whole organization so far had escaped the mercies of the Gestapo, a fair chance existed to continue the work inside the country and to expand carefully into other parts of Germany. They wanted to be ready for any eventuality, still taking a very long perspective. In September Löwenheim left Germany and informed the SPD and the Socialist International that the organization had been dissolved.[38]

About the same time mass arrests began in Berlin and elsewhere. It seems that the Gestapo since 1934 had tried to track the organization, grossly overestimating its strength at about 500. Arrests began in Saxony, and one of the arrested was 'turned round' by the Gestapo, revealing an address in Berlin and what he knew. The Gestapo patiently followed the clues, observed carefully and was greatly helped by the discovery of a suitcase containing archival material, which had been sunk in a Berlin lake and had drifted ashore. Why this mass of material was kept so long in Germany and was not destroyed was a mystery. In any case, at least in Berlin the organization was virtually wiped out, except for a small remnant which remained undiscovered for several more years. In Bavaria and elsewhere *Neu Beginnen* survived in small groups. Outside Germany it remained one of several groups faithful to a policy of revolutionary socialism, with Richard Löwenthal as its theoretician, but in Berlin it no longer existed as a proper underground organization. Löwenheim and his circle of friends retired to London where Löwenheim became a businessman.

The organization which suffered most from the blows of the Gestapo and the severity of the court verdicts was the KPD, partly on account of its mass agitation and its faulty structure, partly because of successful police penetration. In July 1934 the Hamburg police reported that two great trials were pending against about 400 accused of rebuilding the Revolutionary Tradeunion Opposition (RGO), as well as similar large trials in Bremen, Oldenburg and Mecklenburg. In and around Hamburg about 800 had been arrested for distributing the RGO organ. The KPD youth organization in Hamburg was hit by waves of arrests in 1934, after which only small remnants remained. It had tried to rebuild the old organizational structure in all quarters of the city, with a political, an organizational and an agitprop leader on each level and instructors responsible for the adoption of the 'right' line throughout. But the desired 'mass offensive' remained on paper, as did the fight against

'counter-revolutionary Social Democracy' and the 'counter-revolutionary knave Trotsky' and his friends. In Leipzig between September 1934
and April 1935 about 2000 arrests were carried out, including the entire
apparatus of the district leadership, due to 'negligence in conspirative
methods'. One of the arrested made damaging admissions and a second
leadership group was also caught. When an imprisoned young Communist returned to Leipzig after his release he found most active comrades either in prison or emigrated. 'Many comrades have given up,
bread pigeons. "Politics? Leave me alone, talk about something else." '[39]
    In Brunswick the last attempt to form a district leadership came to
an end in July 1934. The group tried to find conspirative cover in a
sports club which many members of a workers' club joined. In Bremen,
a new district leader was arrested in November 1935, together with
about 100 party members. More arrests followed in 1936. In
Mannheim, new district leaders were appointed in the autumn of 1934,
but mass arrests followed during the winter, and the former leader
remembered that the KPD was hardly capable of action at that time.
In 1936 there were more arrests. They destroyed the organizational
contacts and the distribution of underground literature practically
ceased, as the public prosecutor reported to Berlin. The same was true
of Hof in Bavaria when the transport of material across the Bohemian
frontier came to an end. In Frankfurt seven successive leadership groups
were caught by 1935. In March the Gestapo was particularly successful.
They arrested some party officials responsible for the whole of south-
west Germany, including the *Oberberaterin* (chief adviser) Maria
Krollmann, the entire group of district leaders for Hessen-Nassau, the
leaders of 'Red Help', the RGO and the 'International Workers Aid',
as well as many instructors for the different Frankfurt districts. Also
caught was the Reich courier for south-west Germany, leading to further
important arrests in Berlin. To recognize each other the leading officials
all wore a certain wartime decoration in their buttonholes.[40] The report
makes it clear that some of the arrested were 'induced to talk'. For the
time being the party's work in the south-west reached its end.
    In Munich, the political police since the end of 1934 knew everything
about the actions and structure of the underground KPD. The top
leader was a police agent, thus the police could direct and control the
party groups, allowing them to work for many months and distribute
literature, so as to be able to spy out all the tentacles: two waves of
mass arrests in 1935 and 1936 finished it. When members of a factory
cell at Agfa were arrested in 1937 it meant the end of KPD activity in
Munich. In Würzburg another police spy was the initiator and organizer
of underground work. He distributed to members illegal literature
which he seemed to have obtained from the police. In Kassel, the

Gestapo reported in August 1935, the KPD was well organized, the members paying their dues and receiving the party literature until June when arrests took place, following many earlier ones. In Stettin, those trying to rebuild the KPD were arrested in 1935, and the Gestapo reported that many of them had 'confessed'. In Cologne, the last KPD organization spanning the whole city came to an end in the spring of 1936 when – after many previous arrests – about 150 were caught and their contacts in the local factories and in the area were liquidated.[41]

The Rhine–Ruhr area had been one of the strongholds of the KPD, and so it was of its underground work. In November 1934 the party reported that it had again 260 members in Essen, 240 in Hamborn, 160 in Moers, 100 in Dortmund. But in the early months of 1935 more mass arrests were carried out, including nearly all members of the district leadership, so that party work came almost to a standstill and only isolated small groups remained. That was partly due to the massive import of KPD literature across the Dutch frontier. Late in 1934 the Gestapo found near the frontier a depot of ten hundredweights, and in February 1935 another four containing 5669 pamphlets. Whole columns of smugglers were employed. In March 1935 the loads were transferred to a car from Essen which was supplied by the Gestapo and driven to a tobacconist in Essen whose shop was under observation, so that the couriers collecting the parcels could be followed to other towns. The quantities were so colossal that the Essen Communists were quite unable to cope with them. Mass arrests took place repeatedly in many towns. In Krefeld they were due to treason. The local treasurer was responsible for the arrest of the district treasurer and of many others. In November 1934 the printing shop of the *Rote Fahne* was discovered in Solingen; three months later, another in Cologne. In Duisburg and Hamborn three great police actions virtually annihilated the local party groups; all that remained was a handful of youngsters.[42]

What made matters worse for the party was that its technical apparatus was destroyed in many areas of Germany, and with it the network of distribution. In November 1934 and January 1935, owing to carelessness and faulty methods, most of the 'technicians' in west and south Germany as well as Berlin were arrested. Soon after, three couriers were caught in Saxony transporting between four and five hundredweights of literature across the frontier, to take them by car to Berlin. In consequence of their arrest the technical apparatus of the Berlin–Brandenburg district was 'almost completely' wiped out, with ramifications as far as Magdeburg, Hamburg and Stettin, to where the material was to be sent. From these blows it was almost impossible to recover. But it also demonstrated the size of the party apparatus after two years of the Nazi regime. In Berlin alone, until March 1934, the Gestapo dis-

covered ten printing shops which were used by the KPD for the production of its illegal material, 'its Reich printing apparatus'.[43]

The KPD aimed at maintaining in Berlin a central leadership for the
whole of Germany, but under the conditions of the Third Reich this
eventually proved impossible. Much later Franz Dahlem, one of the
leaders, claimed that early in 1934 he was sent to Berlin with false
papers so as 'to decentralize the party', so that the various districts
would have separate contacts with frontier leaders established all
around Germany. But that certainly was not the case in 1934. In the
spring of 1935 a new all-German leadership group was sent from
Prague to Berlin. But it had only existed for three weeks when they
were all arrested in a conference with emissaries from the provinces.
After that débâcle the leadership was transferred to Paris where some
of the leaders had been installed since 1933. As the party's leader,
Wilhelm Pieck, admitted in October 1935, the majority of party districts
then had their fifth leadership group, southern Bavaria its sixth, Hesse,
the Ruhr and North Germany their seventh, and Baden its eighth.[44]
These continuous disasters finally forced the KPD to a change of tactics.
The party groups in Germany were instructed to establish links with
frontier offices close to the German frontiers – as the SPD had done
since 1933.

The party line remained unchanged until the Seventh Congress of
Comintern in the summer of 1935, when the policy of 'united front
from below' was officially given up. The old illusions remained. In June
1934 the Central Committee issued a proclamation urging the 'masses'
not to pay any rent, tax, interest or gas and electricity bills, but to
march to the town halls and revenue offices. In August another appeal
was published to all comrades of the SPD to unite in 'one revolutionary
mass party', to forge the 'great united front for resistance and strike
action'. For the plebiscite of August 1934 a leaflet declared that a new
world war was imminent: 'And now the Nazis want to hear that you
consent to everything, to hunger, misery and death for the profit of
monopoly capitalism'. But the workers would reply: 'Fight with the
KPD for Soviet power!' A leaflet issued for the *Vertrauensrat* elections
of 1935 in Dortmund urged the rebuilding of free trade unions and
'the restoration of working-class unity on a revolutionary basis'. The
class forces were to be organized 'on the basis of proletarian
democracy ... for the fight against economic and political enslavement
of the worker by Fascism'. But it remained without an echo. For
MayDay 1935 slogans such as 'Free the streets for peace!' and 'remind
Ley on 1st of May: higher the wages!' were issued in Berlin, slogans
were painted on walls and red flags hoisted. According to a leading
party official, it was 'a high point of antifascist agitation'.[45]

At the Seventh World Congress held in Moscow in 1935, Pieck admitted that the German proletariat (meaning the KPD) had suffered a defeat; the party did not want that 'the revolutionary cadres should die out of pure heroism. That is not the greatest heroic courage!' The party secretary, Walter Ulbricht, saw the cause of lack of 'mass resistance' in the 'sectarian traditions' of the party which had not succeeded in organizing a united front with Social-Democratic and Christian workers; he now urged the conclusion of agreements with other organizations which would form a strong motor to antifascist action. The old aim remained unchanged. As a resolution of the 'Brussels' party conference (held near Moscow) put it in the same year, the bitter experiences suffered by the German working class by defeat 'have called forth the will to reunification in a united political mass party. But such a mass party can only fulfill its task . . . if it recognized the necessity of the revolutionary overthrow of the bourgeoisie and the establishment of the dictatorship of the proletariat in the form of Soviets . . . and is built on the basis of democratic centralism.' It was completely unlikely that the SPD leaders in Prague or Social-Democratic groups in Germany would accept such a programme and such aims. It was equally unlikely that leaders of the former Centre Party, such as Heinrich Brüning or Joseph Wirth, would accept Pieck's proffered hand to form a 'united battle front against Hitler'.[46]

Soon there were spurious 'United Front Committees' in different parts of Germany which issued appeals to take action 'against Hitler's Fascism and war', for the fight must no longer be conducted, as in the past, alongside each other: 'Only united will we be victorious!' From Höchst near Frankfurt it was reported that in one compartment of a chemical factory 80 per cent of the workers were pro-Communist and that several small KPD cells existed. One former SPD councillor cooperated closely with them but he was dismissed because he alone refused to give the Hitler salute. An emissary of the KPD was sent to Freiburg in the Black Forest where traditional small groups of KPD and SPD existed relatively unharmed. He addressed a small meeting of members of both parties on the new 'united front' tactics and they agreed to a resolution of approval and appealing to all to close ranks.[47] Otherwise the new tactics had very little success.

What did the KPD organization look like at the basis? In the summer of 1934 an instructor sent to the Lower Rhine district reported to the Central Committee: 'Unfortunately the great weakness is that we don't possess any figures and no exact survey about our lower units in the factories and above all in the living quarters.' It was impossible, he continued, to speak of 'an independent leadership and accurate political work down below. In almost all subdistricts the leading groups are extremely weak.' They tried in vain to obtain *Rote Fahne, Inprekorr* and other party papers, doing all that they could to get them and needing them badly because the lower officials were 'politically very weak' and had no money to issue a weekly paper at regular intervals. Interestingly enough, the same instructor reported on his experience in Solingen that a leaflet calling for a strike had been issued. This caused a sharp discussion 'because the preconditions for a strike did not exist'. On the other hand, 'the comrades talked about arms and believed that we were in a revolutionary situation. There was much confusion whether we had to reckon with a short or a long duration of Hitler's Fascism and how the dictatorship could be terminated.' From the same area a former party official recorded later: 'We were convinced that the elections were falsified and in reality the majority of the people were against Hitler . . . And in spite of all mistakes the party remained the great motor.' Another official talking to the comrades told them: 'The work must be done. Again I heard: must, must and must.'[48] It was a call to duty, and innumerable loyal members obeyed it.

If the KPD preserved its rigid structure and working methods, at least the collection of membership dues with stamps was given up, as the Hanover Gestapo reported in February 1934, 'owing to the heavy losses in members and officials'. These also tried to work without written materials and evidence of identity as far as possible But dues were still collected: in Hanau, for example, 50 pfennigs a month in 1935. According to another report, the Gestapo estimated that in the autumn of 1934 50,000 members were paying dues – a surprisingly high figure – and the KPD had succeeded in reforming all its satellite organizations, the RGO, 'Red Help' and the KJVD. The greatest danger the Gestapo saw was the recurrence of partial political strikes, public demonstrations and active defence against measures of the authorities 'by incited working people' and fomented by the KPD. What surprised the Gestapo was how quickly the positions of officials just arrested were filled again. When the last remaining leader in South Bavaria was arrested in February 1934, together with the whole apparatus of distribution of a paper, and many other officials, the party was without leaders in the district. But the vacant posts were quickly filled and preparations made to form a new leading group. The Münster Gestapo stated in October 1935 that the party members 'were always willing to fill the gaps created and to take the places of arrested comrades, without being deterred by the heavy sentences. The readiness to suffer for the Communist idea goes so far that convinced Communists time and again sacrifice their lives so as not to betray their comrades.'[49] It was recognition from an unexpected side.

Ocasionally demonstrations took place under Communist influence.

When 300 workers were dismissed by a factory in Hildesheim in the autumn of 1935, Communist slogans appeared on its walls and the workers demonstrated singing the 'Internationale'. They blamed the government for the dismissals because it insisted on the fast fulfilment of all orders which could have been extended over a longer period. When the well-known communist Karl Hoffmann who died under arrest was buried in Essen in March 1935, over a thousand men and women came to the funeral; 18 were arrested, among them several women. Interrogations continued until May but nothing could be proved against them. Even in the small university town of Marburg Communist slogans were painted, such as 'Communism is immortal' and 'Adolf Hitler, a 77-fold murderer' (presumably referring to the purge of June 1934). The Gestapo noted that the workmen building the Autobahnen, with their low wages and heavy work in bad weather, provided a breeding ground for Communist propaganda, and indeed many small strikes took place on these sites.[50] But all these events presented no danger whatever to the stability of the Third Reich.

Nor did Communist efforts to infiltrate the DAF – the tactics of the Trojan horse – according to the party directives. Early in 1934 the district leadership of Lower Saxony issued a circular: 'We must, without canvassing for the DAF . . .send all suitable forces into the DAF', with the aim 'to make it clear to all former trade unionists and those forced to join it that the destruction of the trade unions was only possible on account of the anti-worker policy of the union bosses pursued over decades, who engaged in a ferocious fight against the Marxist trade unionists and prepared the way for Hitler as his pacemakers and stirrup-holders.' Other comrades were to be sent into the NSBO 'to thwart the fascist education, to steer the discontented in the direction of the class struggle'. How all this was to be achieved within the tightly controlled Nazi organizations was not explained. Massive discontent existed among industrial workers, especially the 'emergency workers' on the building sites, but the KPD was unable to capitalize on it. In 1935 the Frankfurt Gestapo reported that workers in many factories resented the piece rates they were condemned to which were 'super-human' and could not be kept up for any length of time.[51] There was a great gap between this widespread mood and the activities of the KPD which cannot be explained alone by the terror. But many of the lower party organizations and groups were isolated, and many members gave up the unequal fight. Many were languishing in prisons and concentration camps and the number of victims was forever growing.

The Socialist Workers Party (SAP) also suffered badly from arrests: a target of a special section of the Gestapo. In Berlin, Breslau, Dortmund,

Duisburg, Frankfurt, Mannheim and Munich the membership was deci-
mated; in Dortmund it was the work of a spy. In Mannheim the SAP
carried out a successful action when Hitler spoke for the 'elections' of
1936 in Ludwigshafen. In both towns hundreds of red stickers
appeared: 'Who votes for Hitler votes for war. Therefore no vote for
him and his clan!' Only small SAP groups survived. The Gestapo considered the party especially dangerous because, like most splinter
groups, it contained 'a large percentage of intelligent people', most of
them in good positions. When a party conference met in Moravia in
1937 the SAP had only three functioning districts left, Berlin, Mannheim
and North Germany, and barely a thousand active members. In March
1938 the Berlin group wrote to the party leaders in Paris: 'Work inside
the country has on the whole been aborted . . . Our contact more and
more becomes a traditional one, the relationship of our organization
to the present more and more abstract.'[52] All the remaining small groups
could do was to try and survive until the end of the Hitler regime.

During its campaign against the KPD the Gestapo of Kassel acciden-
tally encountered in 1935 a group of the ISK (International Socialist
Fighting League), consisting mainly of intellectuals. They also found a
pamphlet 'How do I conduct myself in the factory?' The ISK group in
Frankfurt survived until 1936, and some others even longer. They were
protected by their small size and careful conspirative methods. They
continued to cooperate closely with the ITF in Amsterdam. The material
was dispatched from Holland by motorcycle – until a frontier control
found a copy hidden on the driver's seat. Dangerous too was cooperation with the KPD in Kassel and Hannoversch-Münden, for the Communist group contained a policy spy. The Gestapo appointed a special
section to deal with the ISK, and after long preparation and observation
it pounced at the end of 1937. During the following months about 100
people were arrested in many parts of Germany and many of the groups
were virtually liquidated, in towns as far as Augsburg and Frankfurt in
the south and Bremen, Hamburg and Hanover in the north.[53] It proved
that it was impossible to maintain a unified underground organization,
however good its methods of conspiracy might be. For almost five years
the ISK was successful in preserving its underground network and
distributing its literature in many areas of Germany. It was a considerable achievement.

A syndicalist group in the Rhineland, the *Freie Arbeiter-Union*, also
survived until 1937. The members met regularly for discussions, circulated underground literature, collected dues and money for the Spanish
Republican army. In 1938, 88 of them were tried and received comparatively mild sentences.[54]

Opposition also appeared from an unexpected quarter, that of

German youth. Before 1933 there had been many wild 'cliques', mainly consisting of young workers who did not fit into the traditional working-class youth organizations. After 1933 such cliques continued to exist, of boy-scouts, former members of the SAJ and KJVD, and similar organizations which had been dissolved by the National Socialists. They continued hiking and tenting and were often quite unpolitical. Some joined the Hitler Youth (HJ) but were soon disappointed by its strict discipline. They were soon joined by former members of the *Bündische Jugend*, the German youth movement, when their groups were driven underground by the monopoly claim of the HJ. The *Nerother*, for example, who at first tried to reach accommodation with the HJ, after their dissolution continued underground. They were a purely middle-class association, specializing in long-distance hiking trips, but their composition, like some of the others, changed and became more working-class. Initially the many small youth groups remained separate, but later some merged and formed an attractive alternative to the HJ with its military drill which was resented by many youngsters.[55]

A special group was formed by the so-called 'Kittelbach Pirates' in Düsseldorf who wore black shirts and white scarves with a death-head ring. In 1933 they were taken over by the HJ as a group and at first permitted to wear their own distinctive garb. But soon differences and friction developed and at the end of the year they were dissolved by the HJ leaders. But they continued to meet and, as with other cliques, conflict with the HJ soon arose. Conflict also arose with the Catholic *Sturmscharen* which existed legally until 1936. They strongly opposed the measures of the Nazi authorities which tried to hinder their work, and began to discuss political issue such as the danger of war and what could be done about it. There was constant friction with the HJ which tried to provoke the members whenever they camped or met.[56] The conflict became much more serious when the HJ in December 1936 became a compulsory youth organization for all young Germans between the ages of 10 and 18.

Yet another group were the 'Navajos' in Cologne who wore very short black trousers, highly coloured checked shirts, blue caps and long white stockings with tassels, while the girl members wore white blouses with coloured scarves and boots. They attacked members of the HJ, in particular its *Streifendienst* (special patrol service). As one of the HJ statements put it in July 1936: 'Time and again these gangs appear, sometimes stronger, sometimes weaker, to chase the HJ'. The clique members looked at the patrol service as a kind of police for the young; their hostile attitude to it was to become much more intense during the following years. The patrol service in its turn kept a special eye on all 'hostile youth groups', especially those of the *Bündische Jugend*, as was stated very significantly, 'in close cooperation with the Security Service of the SS'.[57]

There was quite considerable leftwing opposition to the regime in the years 1934–36, but it was fragmented, unsure of itself, politically disunited, unable to take any significant action. In any case, as the economic situation began to improve, the conditions under which it developed ceased to exist. This of course did not mean that a united opposition could have overthrown the Nazi regime, but it could have made its life more difficult.

Notes

1. Mammach, *Widerstand 1933–1939*, p. 91.
2. *Deutschland-Berichte*, i, 1934, no. 7, p. 660; Ian Kershaw, *Popular Opinion and Political Dissent in the Third Reich*, Oxford, 1983, p. 82; Vollmer, *Volksopposition*, pp. 106f., 110.
3. Wisotzky, *Ruhrbergbau*, pp. 51f., 56.
4. *Deutschland-Berichte*, ii, 1935, no. 1, p. 45, no. 5, pp. 553f.; Margot Pikarski and Elke Warning (eds), *Gestapo-Berichte über den antifaschistischen Widerstandskampf der KPD*, i, Berlin, 1989, pp. 130ff.
5. Friederike Reutter, 'Verfolgung und Widerstand der Arbeiterparteien in Heidelberg', in Jörg Schadt and Michael Caroli (eds), *Heidelberg unter dem Nationalsozialismus*, Heidelberg, 1985, p. 516; *Deutschland-Berichte*, ii, 1935, no. 7, pp. 779f.; Stoop, *Geheimberichte*, p. 185; Mallmann and Paul, *Herrschaft und Alltag*, p. 364.
6. *Deutschland-Berichte*, iii, 1936, no. 1, p. 87, no. 3, pp. 483f., no. 9, pp. 1171ff.; Wippermann, *Leben in Frankfurt*, iv, pp. 52f.; 102; Voges, 'Klassenkampf in der Betriebsgemeinschaft', p. 352; Günter Morsch, 'Streik im Dritten Reich', *Vierteljahrshefte für Zeitgeschichte*, xxxvi 1988, p. 675.
7. Mallmann and Paul, *Herrschaft und Alltag*, p. 365; Klein, *Lageberichte*, p. 388; *Bayern in der NS-Zeit*, i, p. 256; Pikarski and Warning, *Gestapo-Berichte*, i, pp. 167f., 173; idem, 'Über den antifaschistischen Widerstandskampf der KPD', *Beiträge zur Geschichte der Arbeiterbewegung*, xxvi 1984, pp. 558, 560.
8. Nitzsche, 'Deutsche Arbeiter im Kampf', pp. 144, 146; Pikarski and Warning, *Gestapo-Berichte*, i, p. 154; idem, 'Über den antifaschistischen Widerstandskampf' p. 407.
9. Morsch, 'Streik im Dritten Reich', pp. 683ff., with detailed figures for participation and duration of strikes; Nitzsche, 'Deutsche Arbeiter', p. 147.
10. Pikarski and Warning, *Gestapo-Berichte*, i, p. 157; Hetzer, *Industriestadt Augsburg*, p. 119.
11. Lutz van Dick, *Oppositionelles Lehrerverhalten 1933–1945*, Weinheim, 1988, p. 239; Eiber, *Arbeiter unter NS-Herrschaft*, pp. 121f.; Klein, *Lageberichte*, pp. 83, 204.
12. Marssolek and Ott, *Bremen*, p. 151; Mlynek, *Gestapo Hannover*, p. 169; Kershaw, *Popular Opinion*, pp. 77, 80; Schadt, *Verfolgung und Widerstand*, p. 141. Both songs were well-known working-class songs.

13. Rossaint and Zimmermann, *Widerstand*, p. 97; *Deutschland-Berichte*, ii, 1935, no. 1, pp. 55f., no. 6, p. 658, no. 11, pp. 1314, 1317; Duhnke, *KPD*, p. 208 n. 106; Voges, 'Klassenkampf in der Betriebsgemeinschaft', p. 379; Hüttenberger, 'Heimtückefälle', *Bayern in der NS-Zeit*, iv, pp. 446f.

14. *Deutschland-Berichte*, iii 1936, no. 3, p. 317, no. 4, pp. 449, 510, no. 12, p. 1582.

15. Ibid., no. 1, p. 89, no. 6, p. 739, no. 12, pp. 1561, 1563, 1591.

16. Pikarski and Warning, *Gestapo-Berichte*, i, p. 161.

17. *Deutschland-Berichte*, iii 1936, no. 4, p. 481.

18. Ibid., i, 1934, no. 4, p. 434; Mlynek, *Gestapo Hannover*, p. 287; Zorn, *Widerstand in Hannover*, p. 164.

19. Marssolek and Ott, *Bremen*, pp. 151–55.

20. *Deutschland-Berichte*, iv 1937, no. 1, p. 17; Hochmuth and Meyer, *Streiflichter*, p. 189; Marssolek and Ott, *Bremen*, p. 269; Gitte Schefer, 'Wo Unterdrückung ist, da ist auch Widerstand', in Frauengruppe Faschismusforschung (ed.), *Mutterkreuz und Arbeitsbuch*, Frankfurt, 1981, p. 285; Pikarski and Warning, *Gestapo-Berichte*, i, pp. 163, 169; *Bayern in der NS-Zeit*, i, p. 260; Werner Maser, *Das Regime. Alltag in Deutschland 1933–1945*, Munich, 1983, p. 170.

21. William Sheridan Allen, 'Die sozialdemokratische Untergrundbewegung' in Jürgen Schmädeke and Peter Steinbach (eds), *Widerstand gegen den Nationalsozialismus*, Munich, 1985, pp. 855f.; Fischer-Defoy, *Arbeiterwiderstand*, p. 105.

22. Bohn, *Stuttgart: Geheim*, p. 78.

23. *Deutschland-Berichte*, ii, 1935, no. 6, p. 666.

24. Matthias and Weber, *Widerstand*, pp. 158, 174; Reutter, *Verfolgung*, pp. 524–31.

25. Hetzer, *Industriestadt Augsburg*, pp. 193f., 197; Matthias and Weber, *Widerstand* pp. 162ff.; Mehringer, *von Knoeringen*, pp. 105–8.

26. *Deutschland-Berichte*, ii, 1935, no. 4, p. 430, iii, 1936, no. 1, p. 16.

27. *Widerstand und Exil der deutschen Arbeiterbewegung*, Bonn, 1982, pp. 627ff.; Matthias, *Sozialdemokratie und Nation*, p. 36.

28. *Deutschland-Berichte*, i, 1934, no. 7, pp. 736f.; Marssolek and Ott, *Bremen*, p. 212; Bajohr, *In doppelter Isolation*, p. 21; Paul Sauer, *Würtemberg in der Zeit des Nationalsozialismus*, Ulm, 1975, p. 173.

29. Mehringer, 'Bayerische Sozialdemokratie', pp. 386f.; Hochmuth and Meyer, *Streiflichter*, pp. 47, 118; Bajohr, 'In doppelter Isolation', pp. 21f.; Wippermann, *Leben in Frankfurt*, iv, p. 47; Matthias and Weber, *Widerstand*, pp. 195ff.; Eiber, *Arbeiter unter NS-Herrschaft*, pp. 136f.

30. Bludau, *Gestapo – Geheim*, pp. 36f.; Aurel Billstein, *Der eine fällt, die andern rücken nach*, Frankfurt, 1973, p. 107; Peukert, *Ruhrarbeiter*, p. 118; Zorn, *Widerstand in Hannover*, p. 122.

31. Mlynek, *Gestapo Hannover*, pp. 150, 442; Barbara Beuys, *Vergesst uns nicht. Menschen im Widerstand 1933–1945*, Reinbek nr. Hamburg, 1987, p. 308.

32. *Deutschland-Berichte*, iii, 1936, no. 9, p. 1093.

33. Helmut Esters and Hans Pelger, *Gewerkschafter im Widerstand*, Bonn, 1983, pp. 32f., 127, 129, 132–39, with Oldenbroek's undated report.

34. Ibid., pp. 36f., 39ff.; Foitzik, *Zwischen den Fronten*, p. 209; Peukert, *Ruhrarbeiter*, p. 149; personal recollections, especially of Edo Fimmen.

35. Esters and Pelger, *Gewerkschafter*, pp. 44f., 142, 145, 147; Hochmuth and Meyer, *Streiflichter*, pp. 104f.; Foitzik, *Zwischen den Fronten*, p. 209; Thévoz, Branig etc., *Pommern*, p. 100; Pikarski and Warning, *Gestapo-Berichte*, i, p. 160; personal recollections: Jahn's quick release was due to a sympathetic Staatsanwalt with leftwing sympathies.

36. Esters and Pelger, *Gewerkschafter*, pp. 152ff.; Mammach, *Widerstand*, pp. 138, 269; Gerhard Beier, *Die illegale Reichsleitung der Gewerkschaften 1933–1945*, Cologne, 1981, p. 42.

37. Ibid., pp. 37, 59, 66; Hans Gottfurcht, 'Als Gewerkschafter im Widerstand', in Richard Löwenthal and Patrick von zur Mühlen (eds), *Widerstand und Verweigerung in Deutschland 1933–1945*, Berlin–Bonn, 1984, pp. 52ff.

38. This and the next paragraph are written from personal recollections. See also Bry, *Resistance*, pp. 128–34; Richard Löwenthal, *Die Widerstandsgruppe 'Neu Beginnen'*, Berlin, 1982, pp. 8ff.; Foitzik, *Zwischen den Fronten*, p. 81; Manfred Overesch, *Hermann Brill in Thüringen 1895–1946*, Bonn, 1992, p. 241.

39. Hochmuth and Meyer, *Streiflichter*, pp. 93f.; Bajohr, 'In doppelter Isolation', pp. 23f., 29; Mammach, *Widerstand*, pp. 52f.; Stern, *In den Netzen*, p. 139.

40. Bein, *Widerstand*, pp. 98f.; Marssolek and Ott, *Bremen*, pp. 255, 267; Matthias and Weber, *Widerstand*, pp. 269f., 287f.; Eiber, *Arbeiter*, p. 151; Wippermann, *Leben in Frankfurt*, iv, p. 38; Klein, *Lageberichte*, pp. 428f.

41. Mehringen, 'KPD in Bayern', pp. 132, 135, 148, 229; Fischer-Defoy, *Arbeiterwiderstand*, p. 152; Thévoz, Branig etc., *Pommern*, pp. 132, 149; Viebahn and Kuchta, 'Widerstand . . . in Köln', pp. 307, 312.

42. Peukert, *Ruhrarbeiter*, pp. 83, 166; idem, *KPD im Widerstand*, pp. 145, 155, 189; Günter Plum, 'Die KPD in der Illegalität', in Hermann Graml (ed.), *Widerstand im Dritten Reich*, Frankfurt, 1984, p. 170; Bludau, *Gestapo – Geheim*, pp. 106, 117, 123, 141.

43. Peukert, *KPD im Widerstand*, p. 186; Pikarski and Warning, *Gestapo-Berichte*, i, pp. 102, 124; reports of March 1934 and September 1935.

44. Franz Dahlem, *Am Vorabend des Zweiten Weltkrieges*, Berlin, 1977, i, p. 110; Duhnke, *KPD*, p. 190; Hermann Weber, 'Die KPD in der Illegalität', in Löwenthal and zur Mühlen (eds), *Widerstand und Verweigerung*, p. 92; Hans J. Reichhardt, 'Möglichkeiten und Grenzen des Widerstandes der Arbeiterbewegung', in Walter Schmitthenner and Hans Buchheim (eds), *Der deutsche Widerstand gegen Hitler*, Cologne, 1966, p. 190; Fischer-Defoy, *Arbeiterwiderstand*, p. 138.

45. Bahne, 'Kommunistische Partei Deutschlands', p. 735; Peter Dohms (ed.), *Flugschriften aus Gestapo-Akten*, Siegburg, 1977, p. 470; Kuropka, *Meldungen*, p. 264; Klotzbach, *Gegen den Nationalsozialismus*, p. 197; Ackermann, 'Ich kam aus der illegalen Arbeit in Berlin', p. 830.

46. Arnold Sywottek, *Deutsche Volksdemokratie*, Düsseldorf, 1971, pp. 40, 52, 60; Ursula Langkau-Alex, *Volksfront für Deutschland?* Frankfurt, 1977, p. 109.

47. Margot Pikarski and Günter Übel (eds), *Die KPD lebt*, Berlin, 1980, pp. 148f.; Gerhard Nitzsche and Günter Übel (eds), 'Die KPD – führende Kraft', *Beiträge zur Geschichte der Arbeiterbewegung*, xx 1978, p. 695; Franz Feuchtwanger, 'Der militärpolitische Apparat der KPD', *Internation-*

ale Korrespondenz zur Geschichte der deutschen Arbeiterbewegung, xvii 1981, p. 524.

48. Günter Plum, 'Die KPD in der Illegalität', *Vierteljahrshefte für Zeitgeschichte*, xxiii 1975, pp. 230f., 234; Inge Sobosny and Karl Schabrod, *Widerstand in Solingen*, Frankfurt, 1975, pp. 38f.; Peukert, *Volksgenossen*, p. 148; Dorn and Zimmermann, *Bewährungsprobe*, p. 156.

49. Mlynek, *Gestapo Hannover*, p. 96; Klein, *Lageberichte*, p. 234; Pikarski and Warning, *Gestapo-Berichte*, i, p. 103; *Bayern in der NS-Zeit*, i, p. 232; Beuys, *Vergesst uns nicht*, p. 296.

50. Mlynek, *Gestapo Hannover*, p. 441; Ernst Schmidt, *Lichter in der Finsternis. Widerstand und Verfolgung in Essen*, Frankfurt, 1980, pp. 77–84; Ulrich Schneider, *Marburg 1933–1945*, Frankfurt, 1980, pp. 89ff.; Klein, *Lageberichte*, p. 331.

51. Mlynek, *Gestapo Hannover*, pp. 108f.; Klein, *Lageberichte*, p. 461.

52. Högl and Steinmetz, *Widerstand*, p. 159; Matthias and Weber, *Widerstand*, pp. 220, 227ff.; Wippermann, *Leben in Frankfurt*, iv, p. 43; Bremer, *Sozialistische Arbeiterpartei*, p. 214; Foitzik, *Zwischen den Fronten*, pp. 51, 201, 220.

53. Klein, *Lageberichte*, p. 345; Esters and Pelger, *Gewerkschafter*, pp. 59ff.; Bein, *Widerstand*, p. 119; Bernd-Anton Tapken, 'Die Auseinandersetzung des ISK mit der KPD und der KPdSU in der Zeit des Exils', Ms. 1984, p. 29; Foitzik, *Zwischen den Fronten*, p. 88; Hochmuth and Meyer, *Streiflichter*, p. 150; Zorn, *Widerstand in Hannover*, p. 204.

54. Mann, *Protest und Kontrolle*, p. 218.

55. Bernd-A. Rusinek, 'Desintegration und gesteigerter Zwang', in Wilfried Breyvogel (ed.), *Piraten, Swings und Junge Garde*, Bonn, 1991, p. 280; Arno Klönne, 'Bündische Jugend, Nationalsozialismus und NS-Staat', in Schmädeke and Steinbach, *Widerstand*, p. 188; Matthias von Hellfeld and Arno Klönne, *Die betrogene Generation*, Cologne, 1985, p. 269.

56. Karl Schabrod, *Widerstand gegen Flick und Florian*, Frankfurt, 1978, pp. 61f.

57. von Hellfeld and Klönne, *Betrogene Generation*, pp. 79f., 301; Alfons Kenkmann, 'Navajos, Kittelbach- und Edelweisspiraten', in Breyvogel (ed.), *Piraten, Swings und Junge Garde*, p. 147.

CHAPTER FIVE

The last years of peace

The years 1936 to 1938 brought the Hitler regime not only great successes in the field of foreign policy – the occupation of the Rhineland, of Austria and the Sudetenland – without a shot being fired. They also saw consolidation and success on the home front. There was an armaments boom, and mass unemployment came to an end. On the contrary, there was a growing shortage of skilled industrial and building workers, and their living standards improved steadily, even if other categories were left behind. The regime seemed to be established for ever and this naturally affected the workers' mood. The opposition declined. Many leftwingers were safely behind bars, many of the survivors gave up the struggle as hopeless or were won over by the undoubted successes of Hitler. His position at home and abroad was unassailable. There developed what has rightly been called 'a passive consensus with the regime'.[1] The reports of the exiled SPD leaders also admitted that Hitler became more popular with the workers, more popular than his party – he could do no wrong.

From Saxony it was reported in March 1938:

> It cannot be denied that Hitler has regained enormously in confidence and prestige among all social groups, and perhaps most among the workers. That Austria has been subjugated by force counts for little or nothing at the moment. What is decisive is *that* Austria has been incorporated, not how.

A report from the Palatinate spoke of 'dismay and depression' among Social Democrats. The comrades were saying resignedly: 'Hitler succeeds in everything, he can do as he likes because all give way.' From Bavaria it was said, a little more cautiously, that the change in the general mood was not so much due to the *Anschluss* of Austria but to the fact that there was no war. But Hitler was generally admired: 'He is after all a man.' On the periphery of the socialist groups the mood was that it was pointless to work against Hitler; if Britain could not act: 'how could we do anything?' According to the report, this general depression was continuing. In Saxony, however, according to another report the exaltation did not last; the mood changed unexpectedly after only two weeks. 'Suddenly the whole Austrian adventure does not interest many people all that much. It is hardly mentioned any more, in spite of the feverish propaganda for the "election" of 10th April . . .

Only the young are still excited and full of enthusiasm.'² Clearly, national enthusiasm could not last for ever, and day-to-day worries reasserted themselves.

From a factory in south-west Germany it was recorded in the spring of 1938 that 'the great events of the past months' left little trace among the workers; they created 'momentary enthusiasm and wavering', but then the proletarians had to cope with their everyday problems. The majority of the workers had long wanted to change their jobs but all attempts were without success, for the management did not allow anyone to leave and, even if it did, the labour exchange would object; all sorts of means were tried to obtain a dismissal but all in vain. When the Munich agreements were signed in September 1938 and the Sudetenland was handed to Hitler on a platter the reactions were similar. Large sections of the working class, it was reported from south-west Germany, felt 'that in future Hitler would be able to get everything'. Many were satisfied that the Sudeten Germans would join the Reich. But 'our comrades do not believe in a lasting peace but see only an armistice which would last some months or perhaps one or two years'. From the Ruhr it was similarly noted that people were greatly relieved when it became certain that 'the great slaughter' was postponed. It was clear, however, that war was not avoided on account of Hitler's love of peace but by 'a heavy defeat of democratic policy', for war would come nevertheless. Even good old comrades were saying: 'What sense does all this make? Hitler forces them all to their knees. Democracy capitulates everywhere. What can we in Germany do if the whole world is frightened by Hitler?' In Munich too there was 'deep disappointment' with the negative attitude of the democracies, not only of their politicians but also the labour parties and the Socialist International.³ Interestingly enough, most do not seem to have believed in a lasting peace – as so many outside Germany did – but only in a postponement of the inevitable war.

Indeed, already at the beginning of 1937 one reporter in Berlin found that all the people he talked to reckoned with war in the near future, and no one reckoned with a German victory or was in favour of war, while many socialists welcomed a war which would do away with 'the spectre of National Socialism'. At Christmas 1936 many Berlin housewives spoke of the coming war which would bring hunger. The pessimistic views were caused by the news in the papers, above all the news from Spain. 'The people stood about in groups and argued; especially in front of the newspaper kiosks there were bunches of people.' From the Palatinate it was reported in the summer of 1937, while some time ago many believed in a German victory, now the majority expected a defeat. This was apparently due to Nazi propaganda which continuously described in the 'blackest colours how the other nations rearmed', and people concluded that Germany must lose if it had to fight against all these powerful states. Twelve months later this pessimistic view was surprisingly confirmed by a report of the Armaments Inspectorate of Bavaria that large sections of the people thought a war would put an end to the economic prosperity and reach 'a terrible end for Germany'. Members of the older generation, among them many workers, silently compared the situation with the years before 1914 when there was general prosperity 'until finally the terrible catastrophe broke over Germany in August 1914'.[4] Coming from this source it was an admission full of pessimism.

In the summer of 1938 the people's mood was described in reports reaching the SPD leaders from Saxony as fear of war, above all by those who had participated in the last war. The enemies of the regime looked at war 'as the initiative for liberation from the fascist dictatorship'. In general people were convinced that Germany would lose if the war did not end in the shortest time: 'everybody knows that Germany cannot sustain a long war.' Nobody knew what would come after Hitler, 'one only expects that Germany will suffer a disastrous defeat and will then be divided up'. From the south-west it was written that Hitler's enemies – not only socialists but also Catholics – hoped 'if only war came'. 'It is like the illusion about the army: the politically uneducated above all hope for a war, those who years ago hoped that one day the *Reichswehr* would overthrow Hitler.' In September 1938 the Central Committee of the KPD instructed its subordinate sections to counter the mood of fatalism permeating Germany: 'Hitler achieves everything without a war on account of the cowardice and weakness of the democratic countries.' The Communists had to show that such partial successes did not solve the difficulties of the regime, that the danger of a general war did not disappear, for the 'liberation' of the Sudetenland was only Hitler's pretence in order to achieve his domination in south-eastern Europe and preparation for the assault on Czechoslovakia. There is even some evidence that in Silesia – close to Poland – the violent anti-Polish propaganda preceding the outbreak of war found an echo among the workers. In the spring of 1939 the SPD recorded that 'our friends in the factories' thought in case of war the 'great masses' would follow Hitler; the anti-Polish agitation was influencing people with leftwing views and some even believed that Poland, with British money, was preparing a war against Germany.[5]

The Nazi organization the workers were confronted with in the factories and mines was the German Labour Front. It was not a trade union and its principal aims was to preserve 'work peace'. It nevertheless fulfilled certain functions of the dissolved unions and to some extent represented the workers' interests. Its legal advice centres tried to mediate in cases of conflict, for example in 1936 in the Palatinate in 8222 cases. In the Ruhr it achieved that the miners, against the employers' opposition, were given more leave and leave money. The DAF office for women conducted a tenacious struggle to improve the position of working women and obtain better wages, as well as compaigning against their work on certain machines and in brick-kilns, and for the payment of better support after childbirth, etc. Yet many working women did not want to have their free time organized by Strength through Joy. The DAF also met opposition when it tried to interfere with the running of the factories. At Siemens its officials were curtly told: 'There is nothing you can obtain here, at most you can learn something.' Many employers complained to their association about interference by local DAF officials, and in 1935 the employers established a special working group, 'Social Factory Work', to ward off encroachments. Yet many enterprises responded to DAF initiatives by allowing their female workers some free days for their household chores, giving pregnant women lighter work, establishing crèches, helping with the payment of kindergarten fees, etc.[6] As the employers made enormous profits they could well afford such small concessions, as long as they remained 'master in the house'.

Many workers looked at the DAF with great suspicion. From an iron foundry in Chemnitz it was reported in 1937 that the workers knew full well they no longer had an organization to represent their interests. 'If we only still had our old unions', many Chemnitz metal workers often said, 'then things would be different.' In central Germany, another report said, most workers considered the DAF superfluous, especially because employers and employees had to be in the same organization; the dues were a kind of tax that had to be paid. If they complained the answer usually was: 'Settle it in the factory and reach agreement!' A worker in a joinery complained to the DAF about accidents; its representative negotiated with the employer and demanded to know the name of the complainant. He asked whether he was a DAF member, and when the answer was negative he called the complainant insolent and demanded to know why he was not a member. He then lectured the workers about their duties under the Four-Year Plan and towards 'nation and state'; no incitement would be tolerated. At an Upper Silesian mine the burial fund of the miners, which had always been administered by them, was to be transferred to the DAF. But the miners declared they would no longer contribute if the DAF took over. A miners' meeting opposed the transfer which would exclude the Polish miners from getting benefits. There were hostile interruptions, the meeting was dissolved but the fund continued to be administered by the miners. In 1937, according to a Gestapo report, a DAF speaker in a large Düsseldorf factory greeted the assembled men with the Hitler salute to which they replied by murmuring. At the end of the 'factory appeal' they did give the required salute distinctly and clearly, but only because the appeal was now finished.[7] Obviously, the workers were not interested in listening to a boring speech. Even the Gestapo found that DAF speakers often conducted themselves 'clumsily'.

If DAF officials by their 'bossy' attitude found it difficult to gain the workers' confidence, the same was true of the *Vertrauensräte*, the factory appointees who depended on the goodwill of the employers. From Saxony it was reported in 1937 that the postponement of the elections aroused little interest in most factories. Many workers thought that the elections served no purpose because the candidates were selected by the employers and their main task was to organize Nazi spectacles in the enterprise. But in the same year it was also stated that some *Vertrauensräte* 'really tried to represent the workers' interests'. That never lasted long, however, because it lacked a legal basis: 'either the man in question has to leave the enterprise or he becomes indifferent and lets things slide.' When a *Vertrauensrat* did not possess the workers' confidence, as in a Bavarian transport enterprise, the men tried to sabotage his work or to manoeuvre him into unpleasant situations.[8]

For the employers' side the *Vertrauensrat* fulfilled an important function in combating the spread of *Bummelei* – absenteeism on account of ill health or without an obvious reason. In the Ruhr mines, for example, on an average working day 7.4 per cent of the workforce were absent in 1938. In September 1939 the *Vertrauensräte* of some mines demanded measures be taken 'to force these *Bummelanten* to fulfil their duty'. In general, according to the DAF paper of June, in most enterprises the *Vertrauensrat* only led 'a shadowy existence' and was not consulted at all or only on minor issues.[9] Given its dependent position and lack of legal rights this weakness was quite inevitable.

In a Bavarian transport firm the workers' attitude to their *Vertrauensrat* in 1937 was that they could not always avoid approaching it, but whenever possible they went to the members of the former factory council which then negotiated with the management. Even Nazi workers did so and the old councillors acted for them. In consequence all *Vertrauensrat* members resigned and left the field to the old factory council. From a Ruhr mine it was reported in 1938 that the authority of the old councillors was greater than it had been when they functioned officially, owing to the complete inactivity of the DAF. The Düsseldorf Gestapo noted in 1937 that many workers did not approach the DAF with their wage problems but went to the old union representatives who were often elected to the *Vertrauensrat* and saw to it that their comrades as well got the better posts in the enterprise. When a leading economic paper announced in February 1936 that in the long run it would be impossible to pay invalidity rents after ten years of contributions to the insurance and that the period would have to be increased to 20 years, such widespread indignation arose about the announcement that large numbers wanted to terminate their DAF membership. This the Gestapo termed 'propaganda against the government in a Marxist sense', but the waiting period was not extended.[10] Small successes could be gained if excitement and indignation became sufficiently widespread and the authorities got worried.

Certainly widespread – and worrying to the authorities – was the *Bummelei* which started fairly widely in 1936 and increased during the following years. As such it was not a new problem because already before 1933 absenteeism was widespread among the Ruhr miners, mainly owing to sickness. When some Ruhr mines investigated the causes of absenteeism in the late 1930s the reasons given by the miners varied from old age and overwork to house repairs and work on the allotment, and by women from household work to looking after sick people, bad health and husband's leave. The employers reacted with public reprimands, deductions from wages and leave, to threats of imprisonment and other punishments, but with little success. Because of the growing labour shortage dismissal was no longer a threat, and all penalties proved ineffective. On the contrary, many workers wanted to change to better-paid jobs and, if the employer refused to let them go, resorted to malingering or provoking illness. As a report of May 1938 put it: 'The one is absent for a week without excuse, the other works badly . . . but the hoped-for dismissal does not happen.' At the Concordia mine the wage was cut by half a day for the first case of absenteeism, by a full day for the second, and by dismissal for the third. If leave was not granted the workers simply stayed away. Significantly the rate of absenteeism increased markedly during school holidays and at harvest time.[11]

As to the length of the working day, the eight-hour day remained legally in force, but since 1934 the *Treuhänder* were empowered to stipulate exceptions from that rule and made use of it on a large scale because of the labour shortage. Overtime of one or two hours a day became quite common. In the aviation industry a 60-hour week was worked in 1938. The report of the *Reichstreuhänder* for the last quarter of 1938 stated that the labour shortage led to 'a further extension of working time', which many workers found 'oppressive', and caused a decline of performance. In especially urgent cases continuous working time reached 26 and even 36 hours. The *Treuhänder* also recorded a worrying increase in absenteeism and illness. A Thuringian metal factory found that absenteeism had a tendency to grow the further the worker's domicile was away from the factory, which made control more difficult; after the Christmas holiday of 1938 the sickness figures increased sharply. In the Thuringian lignite and potash mines up to 30 per cent of the men were absent after Christmas. In the chemical industry, too, absenteeism was growing considerably and complaints about slack work discipline were increasing. In November 1938 several *Treuhänder* reported that, because of continuous overtime, many workers would not work longer than 48 hours a week. If their wish was not fulfilled a drop in output would result. On several building sites the men went home after payday on Friday to reappear only on Monday or Tuesday. Women whose husbands were earning well often appeared for work even more irregularly.[12]

As far as the miners were concerned, a medical report of August 1938 found that the excessive demands for more work 'could not possibly continue for any length of time without a danger that, apart from damage to the individual's health, economic damages will appear in the near future'. The employers began to reckon with an increasing exhaustion of the miners. In October one mining group of the Ruhr held a special meeting to discuss the health of their workforce. In spite of this a decree of April 1939 about an increase of production and shift wages provided for an extension of the working shift from 8 to 8¾ hours and high premiums for greater production. In fact, coal production in the Ruhr remained fairly constant at about 127,000 tons p.a. in 1937–38 and increased to 130,000 in 1939. In the workers' settlement of Hochlarmark the decree was received with derision. One comment was: 'They want to have the workers away from the street so that they can no longer see the fat ones drive in their cars.' The older miners were opposed but some of the younger ones were in favour because they would earn more. The workers' mood, according to a report of March 1937, became 'noticeably more restless' because the managements demanded more overtime and refused to pay proportionately more for it. Loud complaints arose about low wages, discontent with the workers' situation and the growing cost of living. Even some *Vertrauensräte* and DAF foremen demanded better pay. By November 1939 more than a thousand Ruhr workers were accused of absenteeism or refusal to work and the courts were unable to cope with the multitude of cases. In April 1939 one manager stated resignedly that no threat of dismissal could be carried out 'because we need every man'. In the Saar the young miners were prominent in absenting themselves. That was the situation shortly before the outbreak of war.[13]

The first signs of a beginning labour shortage appeared as early as the summer of 1935. The vast amount of military construction and of

Autobahn sites made it difficult to find the workers. In September Göring, charged with the implementation of the Four-Year Plan, noticed signs of strain. The first draft of a law concerning labour mentioned 'a noticeable shortage of skilled labour ... in the building, building-materials and metal industries'. For the aviation industry 50,000 more metal workers would shortly be needed, and the introduction of con-scription would further aggravate the labour shortage. Workers were enticed away by the offer of higher wages, and rates of up to three times the tariff minimum were paid, not counting overtime for a working day of up to 14 hours. Many workers left their jobs and so broke their contracts, or they forced 'their employers to dismiss them by behaving in an ill-disciplined way or by putting less effort into the work'. Strikes to gain increases were 'no longer an exceptional occurrence'. In August 1936 the Rhenish labour office stated that skilled workers constantly changed their jobs, that in spite of the official wage-stop higher wages were paid. The SPD reports also noticed that men who had been unemployed in the Rhineland were earning well. Skilled men were enticed away and the position of certain categories grew stronger. They gained self-confidence and used the situation to the full, while the government and employers let the situation drift. From December 1935 to June 1939 the average hourly wage in the armament industry rose by 10.9 per cent, the weekly wage (because of overtime) by 16.8 per cent, thereby reaching the pre-crisis level. In Upper Franconia the wages of skilled men rose by about 5 per cent but those of the auxiliary workers by 15 to 20 per cent because they started from a low level.[14]

As any collective bargaining was impossible, highly qualified workers in 1936 negotiated singly with the management, as at Siemens in Berlin, to obtain better value for their work. At the Henschel aviation works in Berlin one worker would demand to be moved into the next highest category. That achieved, the next man would come with the same demand; 'one relies on the other, without any concerted action for the whole compartment'. In another Berlin factory more than 20 engineers gave notice. They rejected an offer of a five-pfennig increase per hour but accepted ten pfennigs and withdrew their notice. In the Zündapp works at Nuremberg the piece rates were to be cut in 1937 whereupon all workers gave notice; the old rates were restored. In a Berlin electrical firm the men went singly to the foreman demanding better wages and he sided with them. One demand led to the next but all that was achieved was an increase of two to three pfennigs per hour. In the Linke-Hoffman works at Breslau it was proposed to cut the clothing allowance of 1.35 marks of the electrowelders and give them overalls instead. The workers protested to the *Vertrauensrat*; after a long palaver the proposal was withdrawn and over-time payment was increased by

15 per cent. In 1938, however, the piece rates were cut by 25 per cent, causing great embitterment, and only a minority were able to have the old rates restored.[15]

Soon the movement to obtain higher wages spread to other industries. Early in 1938 the *Treuhänder* for Lower Saxony reported that many workers made their starting a job dependent on better payment – a tendency spreading to 'other sections of the labour force'. Workers brought from Silesia to build a canal declared they would not work for 52 pfennigs an hour, and a quarter of them left the site and went home. Elsewhere 140 workers of a construction firm demanded an increase of ten pfennigs an hour, otherwise they would go on strike. A firm in Brunswick which already paid 88 pfennigs an hour – 29 above the legal minimum – found it was daily losing five to seven workers to the building sites of the Volkswagen factory. With the vast amount of building work going on all over Germany the building workers could insist on an improvement of their low wages. In 1938–39 the labour shortage increased further and included all degrees of skill in all trades. But the principal beneficiaries were the iron, metal and building workers; they could simply point to better conditions existing in neighbouring factories or sites, and they were often successful with their demands.[16]

At the MAN factory in Augsburg control clocks were introduced in the summer of 1937 to measure the time required for piecework, whereupon 130 skilled workers refused to start their machines in the morning. The *Vertrauensrat* unsuccessfully tried to mediate, but the clocks were removed. In two halls dissatisfaction with the piece rates was so great that only their contracts prevented the workers from quitting. At a brick-kiln at Kronach in Franconia the men threatened the manager because the labour exchange refused them permission to leave for construction work. In central Germany there were almost daily reports of brickmakers leaving their jobs. At one kiln the workers in 1938 demanded a rise of five marks a week, otherwise they would stop work. After intervention by the *Treuhänder* they continued to work but gave notice. Arrests could not be carried out because an immediate stoppage would have taken place. In the same year the official responsible for the district of Aachen reported that the local factories were outbidding each other to get workers, offering better leave, protection against dismissal, bonuses for separation from the family, etc. Many stopped work in order to get into a better paying enterprise. At the end of 1938 the same official wrote that the wages paid at the Westwall construction were like a magnet attracting qualified workers from the entire local industry; substitutes could not be found; the labour exchanges tried to prevent certain works losing too many men, but they always found ways and means to circumvent this. By working overtime some could earn as much as 80 marks a week.[17]

Not all workers, however, were in such a strong position. In many factories, according to reports reaching the SPD leaders, workers had to accept cuts in piece rates or lower wages. In a Silesian textile factory the men stopped work because of an intended cut in wages and piece rates. The management then abandoned the first but not the second. The Gestapo intervened and the intimidated workers went back to work. A large firm producing wooden barracks wanted to cut the piece rates of the saddlers and upholsterers by 15 per cent. Forty workers stopped work to force the management to negotiate, but the DAF declared the cuts justified: three ringleaders were arrested and work was resumed. The directors of a Silesian glass factory refused to pay overtime of 25 per cent, the workers often had to do repair work at night and demanded to be paid overtime according to the valid tariff. The local DAF official found this justified but the firm refused to budge. At a factory meeting with the *Treuhänder*, a DAF official, the mayor etc., the *Treuhänder* stressed the financial difficulties of the firm and announced stern measures against 'grumblers and criticasters'. The workers could not speak and a second factory meeting, although announced, never took place. In a Saxon factory the piece rates were cut by up to 20 per cent. Two young mechanics refused to accept whereupon the *Vertrauensrat* denounced them for refusing to work. They insisted on dismissal – and were sent to East Prussia to work on fortifications. The management of a Bavarian glass factory promised to increase piece rates by 10 per cent, but then introduced Sunday work and explained to the men that, if they worked on Sundays, their earnings would rise by 10 per cent, and the men had to accept.[18]

In the Upper Silesian coal mines there was an attempt to extend the eight-hour shifts or to introduce Sunday shifts, and this met with strong opposition. At one big mine the miners simply declared they were too weak to work more, they had not seen eggs or bacon for three months. At another mine the *Vertrauensrat* accused the men of sabotage, for food was sufficient; the reply was: 'Certainly, for those with money, but not for us.' At yet another mine it was explained to the *Vertrauensrat* that the quotas could not be achieved because butter was too expensive and lard unobtainable. Elsewhere the men went home after eight hours or agreed not to produce more coal than they considered enough. But at other mines the men duly worked the overtime demanded.[19] The picture varied from mine to mine, depending on age and nationality (many men were Polish) and on their degree of militancy.

In a Bavarian factory producing sports clothing the seamstresses in 1937 had to listen to a lecture on 'blood and race' and were told to produce more children. They had strong objections and the indignation increased when the management announced that the lost hour spent at the lecture would have to be worked: 'Whoever opposed this was a rebel against the state and would have to bear the consequences.' The unrest subsided under this threat. In a Saxon machine tool factory 80 of 400 workers signed a list objecting to a deduction for the Winterhelp. The manager admonished them and the DAF representative called them 'Marxists and enemies of the state'. It was then suggested they should give at least ten pfennigs, but the workers claimed they had already contributed and refused to give more. In 1938 a collector for the Winterhelp in Cologne said that he simply could not repeat what the women told the collectors. It was difficult to collect any money in the factories and the workers called it 'blackmail' when the manager time and again asked them to contribute. But from Saxony it was reported at the same time that the many steep deductions from the wages and the continuous collections were 'only seldom a reason for criticism'. The large majority were not interested in politics and only rarely listened to foreign stations. What counted was that several million unemployed had got work at whatever wages.[20] The large majority were interested in their bread and butter, not in politics.

But they were also interested in freedom of movement and wanted to get better-paid jobs. In June 1939 a Nazi official reported from the Rhineland:

> There is discontent on a large scale about the regulations arising from the Four-Year Plan, restricting freedom of individual movement, like compulsory military service, about the directives fixing maximum wages and the limitation of the worker's right to terminate his employment.

The workers failed to understand why the restrictions should affect them '90 per cent of the time' and the employers 'perhaps 10 per cent and the civil servant not at all'. A report of the Military-economic Inspectorate for Berlin of July 1939 mentioned 'passive resistance' and complained about falling productivity. The owner of a Dresden tannery recorded that, when he asked his workers why they wanted to change their jobs and gave false reasons for doing so, they replied that now everything was camouflaged and so they had to do the same. In September an official of the Ministry of Labour stated in a conference that, on an average, earnings per hour had risen by 10 per cent since 1933, weekly earnings by 20 per cent; at fortification works weekly wages up to 300 marks were paid, at the building site of the Berlin chancery 250 to 300 marks. The discrepancies in wage levels were causing 'serious social tensions and considerably weakened the workers' will to work'. While metal workers on an average gained a rise in their real wages of 12 and building workers of 4 per cent, the real income of textile workers fell by 12 per cent.[21] The discrepancies opened a gulf between the workers able to take advantage of the boom conditions and the disadvantaged poorer workers. Solidarity could not possibly develop under such conditions.

Food prices became more stable and the shortages less severe. But difficulties continued to exist, especially in the provision of fats, and there were temporary shortages of potatoes and eggs. In the autumn of 1937 it was reported from Berlin that a potato shortage caused near-riots in the market, and women were fined for expressing their indignation. A shortage of meat in Berlin meant that workers living at a distance from their workplace experienced great difficulties in getting the cheaper cuts, for demand increased on paydays and when they reached home only the more expensive varieties were available. From Saxony it was reported in the same year that women openly expressed their indignation in the shops because of the meat and fat shortages. In Königsberg in East Prussia women were equally prominent in the spring of 1939 in demonstrating against the shortages, when the fish available was not fresh or when they were forced to buy food of poor quality. In the summer there were more reports from West Germany of women showing deep resentment in the shops on account of the short supply and bad quality of the goods on offer.[22] However, with almost full employment and wage rises for many workers the discontent was less of a problem for the Nazi regime than it had been in the earlier years.

The mood of the working class in the years before the war varied very considerably from place to place. Early in 1936 the *Treuhänder* for Hesse spoke of an 'apparent quietness' of the workers, an attitude of 'resignation and renunciation'. It was widely believed that the measures to create work had only helped the employers to recover from their economic decline, 'but that the worker was excluded from the successes'. In October 1936 the administrative head of the Bavarian district of Swabia recorded that, according to many local reports, there was widespread dissatisfaction with the government and the Nazi party. The workers could not understand the rise in the cost of living when wages remained stationary or were falling, as in the textile industry. The opinion was gaining ground that the other social classes were helped more than the workers. A sketch of the mood of the Ruhr miners by one of their former union officials noticed that they did not demand higher wages or more rights, did not dispute the necessity of rearming if all other countries were armed; but what they discussed constantly was who had to make the sacrifices, comparing the directors' salaries and the profits with their own wages. Those issues really excited the miners. Early in 1937 the leaders of the Westphalian Nazi women found that the 'glad approval' the people had shown for the *Führer* and the movement had been 'in part seriously destroyed'; any pessimistic remark 'about a coming war, about great food shortages and other catastrophes finds a well-prepared soil'.[23]

The reports received by the SPD leaders in Prague reflected the different trends of opinion. From Berlin it was written in 1937 that many of those who had not belonged to a union tended 'to discover and "appreciate" certain achievements of the Nazi regime in the field of social policy, for the simple reason that they have no idea what the old unions achieved'. A Bavarian building worker stated that among his colleagues there was hardly a convinced Nazi. He did not believe in the people's community: to the old rich, new ones were added – the *Bonzen* of the regime. Or, as the Nazi leaders of Augsburg put it later: the workers do not understand how one can talk of 'the greatest possible austerity' while on the other side a luxury existed which must astonish every simple human being. From the Rhineland it was reported that 'the great mass is indifferent, accepts everything and only occupies itself with personal matters': they take part in factory functions out of curiosity, contribute to collections, have no political interest, are satisfied if they can work on their allotments in the evenings and on Sundays, they are not Nazis, nor are they anti-Nazi. This was confirmed from Saxony at the end of 1937: 'the real wage has become lower but the employer's dividend higher ... The present attitude of the German worker must be seen as similar to the way the soldier installed himself comfortably in the trenches so as to make that life if possible tolerable.' What depressed them most was the outlook for the immediate future; it made them fatalists. In an armaments factory of the south-west, it was noted, two camps existed: the weaklings and sneaks and those demanding a proper wage for their work who formed the majority.[24]

Early in 1938 it was recorded from Saxony that the mass of the people were 'dominated by a frightening fatalism'. If the food supply functioned they were 'quiet and content', if shortages occurred they grumbled. In a large Bavarian armaments factory the mood was one of 'severe depression', like that in a doctor's waiting room; no one knew what was coming and what would happen to him: 'because nothing good could be expected of the future he does not want to think about it'. In North Germany the 'great mass of the people are completely indifferent' and do not want to hear anything about politics; they 'grumble everywhere and about everything, but no one wants to criticize the regime with that grumbling'. Even a leading Communist had to admit that the growing dissatisfaction did not indicate any willingness to do something against the regime. The ever growing terror induced many of the dissatisfied to tolerate the regime out of fear, and not a few 'were prepared to give open or secret hints about oppositional tendencies to the terror apparatus'. A DAF memorandum, on the other hand, stated in May 1939 that the eight-hour working day was the most favoured time, for there existed among the workers a mood of disquiet and in large factories of the Rhineland, Silesia and central Germany productivity had declined by 15 to 25 per cent. When punitive measures were taken the result was a rapid increase in the number of those reporting sick.[25]

What most workers disliked heartily was compulsory attendance at the MayDay rallies organized by the authorities. As one participant remembered, they had to march in columns to the assembly places and were watched so that no one disappeared *en route*. But when they reached the meeting place, 'not five minutes and we disappeared'. In Brunswick, the Gestapo reported in 1938, the different marching blocks dispersed when they got near the square where the meeting took place and returned to town without entering the square. 'Then a general floating back of the masses from the square started so that at the beginning of the *Führer*'s speech only about one third of the participants was left.' Clearly, the control measures proved faulty. In 1937 some forest workers threatened with dismissal were told they could keep their jobs if they went on the MayDay parade: those unable to prove it were discharged.[26]

In general it can be said that the vociferous propaganda of the 'people's community' made little impression on the workers, for the gulf between them and the rich – whether employers or Nazi bigwigs – was too wide. The mood was one of passivity and resignation, not of defiance. Small opposition groups continued to exist but their effect was negligible. Workers were interested in their wages and living conditions, which continued to be very poor. They grumbled and the Ruhr miners often asked: 'When will I finally earn more?' So did of course most others. Yet at the Ruhr another tendency remained alive. In the autumn of 1939 the Military-economic Inspectorate of Münster launched an enquiry about the wishes and complaints of the armament workers. The result was that they did not only desire higher wages, lower prices and shorter working hours, but also freedom to change jobs as well as freedom of opinion and of the press.[27] These relatively well-paid workers had not forgotten what the regime deprived them of and resented the fetters with which they were bound. This does not mean that all workers thought so. Many of the young who got their first jobs under Hitler would have thought differently. In July 1939 the reports received by the SPD leaders noted:

> The great mass is overtired and indifferent . . . Those who did think previously still think, and those who previously did not think think even less today, with the difference that today the first lot are no longer able to lead the others.[28]

This allowed the Nazi authorities plenty of opportunity to lead the unthinking, to keep them quiet and obedient.

Deep resentment, however, was caused by the compulsory assignment of many thousands, not only of unemployed but also of employed men, to priority undertakings, such as road and Autobahn building and later the construction of the Westwall and other fortifications. According to one estimate, about 1,300,000 workers were sent away from their homes, almost 400,000 to the Westwall, most of them for limited periods. They were housed in barracks in rather primitive conditions and received little compensation for low wages and separation from their families (which was improved in 1939). From Silesia, according to the SPD reports, many hundreds were sent in 1937 to Pomerania, Mecklenburg and East Prussia. They grumbled but did not resist. But after a short time many returned because the wages were too low (often only 35 to 45 pfennigs an hour), they were housed in sheds and barns, the work was too heavy, and their families received little support. Some claimed that in East Prussia they were treated like cattle. After their return, they were refused benefits and policemen were used to conduct them back to the places assigned to them. The wives threatened to go with them but were removed by the police. From the Lower Rhine workers were sent to the ore mines of Württemberg, but they were unable to send money to their families – which suffered badly for weeks, until they received additional support. From Hamburg unemployed men were sent to Mecklenburg to work on military undertakings.[29] Yet these compulsory assignments – and conscription for the armed forces – reduced the unemployment figures.

In April 1937 a conference took place in the Ministry of Economics to discuss the assignment of miners from the Saar region to work outside because, at the time of administration by the League of Nations, they had allegedly shown an anti-German attitude and would 'represent a danger to the Reich if they remained in the Saar (frontier region)'. To avoid unrest the transfers were to take place in small groups and in different localities. In the spring of 1939 the Gestapo complained about low morale among the Westwall workers which it attributed to incorrect treatment and bad selection. The 'dissatisfied elements' were putting forward more and more demands so that 'new centres of dissatisfaction' were created by radical workers. Other Gestapo reports confirmed the low morale and embitterment of the workmen employed far from home at low wages on military construction projects, for example at Emden

and Wilhelmshaven on the North Sea. Early in 1939 the mood deteriorated to such an extent that many refused to sign their contracts, sought
different jobs or returned home without permission, especially when
promises of leave were not kept for 'state-political reasons'. In the early
years of the war about 15,000 miners were transferred from Upper
Silesia to the Ruhr, and once more endless complaints arose about low
wages, insufficient family support and bad accommodation, so that
finally they were allowed to return home.[30] During the war, mass alien-
ation of thousands of workers could not be risked so easily.

In spite of the violent anti-Semitic propaganda of the regime Germans
of all social classes continued to frequent Jewish shops. In Munich, the
police recorded, the throng in a Jewish department store before Christmas 1936 was so great that the personnel, increased by additional help,
was unable to cope with the customers, consisting of workers as well
as country folk. The Bavarian peasants continued to trade with Jewish
cattle dealers as they paid well and in cash. Some peasants were classified as 'pro-Jewish', and the Munich Gestapo found that the peasants
were lacking 'all racial consciousness'. From Münster too it was
reported early in 1937 that the Jewish shops had more customers. In a
Protestant elementary school in Hanover, as a teacher remembered, the
Jewish pupils were treated very well, 'no hair on their heads was to be
touched'.[31]

While these few reports do not permit any general conclusion, it was
quite different with the terrible pogroms of November 1938 and the
accompanying looting and vast destruction which caused general indignation in many parts of Germany. This applied above all to Hamburg.
Whoever returned home with the harbour and dock workers in the
November evening 'heard nothing but imprecations and curses about
these manhunts'. In one case workers witnessing the looting of a Jewish
jewellers pursued the looters and returned the loot to the owner with
the acclaim and protection of the onlookers. Other reports spoke of
policemen protecting Jewish shops and their owners, while the participants in the pogroms were classified as juveniles from the HJ and the
scum of the lowest classes. From a place in the Upper Palatinate
the police reported: 'Up to now not one person has said that the Jews
got what they deserved.' On the Sunday after the pogrom the Catholics
of a village near Ulm made a pilgrimage to a burnt-out synagogue.
People from other villages boycotted a pub in Ochsenfurt because the
owner's son had participated in a pogrom. In Munich, the mood of
the people was 'wholly against the action', bakers delivered bread to
Jews and grocers enquired whether they needed anything, in spite of
the ban on sales to Jews; and there were acts of solidarity with the
persecuted in other Bavarian towns. The administrative official respons-

ible for Lower Franconia reported that many people declared they would not give anything for the collections after the wilful destruction of so much property. In an aviation factory near Berlin the workers' attitude to the pogroms was negative and indignation increased when it became known that local SA men had been arrested because they had enriched themselves – as the wits would have it, 'due to a misunderstanding'. But there also was a report from the south-west that the indignation was not all that 'uniform', that some working-class people did not defend the Jews.[32]

The Communists of the Rhine–Ruhr area issued a leaflet 'Against the Jewish Pogroms' which mentioned the 'general indignation and revulsion of the overwhelming majority of the population', especially about the vast destruction of property. They received many eyewitness reports from the area about the 'methodical' action of the SA and SS units against Jewish shops, flats and synagogues, the cruel treatment of men and women and the personal enrichment of members of the SA, SS and HJ. The Gestapo commented that the Communists, together with bourgeois and clerical circles, undoubtedly succeeded in 'considerably influencing public opinion' – a remarkable admission.[33] If the Gestapo attributed this to 'circles hostile to the state' they were mistaken, for in this case indignation was not limited to these groups but was much more general. In some cases it had political consequences. In Cologne, an 11-year-old working-class boy witnessed the murder of a Jewish hairdresser by Nazi thugs, and his father was unable to help the man. The boy's sister later testified: in her family 'a hatred developed. We were simply no longer able to say "Heil Hitler" '.[34]

In general, however, the years 1936 to 1939 saw a considerable consolidation of the Nazi regime and, for some sections of the working class, a little prosperity. Unemployment virtually came to an end and this enabled certain sections of the working class to achieve better conditions, but the condition of other sections remained very precarious.

Notes

1. Peukert and Bajohr, *Spuren des Widerstands*, p. 165.
2. *Deutschland-Berichte*, v, 1938, no. 3, pp. 260, 262, 264, 280.
3. Ibid., nos. 4–5, pp. 445f., no. 9, pp. 940–45, no. 10, p. 1064.
4. Ibid., iv, 1937, no. 1, pp. 9, 14, no. 8, p. 1087; *Bayern in der NS-Zeit*, i, p. 277: report of 9 September 1938.
5. *Deutschland-Berichte*, v, 1938, no. 7, pp. 686, 688, 690, vi, 1939, no. 5, pp. 560f.; Klaus Mammach, 'Die KPD und das Münchener Abkommen 1938', *Zeitschrift für Geschichtswissenschaft*, xvi 1968, p. 1038.
6. Mallmann and Paul, *Herrschaft und Alltag*, p. 140; Wolfgang Franz

Werner, 'Bleib übrig'. Deutsche Arbeiter in der nationalsozialistischen Kriegswirtschaft, Düsseldorf, 1983, p. 361; Dörte Winkler, Frauenarbeit im Dritten Reich, Hamburg, 1977, pp. 78ff., 157f.; Rüdiger Hachtmann, Industriearbeit im Dritten Reich, Göttingen, 1989, p. 257.

7. Deutschland-Berichte, iv, 1937, no. 3, pp. 313, 330, v, 1938, no. 11, pp. 1258f., 1273; Tim Mason, Arbeiterklasse und Volksgemeinschaft, Opladen, 1975, p. 380.

8. Deutschland-Berichte, iv, 1937, no. 6, pp. 806, 808, no. 12, pp. 1688f., iii, 1936, no. 1, p. 86.

9. Frese, Betriebspolitik im Dritten Reich, pp. 213, 215, 217; John Gillingham, 'Die Ruhrbergleute und Hitlers Krieg', in Hans Mommsen and Ulrich Borsdorf (eds.), Glück auf, Kameraden! Cologne, 1979, pp. 334f.

10. Deutschland-Berichte, iv, 1937, no. 6, p. 806; Peukert and Bajohr, Spuren des Widerstands, p. 128; Mason, Arbeiterklasse, pp. 295, 386.

11. Gunter May, 'Warum steht der deutsche Arbeiter zu Hitler?' Geschichte und Gesellschaft, xii 1986, pp. 223f.; John R. Gillingham, Industry and Politics in the Third Reich. Ruhr Coal, Wiesbaden, 1985, p. 56; Deutschland-Berichte, v, 1938, no. 4–5, p. 446; Gillingham, 'Ruhrbergleute', p. 336.

12. Mason, Sozialpolitik, p. 280; idem, Arbeiterklasse, pp. 848, 862ff.; Hachtmann, Industriearbeit, p. 52.

13. Gillingham, 'Ruhrbergleute', p. 333; idem, Industry and Politics, p. 58; Zimmermann, 'Ein schwer zu bearbeitendes Pflaster', p. 82; Wisotzky, Ruhrbergbau, pp. 140f., 224ff.; Mason, Sozialpolitik, p. 320; Mallmann and Paul, Herrschaft und Alltag, p. 358.

14. Mason, 'Labour in the Third Reich', Past and Present, no. 33 1966, pp. 126ff.; idem, Sozialpolitik, p. 229; Rüther, Arbeiterschaft, p. 228; Herbert, 'Arbeiterschaft im Dritten Reich', p. 332; Eiber, Arbeiter unter der NS-Herrschaft, p. 177; Voges, 'Klassenkampf', pp. 347, 381.

15. Ibid., pp. 347ff.; Deutschland-Berichte, iv, 1937, no. 3, p. 328, no. 7, p. 1004, v, 1938, no. 8, p. 988, vi, 1939, no. 1, pp. 46f.

16. Mason, 'Labour in the Third Reich', pp. 134f., 138; idem, Arbeiterklasse, pp. 609f.

17. Hetzer, Indsutriestadt Augsburg, pp. 120f.; Mason, Arbeiterklasse, p. 658; Rüther, Arbeiterschaft, pp. 272f.

18. Deutschland-Berichte, iv, 1937, no. 6, pp. 779, 781, v, 1938, no. 3, pp. 289f., 302, 304.

19. Ibid., iv, 1937, no. 6, pp. 826, 1037f., v, 1938, no. 3, pp. 434f.

20. Ibid., iv, 1937, no. 6, pp. 813f., no. 10, pp. 1678f., v, 1938, no. 1, pp. 27, 97.

21. Marlis G. Steinert, Hitler's War and the Germans, Athens, Ohio, 1977, p. 32; Mason, Sozialpolitik, pp. 315f.; Wicht, Glanzstoff, p. 185.

22. Deutschland-Berichte, iv, 1937, no. 1, pp. 47f, no. 10, p. 1434, vi, 1939, no. 5, p. 639; Wisotzky, Ruhrbergbau, p. 151; Dahlem, Am Vorabend, ii, p. 324.

23. Mason, Sozialpolitik, p. 173; Wolfgang Domarus, Nationalsozialismus, Krieg und Bevölkerung, Munich, 1977, p. 57; Franz Vogt, 'Die Lage der deutschen Bergarbeiter', quoted by Peukert and Bajohr, Spuren des Widerstands, pp. 148f.; Kuropka, Meldungen, p. 181.

24. Deutschland-Berichte, iv, 1937, no. 2, p. 142, no. 3, p. 316, no. 9, pp. 1239, 1244, no. 12, p. 1670; Domarus, Nationalsozialismus, p. 59.

25. *Deutschland-Berichte*, v, 1938, no. 1, p. 27, no. 4–5, p. 451, no. 7, p. 697; Dahlem, *Am Vorabend*, i, p. 182, ii, p. 170.

26. Alexander von Plato, '*Der Verlierer geht nicht leer aus*', Berlin-Bonn, 1984, p. 21; Bein, *Widerstand*, p. 123; *Deutschland-Berichte*, iv, 1937, no. 6, p. 810.

27. Wisotzky, *Ruhrbergbau*, pp. 242f.; Mason, *Sozialpolitik*, p. 285.

28. Kershaw, *Popular Opinion*, p. 109; idem, 'Alltägliches und Ausseralltägliches', in Peukert and Reulecke (eds), *Die Reihen fast geschlossen*, Wuppertal, 1981, p. 284.

29. Mason, *Sozialpolitik*, pp. 290ff.; Eiber, *Arbeiter*, p. 183; *Deutschland-Berichte*, iv, 1937, no. 2, pp. 177–80, no. 10, p. 1490.

30. Mallmann and Paul, *Herrschaft und Alltag*, p. 50; Pikarski and Warning, *Gestapo-Berichte*, i, p. 210; Gillingham, 'Ruhrbergleute', p. 338; Mason, *Arbeiterklasse*, pp. 635, 941.

31. *Bayern in der NS-Zeit*, i, p. 464, ii, pp. 300f.; Kershaw, *Popular Opinion*, p. 241; Kuropka, *Meldungen*, p. 288; van Dick, *Oppositionelles Lehrerverhalten*, p. 250.

32. *Deutschland-Berichte*, v, 1938, no. 11, pp. 1352, 1356; *Bayern in der NS-Zeit*, i, p. 475, ii, pp. 329ff., 335; Robert Gellately, *The Gestapo and German Society*, Oxford, 1990, p. 210; *Deutschland-Berichte*, vi, 1939, no. 3, p. 364.

33. Copy of leaflet in Pikarski and Warning, *Gestapo-Berichte*, i, p. 194; Rossaint and Zimmermann, *Widerstand*, p. 145.

34. Family of the roofer-apprentice Bartholomäus Schink (who was executed): Matthias von Hellfeld, *Edelweisspiraten in Köln*, Cologne, 1981, p. 13.

CHAPTER SIX

Decline of the opposition

All acts of defiance or opposition (or what was perceived as such) were carefully recorded by the authorities, but the number was not very large. In July 1936 the Gestapo of Halle in central Germany complained that 'the lack of discipline among the workers of the Bitterfeld industrial area in political ways has increased fairly seriously'. It was noticed that, at the celebration of the building of a local film factory, a large section of the workers did not participate in the singing of the Horst-Wessel Song and the national anthem. In two compartments of the MAN at Augsburg (a factory known for oppositional attitudes) the men declined several times to take part in a Nazi function or to buy Winterhelp badges. To break the opposition some Nazis were added to the old crews, but the older workers made it clear to the new men that they had to conform. In a Silesian metal factory the workers took defensive action against the high speed of work and compulsory overtime. In some compartments they agreed among themselves to reduce the tempo, pretending they were exhausted. When the engineer failed to achieve better results and to increase the speed he classified the slackening as 'organized sabotage' which he would have to report to the managers. In eastern Bavaria, according to a DAF report, workers who were given free tickets for an anti-Bolshevist exhibition in 1937, tore them up and declared: 'The Soviet paradise we have got here.' They added offensive remarks about the DAF leader Ley. What happened to them was not stated. In the summer of 1936 the Augsburg police noted 'increasing unrest' among the textile workers. 'Their enthusiasm for state and party is not great and bitter remarks are not rare.' In 1937 the workers' mood in one local textile factory was described as 'explosive'; none of the few Nazi workers would risk to open his mouth.[1]

At the end of 1936 it was announced that from 1 February 1937 the regulations for the transfer of German wages from abroad were to be changed. This caused grave disquiet among the 6000 Saar miners who worked in French mines across the frontier, for the new rules meant the loss of one third of their earnings. The DAF summoned a meeting at which the NSDAP district leader was heckled when he refused to make any concession to the miners. On 14 February the miners of one shift crossed the frontier jointly after changing their wages in France in violation of the new regulations. The Nazi *Gauleiter* Josef Bürckel then declared the new rules would not be applied; but at the end of February the miners were informed they would have to change two thirds of their wages at the frontier at the official German exchange rate, which meant a big loss. On 27 February 800 crossed the frontier together, *after* changing their wages in France into marks. The Gestapo investigated the local pubs looking for 'ringleaders'. Hundreds of miners were interrogated, 28 were arrested, the punishments varied from six weeks' to eleven months' detention to fines of 130 marks, but all were freed soon. In March 1938 there were more protests and arrests. One miner was battered to death in prison. At his funeral in Lauterbach large numbers of miners and other inhabitants took part. In August – after a change of the exchange rate to the miners' disadvantage – a considerable financial compensation was granted to them.[2] Clearly, concessions were made when it was impossible to enforce a hard course.

From a Ruhr mine it was reported in 1938 that one team had their shift wages cut because the foreman thought that they produced too little coal. Thereupon the miners resorted to passive resistance – they worked but produced only half the amount of coal they had produced before. On the fourth day the foreman announced that the cut of the previous month was cancelled. In Penzberg in Upper Bavaria the miners adopted a policy of passive resistance, and production declined. Strong measures were taken against absentees. In May 1939 two popular foremen were arrested for alleged fraud in calculating the wages, and were later sent on leave. But in August 350 miners refused to start work unless one of the two men was reinstated. The management gave way and the miners marched to fetch the foreman from his house. The old solidarity still existed but it was not political opposition. In June 1939 the Military-economic Inspectorate of Nuremberg reported deep resentment of the workers about the 'enormous strain' at work; in two local armament factories this led to 'open resistance or sabotage and sabotage attempts'. Workers were arrested for attempted sabotage and two more for 'incitement'. Sabotage was exceptional and the authorities were clearly worried. In the same year 15 workers were dismissed in an Upper Silesian factory because of lack of material. Thereupon a chalk drawing appeared on the door of a toilet showing the director hanging from a gallows and the words 'That will be your fate and that of Adolf Hitler!' The Gestapo took the door away and many workers had to give their signatures in chalk, without any success. On another door someone wrote: 'You are much too stupid to catch the guilty! Workers, spread the slogan: Adolf and our director will be hanged!'[3]

Many strikes occurred in the years 1936 to 1938, more than can be mentioned here. But the majority were still very small and were settled

after a few hours. For the 18 months from February 1936 to July 1937
the DAF counted 192 strikes and work stoppages, but in only six cases
more than eight men participated in them. Most of them were for better
wages and working conditions, some defensive, others offensive. In
October 1936 the Gestapo sent a circular to the Bavarian authorities
warning them of an increase in work stoppages due to poor labour
relations. A Gestapo report of July 1936 listed a larger strike at the
Auto-Union works in Berlin and several small ones at construction sites
in Saxony and Schleswig as well as among agricultural workers. The
strike at the Auto-Union included about 500 to 600 men of the saddlery
who objected to a new wage arrangement. They assembled in the
factory yard and responded to demands that they should resume work
with shouting and yelling. The management denied that the new
arrangement meant a wage cut; we do not know the outcome. At a
Ruhr mine the miners successfully rejected the demand of the management that they should build a hydrowork without receiving overtime
payment. Most of the other strikes concerned men on Autobahn and
other building sites.[4]

Early in 1937 it was reported from a glass factory in eastern Bavaria
that on every payday bitter debates erupted about wage differentials.
One day, when the sirens signalled the resumption of work no one
moved. Then two uniformed officials and the manager appeared. One
of them shouted 'Strike!' who was the instigator? 'Without a reply there
will be no negotiation!' He threatened that, if work was not started
within the hour, half the workers would be arrested. The majority then
decided to resume work; the search for a 'ringleader' proved fruitless,
as did the negotiation of the DAF with the manager. In the summer of
1937 there was a grave danger of a strike at the Hoesch steel works in
Dortmund which was only overcome with the 'greatest efforts', and
again no 'instigator' could be found by the Gestapo which noted that
the workers earned as much as 220 to 340 marks a month. In a
Thuringian glass factory a strike of 150 men lasted only half an hour,
caused by differences over piece rates. As usual the Gestapo suspected
'Communist influences' but this was not confirmed. A go-slow of 600
Autobahn workers in the Rhineland over wages rates achieved its aim
after five weeks: as the firm in question was tied to the agreed dates, it
had to give way. Several smaller strikes of Autobahn workers, however,
were unsuccessful; the police made arrests and the other men resumed
work. In a case near Korbach in Hesse the firm, pressed for time, had
to agree to pay 180 men four pfennigs above the tariff and more for
overtime.[5]

In the Ruhr mines only one case of work stoppage was recorded in
1937–38. In February the miners of Friedrich Thyssen noticed below

too high a temperature and 47 of them ended work prematurely because, according to the contract, work was to last only six hours if the temperature rose above 28 degrees: all were fined three marks. The workers of a construction firm near Nuremberg tried to achieve their dismissal by slow work, absenteeism and drunkenness but were not dismissed. Whereupon they declared: 'We do not work, we strike!' Five of them were arrested. The same was the fate of Autobahn workers near Nuremberg who tried to induce their colleagues to stop work, as it seems with partial success. There also was widespread passive resistance of many miners against the demand to work on Sundays and New Year's Eve so that the managements had to cancel special shifts. Elesewhere miners simply took another day off because they were paid 50 per cent more for Sunday work. As all men were needed, no punitive measures were taken against miners who were absent or reported sick. In the summer a thousand fortification workers struck in the Saar, demanding more money and better food, and were partly successful.[6]

In the spring of 1939 a short strike occurred at the Opel works in Brandenburg. The management levied small fines for the loss of tools or faulty use of material. The money was to be distributed among the workforce but then it was announced that it was to be sent to Slovakia as a 'Hitler gift'. Work was stopped spontaneously and successfully; only ten marks a head went to Slovakia and each man received 30 marks. At an Upper Silesian mine the production quota per shift was increased so that wages dropped by 10 to 15 per cent. Work stopped and the DAF district leader took the miners' side. Nazi workers participated in the stoppage, and the old wages were restored. At a Saar mine 140 men stopped work for a day when a wage cut was announced, apparently without success. In Bavaria several small strikes took place, mainly on Autobahn sites and at military projects, and men were arrested for refusing work or creating unrest. The Westwall workers were more successful. In June 1939 it was announced on the radio that their massive requests would receive a positive answer, they would get better food and wages, separation allowances and an 'equalization' grant for working 60 hours per week.[7]

Even in the Third Reich not all strikes were met by calling in the Gestapo and the arrest of alleged 'ringleaders'. By 1939 so many of the construction and armament projects were so urgent and received such priority that the workers' demands were partially conceded. They could use the ever growing labour shortage to press for better conditions, exactly like the skilled workers of the armament industry. But the demands were not political and remained within the basic features of the Nazi regime. It was strong and the workers isolated and weak, in spite of the conditions of the boom. There is no evidence that large groups – apart from the small underground cells – desired a change of the regime. More political were some comments on the civil war in Spain. In the autumn of 1936 the public prosecutor of Baden reported that the activities of the leftwing groups had sharply declined but that the whispering propaganda of circles 'hostile to the state' often referred to the events in Spain and received 'a certain impetus' from them.[8]

Interestingly enough, the only mass opposition action during these years was not one of the working class but of the rural people of the small state of Oldenburg by the North Sea. There the Minister of Church and Schools, Julius Pauly, in November 1936 issued a decree that no church emblems were permitted in public buildings and the existing ones, such as crucifixes, were to be removed by December. This around a protest storm among the entire population of strictly Catholic areas. The mayor of Essen replied it was so strong that he could not carry out the decree. The official responsible for the district of Cloppenburg reported that the revolt was not limited to the enemies of the party and very pious people but included those who 'do not follow the clergy blindly'; 'a united front of the whole people has come into being, clearly and solely directed against National Socialism'. Several mayors and many teachers refused to remove the crucifixes, and threats of violent resistance were uttered. Another mayor stated that 'the confidence in the state was shaken by the decree in the worst imaginable way', to carry it out was 'impossible if we expect the people's cooperation in future'. Sermons on the issue were read in all churches.[9]

On 25 November 1936 *Gauleiter* Karl Röver spoke in a mass meeting in Cloppenburg. When the SA columns marched in the audience did not raise their right arms as required. Röver tried to skirt the main point and emphasized racial issues such as 'Nordic race', 'breeding' and 'good offspring', but he was soon interrupted by shouts 'get to the point!', 'the crucifix, the crucifix!' He then pulled a sheet from his pocket and announced that the decree would be revoked. Everybody shouted 'Hurrah!' and one man 'We know more about race than you!' People rose to leave but found the doors shut so that Röver could continue his speech. Thanksgiving services were held in all churches. It was a victory but the victory was limited. Early in 1937 two leaders of the revolt were arrested and interrogated at length: one because he had written and circulated a memorandum with more demands relating to Nazi schools policy, the other because he published his notes about an interview with the minister. The first was sent to a concentration camp but released after the death of his wife, the other was only threateneed with the same measure. The crucifixes remained in the schools.[10]

There existed another kind of open opposition, if not to the Hitler regime, then at least to the Hitler Youth and its claim to monopoly. It came from remnants of the German Youth Movement and the youth organizations of the dissolved leftwing parties, and one of the centres was the Lower Rhine area. On Ascension Day 1937 groups of the *Bündische* continued their traditional participation in the procession to the monastic church at Beyenburg. As one participant wrote much later, there he saw for the first time large groups of boys and girls all wearing shirts with large coloured squares, carrying knapsacks and guitars or balalaikas. They were not yet politicized – all they wanted to do was to keep together and continue their hiking. But a boy of the HJ had been killed by a car whose driver had fled and this led to a big police action against the assembled youths. In 1938 this was repeated at Beyenburg. The HJ patrol service supported by policemen confiscated all *bündisch* implements carried by the young and took their names; some were beaten up. In October 1939 they met again to tent together with the remnants of the dissolved *Nerother* association. Again the patrol service went into action, confiscated their equipment and took their names. They were kept overnight, then taken to police head-quarters in Wuppertal, and their schools were notified. They were treated like outcasts, called 'rabble' and 'scum', and this brought about a slow politicization, for the Nazi authorities would not suffer any deviation from their rules.[11]

More political were the *Meuten* (packs) of Leipzig which developed in the same years, largely from remnants of the Communist and socialist youth organizations, but including some members of the HJ. They sang working-class songs and had political discussions but remained rather loose local groups without a tight form of organization. They used the greeting of the Soviet Young Pioneers 'Be ready – always ready' and discussed conditions in the Soviet Union which they compared very favourably with those in Germany with its lack of liberty. The prompt-ings of the Nazi government were to be frustrated by laziness and slow work. They aimed at forming a counterweight to the Hitler Youth and its female counterpart and at dislodging it from the streets: with such success that in certain parts of Leipzig the HJ was unable to show itself. It was estimated that the *Meuten* had about 1500 members. In 1938 eight of their leaders were sentenced to terms in a penitentiary varying from one to eight years.[12]

The mass arrests of 1935–36 virtually destroyed the underground network of the SPD and no attempt was made to rebuild it. As the frontier secretary Hans Dill wrote to the party leaders in July 1937: nothing could be expected from inside Germany, 'our illegal activity of 1933–34 has failed', further efforts to distribute underground literature were in his opinion futile. He did not want to have a large apparatus to control, that would be too insecure; nor did he want to know any names and would only act as the conduit of reports received from his few informants in Germany. Dill admitted that the Gestapo and Nazi propaganda would cause all his efforts to fail. In its report for 1937 the Gestapo described the attitude of the SPD adherents as 'wait and see', the change would come from abroad. 'But one has to be prepared for this eventuality, to resume previous activities in a suitable form'. The socialists avoided all organizational forms and only tried to keep their friends 'loyal'. The Gestapo observed 'many initial attempts to form groups', but all were social gatherings in small circles without any distribution of illegal material 'so that in the large majority of cases police measures would have an absolutely negative result'. They knew that prominent SPD leaders abroad were often very well informed about the economic and military situation in Germany as well as the general mood, but they found it very difficult to catch the reporters because they were individuals who contacted individuals abroad. Many former SPD members were now travelling salesmen in coffee or soap; they visited their former comrades and sold them their wares referring to the old ties. They used this to exchange opinions about the political situation: in this form 'a loose net exists which has only one purpose: not to lose contact with each other'.[13]

This picture is confirmed by reports from many towns. In Mannheim, for example, a small group met regularly in the pub 'Grosser Hirsch' and another in 'Zur Stadt Augsburg', both run by former SPD members, and they deliberated how to find people to fill administrative posts after Hitler. Another loose contact was provided by shops owned by former SPD officials, such as the dairy of a former SPD alderman. All that was recorded by the Gestapo but offered no chance to take action. From the Ruhr area a foreman remembered that they had a 'little circle' meeting regularly, all colleagues of the former mandolin orchestra; they drank coffee or ate together and discussed the events of the day. Another skilled workman spoke of Social Democrats and Communists always sitting together in the factory, during every interval the same men met and 'confabulated'. In Kiel, the former women's groups of the SPD met in three separate circles for coffee and needlework, and also for political discussions. There was an endless variety of such loose circles.[14]

One important exception to this general rule existed. Late in 1936 two former prominent SPD officials, Dr Hermann Brill and Otto Brass, inspired by the Spanish civil war, founded what they called the 'German Popular Front' or, called after its programme, 'The Ten Points Group'. Among these points were restitution of all basic rights, complete self-government 'in a new Reich of political, economic and social democracy', nationalization of the banks, heavy industry and public utilities and very significantly: 'complete reconciliation with France' and 'building a community of European states through honest cooperation in a reorganized League of Nations'. As Brill wrote in 1937 the aim was 'freedom instead of suppression . . . law and justice instead of terrorism, peace instead of threats of war . . . butter instead of cannon'; the popular front was living in the hearts of all who stood for these aims. The members were highly critical of the popular front advocated by the KPD which they considered an 'artificial construction', but also of the policy of the exiled SPD leaders. Brill and Brass soon established contact to the *Neu Beginnen* groups in Prague and in Berlin and cooperated closely with them. But in September 1938 they were all arrested. Brill and Brass were each sentenced to 12 years of penitentiary, and three of the members were killed. The leaders of the Berlin *Neu Beginnen* group, among them Fritz Erler, received similar sentences.[15] That was practically the end of organized SPD activity in Berlin and North Germany.

But the many contacts and small circles of friends continued to exist. As the Gestapo put it in 1938: 'These people are neither organized nor do they issue illegal material . . . On the other hand there are many examples that the contacts of these people are well organized and function well.'[16]

Meanwhile the KPD continued its old ways of distributing propaganda material. According to the report of an instructor sent to Bremen in 1936 by the frontier secretariat in Amsterdam, the material was put into letterboxes or left in trams, and the result was mass arrests in those places and the destruction of underground groups – one of the reasons why Social Democrats refused to cooperate with the KPD. In the same year the Gestapo registered as many as 1350 new *Hetzschriften* (pamphlets, leaflets, etc.) with a combined circulation of 1,500,000 – an enormous figure – and the vast majority of them would have been Communist. In 1936 11,678 members of the KPD were arrested. If the party in 1935 still had about 5000 members in Berlin, at the end of 1936 the Gestapo liquidated many of the groups in the centre, west, north-west, north, north-east and east of the city including the local leaders, and four other districts followed suit in 1937. Only small parts of the organization survived and contacts between them were very precarious. In the Rhineland too, according to an agent's report, the KPD no longer had a 'firm organizational structure'. The reason given was the 'severe treatment' of the arrested by the Gestapo and the heavy sentences meted out which allegedly had a deterring effect. It was also true, however, that the system of frontier secretaries and instructors sent by them into Germany was hardly less cumbersome than the old one, with a central leadership trying to direct the party units.[17]

In Herne in the Ruhr, more arrests in October 1936 meant the end of organized KPD activity; all that was left were loose circles of friends. After 1936 the party groups in Leipzig had the character of discussion groups so as to recover after massive arrests; there was hardly any outside activity. Among the Ruhr miners from about 1937 loose groups were formed to listen to foreign stations and no party dues were collected any longer. In 'red' Penzberg in Bavaria, after many arrests, no actions of the KPD took place; the former members met informally in several clubs. In the Rhenish towns instructors sent in from abroad often found no organization at all and had to make great efforts to find party members willing to revive it – often without success. In Frankfurt, after many mass arrests, no attempt was made to rebuild the organization. In Cologne, there were more mass arrests but for listening in groups to radio Moscow, and the same happened in Augsburg. In Bielefeld the KPD was 'completely destroyed'. In 1936 the party official responsible for the Saar stopped the importation of clandestine literature 'because most arrests of recent times can be traced back to it'. The Gestapo report for 1937 stated that, in contrast with earlier years, no mass import of illegal literature could be ascertained. In spite of the new tactics they claimed to have ferreted out some 'large, well-organized local organizations'. This they attributed to 'the cumbersome ways of the Communist apparatus', the long time it took for the local groups to receive their instructions and a certain passive resistance 'because they cannot see why they should dissolve their apparatus preserved over many years' at great risk.[18]

In fact the organizational structure began to change. As the Düsseldorf High Court found in 1939:

> They formed small groups, met each other on walks or in pubs, spoke about questions of Communism, or they discussed topical political issues in a Communist or Marxist sense. They listened . . . to the programmes of Communist hate stations and discussed what they heard.

In March 1937 the Gestapo 'liquidated' the KPD subdistrict of Schwelm near Wuppertal. They had received the newest instructions through instructors and every few weeks material reached them from abroad. This was then sold for 10 or 20 pfennigs and membership dues of 50 pfennigs were collected, as were separate dues for 'Red Help', all given to instructors for transfer. The members were organized in cells and factory cells.[19] In fact, here the old rigid organizational structure had been preserved, to the undoing of the members, but this seems to have been an exception.

In the Berlin subdistrict of Schöneberg too, a factory cell existed, party dues and dues for 'Red Help' were collected and a factory paper was issued with 30–40 copies. Here 41 people were arrested. A very different form of activity recorded by the Gestapo was the participation of about 800 people, not only Communists but also Social Democrats and Catholics, in the funeral of a Communist killed by the SS at Dachau. A wreath was thrown into the grave, its cost was collected, and eight participants were arrested. In 1937 the Gestapo further reported that 102 people who had tried to rebuild the subdistrict were arrested at Korbach in Hesse. 'The illegal methods were rather primitive, there were no great difficulties in tracing the organization with the help of an agent.'[20]

The reports reaching the exiled SPD leaders in 1937 recorded signs of Communist activity in the Upper Silesian mining district. Leaflets distributed at several mines in April demanded better wages, stopping payments to the DAF, and the formation of a popular front against Hitler, and they urged the miners to join the illegal miners' union. The management made great efforts to seize the leaflets and threatened punishments for retaining them. On a road near Hindenburg slogans were painted 'Freedom for our Thälmann' to commemorate the birthday of the incarcerated Communist leader. At another mine a coal wagon was adorned with the inscription: 'This is the new German deed: the wagons always get bigger and we lose more wages.' Similar slogans appeared at other mines, but the workers thought they were painted by the Gestapo so as to proceed to arrests and find out about underground work. From Saxony the SPD was informed in 1938 that the 'Stalin-Communists' still held the Social Democrats responsible for the advent of Hitler; after him, a Bolshevist Germany would be established. The old conflicts continued.[21]

While in 1936 about 1,500,000 pamphlets and leaflets were produced in Germany and abroad, in 1938 the number shrank to about 100,000. Most of them came from abroad, no longer mainly by courier but by post, sent to addresses taken haphazardly from address books and professional lists. The Gestapo also claimed that the structure of the KPD was 'destroyed and deprived of resources and technical institutions'. But by the spring of 1939 it spoke of 'intensification of the KPD's work in Germany'. Instructors sent by the Central Committee appeared in Munich, Trier, Stettin and Königsberg in East Prussia, and other Gestapo offices also mentioned greater KPD activity. The whispering propaganda was to be intensified and 'united front committees' were to be formed in the factories. At Blohm & Voss in Hamburg leaflets were distributed: 'Dr Ley promised us "just wages" and that "more work meant higher wages" '; therefore the workers must demand the fulfilment of his promises in the local units of the DAF. If his promises remained words without deeds, if they tried to enforce the ten-hour day and ever greater production in spite of tiredness and overwork, then the slogans would apply 'Eight hours – enough swot-ted!' and 'Work more slowly!' Excited discussions followed and there was considerable agreement. In Rostock a leaflet protested against the preparations for war, the talk of cannon instead of butter. Thousands of Antifascists were incarcerated and hundreds executed 'because they fought for national and social freedom': everybody was to enlighten his colleagues about the danger of 'sinking into barbarism'. A Communist paper published in Paris in August 1939 declared very optimistically:

> The German working class was, is and remains antifascist, its resistance movements are already a mass phenomenon creating the greatest worries for the authorities. Larger and larger sections of the middle classes join the opposition. Under the extremely difficult conditions of a barbarian regime of terror not only individuals but *masses* conduct a passionate, tough, sacrificial battle to prevent Hitler from unleashing war.[22]

It was the old Communist legend of the revolutionary masses.

A circular of the Central Committee of July 1938 stressed the necess-ity of fighting for peace and criticized the many Antifascists, including active KPD members, who considered war inevitable, so that sacrifices brought in the daily struggle in the factories and mass organizations were unnecessary. This, the circular stated, was a dangerous opinion, based on lack of confidence in the power of the working class and the role of the KPD; it 'speculates on the intervention of foreign powers and cripples the initiative in the actual daily struggle'. It was essential to conduct a tough ideological fight against these ideas, the party having failed to create the 'necessary clarity' among its own cadres. But the real culprits were, of course, the Trotskyites. In 1938 Wilhelm Florin, member of the Central Committee, wrote:

> In Germany the Trotskyites, far more dangerous than in a country with a legal working-class movement, try to annihilate in alliance with the Gestapo [!] revolutionary groups [and] use the situation among the Social-Democratic workers to increase the desorganiz-ation among the working class.[23]

At the end of January 1939 the leaders of the KPD met the frontier secretaries and other delegates at the so-called 'Bern' conference (actually held near Paris). The principal speech on 'The present situation and the tasks of the party' was given by the veteran party chairman, Wilhelm Pieck. The key question, according to him, was the creation of 'union with the Social-Democratic workers and the united front of the working class', but they were still far from achieving this goal; only very few had 'the courage to stand openly for a united front with the Communists'. He claimed that it was prevented by 'rotten elements' expelled from the KPD who were trying to form a block with the SAP, the ISK and others. In the discussion it was argued that the precondition of a united front was a strong Communist party which would have to establish 'contacts with the SPD'; the united front should not prevent the building up of their own party. Another speaker emphasized that the party had to be cleansed of Trotskyites 'and other disintegrating elements' as they had appeared in the KPD groups in Amsterdam and Brussels, and in the Parisian group the fight must be intensified.[24] Clearly, the KPD had numerous enemies among other left wingers, as well as among its own ranks, who must be fought – all in the name of 'unity'.

A question discussed at the conference was whether at the time of the Munich conference in September 1938 'open actions against Hitler's war policy' were possible, whether the 'masses' would have followed the party in such actions. The answer given by the comrades in Germany was that they would not have done so, the Gestapo's pressure was too strong:

> One of our greatest weaknesses in September was the separation from the existing organizations. A legal and half-legal movement for peace can only come into being if the Antifascists succeed in joining the masses in the fascis organizations and make use of the existing dissatisfaction.

It was essential to have contacts in the DAF, the SA, in Defence against Air-raids, and above all in the HJ. Another contributor to the discussion argued: 'The women spoke more openly in September than the men. Often only an organized initiative would have been required to induce them to prevent their men and sons from joining up.' Allegedly Hitler's war plans were opposed by 'whole offices of draughtsmen, constructers, engineers'. Indeed, at the time of Munich widespread anti-war feeling and fear of war surfaced in Germany; but the very idea of mobilizing the 'masses' in the Nazi organizations for action against the war and the regime was based on illusion – possibilities for a 'legal and half-legal movement' did not exist. Those in Germany who warned against such actions were surely right. Another illusion was that, on account of this widespread feeling, allegedly possibilities existed for 'active resistance' and 'offensive agitation' (whatever that meant), as one contributor to the discussion claimed, for any such attempt would have played directly into the Gestapo's hands.[26]

In reality, the policy of the 'united front' – whether from below or from above – was not a great success, for whatever the KPD claimed, only very few Social Democrats were willing to cooperate with Communists. The developments in the Spanish civil war were another inhibiting factor. With the war taking an unfavourable turn for the Spanish government, the Spanish Communists became very powerful and used their power to fight their enemies on the left. German socialist volunteers who went to Spain to serve the Republic disappeared mysteriously. In a discussion about the united front, held in Amsterdam in 1937, the KPD secretary Walter Ulbricht was confronted with the facts; he feebly promised an investigation. The Social Democrats who took part in the discussion felt that no united front was possible with a party using such methods; they asked pointedly what it would do when it gained power in Germany after Hitler?* There was no answer.[27]

More promising from the Communist point of view was the Free Miners' Union which was founded in Paris in 1936 with the support of the Miners International and its president. Among the founders were Communist officials such as Wilhelm Knöchel and leftwing Social Democrats such as Richard Kirn and Franz Vogt, former leaders of the German Miners Union. Also present were miners from the Ruhr, Saar and Wurm areas. At several mines of western Germany small groups of the underground union came into being; the union's *Bergarbeiter-Mitteilungen* were smuggled into Germany from Holland and reported on conditions in the mining districts. In 1938 the Gestapo stated that the union's special characteristic was 'marked decentralization'. Reports were given by word of mouth to a courier who took them abroad, the local representatives dealt directly with the union officials abroad, and all contacts between the underground groups were to be avoided. But this promising attempt to build a free trade union above party soon suffered from Communist meddling and faction building. In 1937 Kirn protested against Communist activity and soon resigned. Later Vogt reached the same opinion and cooperation came to an end. Early in 1940 Knöchel wrote to a British unionist that he could no longer cooperate with Vogt because he tried to misuse what had been built up over the past years. It seems that the union was somewhat more successful than the underground parties in evading the attention of the Gestapo.[28]

The same did not apply to the railwaymen's union organized by Hans Jahn and others. After many arrests in the years 1935–36, another network was organized by Karl Molt in south Germany, again with the support of Fimmen and the International Transportworkers Federation. But in 1938 the Gestapo discovered the organization and arrests followed. In Saxony, in spite of Gestapo observation, the old links were re-established by 1938 and small meetings were held, but the war ended the activities. From his exile in Luxemburg Jahn tried to keep the organization together and to collect reports, until the Germans invaded the country in 1940. Jahn escaped but his wife and child were caught.

---

* The case I quoted to Ulbricht was that of Mark Rein who was kidnapped in Barcelona and was never found, and his was not the only case.

Unfortunately the Gestapo also found in his flat plans and addresses so that many more arrests were carried out.[29]

By 1939 the organized opposition was defeated. The number of arrested Communists and Social Democrats dropped significantly. In 1936 11,687 Communists were arrested, in 1938 only 3864; for Social Democrats the figures were 1374 in 1936, 721 in 1938. This did not mean that there was less criticism of the regime. The number of people tried in Munich for *Heimtücke* increased sharply during the same period, from 445 in 1936 and 571 in 1937 to 1501 in 1938 and 1445 in 1939. But only a few of them belonged to a forbidden political party: 31 in 1937, 64 in 1938, 60 in 1939. The others were probably ordinary people without political affiliation who fell foul of the regime.

Up to April 1939 112,432 men and women were convicted for oppositional activity, and 27,369 were still awaiting trial.[30] But the opposition was unorganized and disunited.

Notes

1. Nitzsche, 'Deutsche Arbeiter im Kampf' p. 142; Hetzer, *Industriestadt Augsburg*, pp. 119, 135f.; *Deutschland-Berichte*, v, 1938, no. 9, p. 1004; *Bayern in der NS-Zeit*, i, p. 264.

2. Mallmann and Paul, *Herrschaft und Alltag*, pp. 370–76.

3. *Bergarbeiter-Mitteilungen*, September 1938, quoted by Peukert and Bajohr, *Spuren des Widerstands*, pp. 127f.; Klaus Tenfelde, in *Bayern in der NS-Zeit*, iv, pp. 331, 333; Peukert, *Volksgenossen*, p. 133; *Bayern in der NS-Zeit*, i, p. 284; *Deutschland-Berichte*, vi, 1939, no. 3, p. 357.

4. Mason, 'Arbeiteropposition', p. 300; Kershaw, *Popular Opinion*, p. 90; Pikarski and Warning, *Gestapo-Berichte*, i, pp. 153f., 161f., 167f., 173; Nitzsche, 'Deutsche Arbeiter im Kampf', p. 144; Peukert, *Ruhrarbeiter*, p. 221.

5. *Deutschland-Berichte*, iv, 1937, no. 3, pp. 317f.; Mason, *Arbeiterklasse und Volksgemeinschaft*, pp. 290, 294, 424; Peukert, *Ruhrarbeiter*, p. 192; Fischer-Defoy, *Arbeiterwiderstand*, p. 171.

6. Wisotzky, *Ruhrbergbau*, pp. 228ff., 240; *Bayern in der NS-Zeit*, i, pp. 273f.; Mallmann and Paul, *Herrschaft und Alltag*, p. 365.

7. *Deutschland-Berichte*, vi, 1939, no. 3, p. 359, no. 6, pp. 768f.; Mallmann and Paul, *Herrschaft und Alltag*, p. 364; *Bayern in der NS-Zeit*, i, pp. 282, 286; Dahlem, *Am Vorabend*, ii, p. 184.

8. Schadt, *Verfolgung und Widerstand*, p. 241: report of 30 October 1936.

9. Joachim Kuropka (ed.), *Zur Sache – Das Kreuz*, Vechta, 1987, pp. 13, 20, 22, 424; van Dick, *Oppositionelles Lehrerverhalten*, p. 477; Jeremy Noakes, 'the Oldenburg Crucifix Struggle,' in Peter D. Stachura (ed.), *The Shaping of the Nazi State*, London, 1978, pp. 218ff.

10. Kuropka, *Zur Sache*, pp. 107f., 310ff., 323; Noakes, 'Oldenburg Crucifix', pp. 223ff.

11. Paulus Buscher, *Das Stigma – 'Edelweiss-Pirat'*, Koblenz, 1988, pp. 104ff., 126, 139, 200f.
12. von Hellfeld and Klönne, *Betrogene Generation*, pp. 89f.; Peukert, *Die Edelweisspiraten*, Cologne, 1980, pp. 188ff.
13. Beuys, *Vergesst uns nicht*, p. 368; Wagner, 'The Hard Lessons', p. 197; Reichhardt, 'Möglichkeiten und Grenzen', p. 182; Günther Weisenborn, *Der lautlose Aufstand*, Hamburg, 1953, pp. 154ff.; Mlynek, *Gestapo Hannover*, p. 535.
14. Matthias and Weber, *Widerstand*, pp. 200ff.; von Plato, *Verlierer geht nicht leer aus*, pp. 18f., 21; Weisenborn, *Lautlose Aufstand*, p. 156.
15. Ibid., p. 147; Overesch, *Hermann Brill*, pp. 254, 281; Mammach, *Widerstand*, pp. 265f.
16. Bein, *Widerstand im Nationalsozialismus*, p. 81.
17. Marssolek and Ott, *Bremen*, p. 267; Pikarski and Warning, 'Über den antifaschistischen Widerstandskampf der KPD', *Beiträge zur Geschichte der Arbeiterbewegung*, xxvi 1984, p. 60; Duhnke, *KPD*, p. 201; Reichhardt, 'Möglichkeiten und Grenzen' pp. 194f.; Vollmer, *Volksopposition*, p. 343; Klotzbach, *Gegen den Nationalsozialismus*, p. 205.
18. Dorn and Zimmermann, *Bewährungsprobe*, p. 175; Erich Köhn, 'Der Weg zur Gründung des Nationalkomitees "Freies Deutschland" in Leipzig', *Zeitschrift für Geschichtswissenschaft*, xiii 1965, p. 23; Peukert, *Ruhrarbeiter*, p. 190; Tenfelde, in *Bayern in der NS-Zeit*, iv, pp. 343f.; Duhnke, *KPD*, pp. 193f.; Mehringer, 'KPD in Bayern', p. 199; Mallmann and Paul, *Herrschaft und Alltag*, p. 219; Pikarksi and Warning, *Gestapo-Berichte*, i, pp. 176f.
19. Mann, *Protest und Kontrolle*, p. 205; Mason, *Arbeiterklasse und Volksgemeinschaft* pp. 422ff.
20. Ibid., pp. 298, 315f.; Fischer-Defoy, *Arbeiterwiderstand*, p. 171.
21. *Deutschland-Berichte*, iv, 1937, no. 3, p. 338, no. 5, pp. 610f., v, 1938, no. 8, p. 984.
22. Pikarski and Warning, 'Über den antifaschistischen Widerstandskampf', pp. 60, 340; Hochmuth and Meyer, *Streiflichter*, pp. 179, 530ff.; Pikarski and Übel, *KPD lebt*, p. 185; Dahlem, *Am Vorabend*, ii, p. 274.
23. Hermann Wichers, 'Zur Anleitung des Widerstands der KPD', *Internationale wissenschaftliche Korrespondenz zur Geschichte der deutschen Arbeiterbewegung*, xxvi, 1990, p. 533; Duhnke, *KPD*, p. 275 note 157; Florin was a member of the Executive Committee of Comintern, and his article appeared in its journal.
24. Duhnke, *KPD*, pp. 551, 553, 567, 570ff. Pieck's speech with omissions also in Klaus Mammach, *Die Berner Konferenz der KPD*, Frankfurt, 1974.
25. Duhnke, *KPD*, pp. 559, 567; Mammach, *Berner Konferenz*, pp. 109ff.
26. Duhnke, *KPD*, p. 562; Weber, 'Die KPD in der Illegalität', p. 96.
27. Personal recollections.
28. Peukert and Bajohr, *Spuren des Widerstands*, pp. 113, 123, 129ff., 152; Beier, *Illegale Reichsleitung*, p. 52.
29. Müller, *Stuttgart*, p. 171; Esters and Pelger, *Gewerkschafter*, pp. 147ff.
30. Hüttenberger, 'Heimtückefälle', *Bayern in der NS-Zeit*, iv, pp. 446f.; Mammach, *Widerstand*, p. 150; V.R. Berghahn, *Modern Germany*, Cambridge, 1982, p. 131.

CHAPTER SEVEN

Jehovah's Witnesses

Among the opponents of the Nazi regime pride of place in many ways belongs to the religious sect which called itself Jehovah's Witnesses or International Bible Students Association. None had more of its members incarcerated and killed in proportion to its size, none was more efficient in illegal propaganda, none produced more 'martyrs' willing to suffer for their faith. Yet the large majority were humble men and women either from the working class or domestic servants or white-collar workers, while the higher social ranks were hardly represented among their ranks.

The society came into being in America in the late 19th century and spread from there to Europe. In Germany it was founded in the early 20th century on a very small scale, but by 1918 it had 3868 members, and by 1926 22,535. When Hitler became chancellor there were about 25,000 to 30,000 of the faithful, with strong groups in Berlin, Dresden, Hamburg and many other towns. Many of the members were victims of the First World War, of the inflation, of hunger and unemployment. The severe crises of German society in the years after 1914 explain the rapid growth of the society which made it one of the centres of the international movement. The members hoping for a radical change which God would bring about, found among the Witnesses human warmth and willingness to help, and joined so as to belong to the 'chosen', the 'people of God'. Jehovah would bring them salvation, redeem them and solve their problems.[1] What happened to them on this earth no longer mattered, for the end of the old world was near.

For the National Socialists who wanted to mould the people according to their worldly and racialist ideology, these ideas were anathema. The Witnesses refused to obey the laws of the state if they clashed with Jehovah's demands, refused to render military service and to support anything connected with war; they knew only one master – and that was not Adolf Hitler. Already the society's name included the word 'International', indicating that the Witnesses served a foreign power, were subordinate to the Watch-Tower Centre in New York: tenets entirely alien to the National Socialists. The two faiths were totalitarian in their demands; a clash was inevitable. Yet the Witnesses tried to avoid it. In March 1933 they founded two separate Bible Associations for north and south Germany. The bylaws underlined that they were purely religious and respected the laws of the state. A mass meeting held in Berlin in June with five to six thousand participants began with the singing of the German national anthem and the hall was decorated with swastika flags. The patriotic course was defended against those Witnesses who had good reason to doubt its success.[2] At first the American links provided some protection by American diplomats, for the new regime had to tread carefully in the field of foreign policy.

It was all in vain. To the Nazis, Jehovah's Witnesses were an alien, pacifist, pro-Jewish organization directed from abroad. In April 1933 the association was dissolved in Bavaria and Mecklenburg, and on the 24th its headquarters at Magdeburg were raided and searched, but its American centre intervened via the American consul in Berlin. Its German leaders described the society as 'completely unpolitical and opposed to Communism as ungodly and dangerous to the state'. For the time being the Magdeburg premises were restored and the confiscation of all the printed material was revoked. But two months later a decree of the Prussian Minister of the Interior dissolved the association and confiscated its property because

> under the cloak of allegedly scientific bible research it leads in words and writing an unmistakable campaign of hatred against the institutions of state and church. In describing both as organs of Satan it undermines the basic tenets of *völkisch* community life. In its numerous publications it . . . pours scorn on the institutions of state and church.

That was one day before the mass meeting in Berlin at which the leaders tried to make their peace with the Hitler government. In August the Magdeburg premises were closed for good. Twenty-five lorries took away the confiscated publications which were publicly burnt, including the bibles found there. In some towns the forbidden missionary activities continued, in others only religious services and bible studies were held privately. A circular of the society's Central European leader, a German American, stressed: 'We want to be good citizens of the country and by our attitude and our style of life give eloquent testimony to the honour of God.' But this met with severe criticism.[3]

To the Witnesses who were unwilling to obey the order of prohibition Hitler appeared as Antichrist, in alliance with their arch-enemy, the Pope; his rule was that of the Devil, and the government demands, such as the rendering of the Hitler salute and the singing of the Horst-Wessel Song were incompatible with a Christian life. They were determined to continue their missionary work, determined 'to fight for truth'. Towards the end of 1933 duplicating machines and a courier network were organized, articles of the forbidden *Wachtturm* were duplicated locally as its delivery by post proved too risky. Illegal literature was smuggled into Germany from Czechoslovakia, one pamphlet with the title 'Until what date will Hitler govern?' By the autumn of 1934 several thousand Witnesses were active, not only selling the bible and permitted calendars but also the publications of the Watch-Tower society, and illegal publications began to appear. They refused to participate in the plebiscite of November 1933 sanctioning Germany's exit from the League of Nations. SA men then invaded the Witnesses' flats, insulted them and tried to force them to vote. In some places they were frogmarched through the streets carrying placards 'We are traitors, we have not voted'. Farms belonging to Witnesses were burnt down. One invalid died as a result of beatings he received.[4]

Employers used the refusal to give the Hitler salute or to participate in the MayDay demonstrations to dismiss Witnesses, even after many years of service to the firm in question. They were not given any new jobs nor were they paid any benefits. As it was put in 1938 by the president of the Rhenish Labour Office, they were 'asocial elements' and had 'to be denied recognition as unemployed in principle and without exception'. In 1935 the insurance agent Fritz Winkler was charged with the supervision of the society's work in Germany. He divided the country into 13 districts, each with a district leader, mainly younger men, and under them group leaders, all appointed from above. Until August 1936 the *Wachtturm* was clandestinely printed in Bremen but then the printing shop was discovered by the Gestapo. It was replaced by a duplicating machine in Hamburg which printed 250 copies, later 500, many of which were sent to Bielefeld, Bremen and Hanover. The work was financed by the 'Good Hope Chest' which provided support for those living underground and the families of the imprisoned. In this way a large, efficient illegal apparatus was created.[5]

At first persecution was not so severe – far less so than that of the hated Communists. In the summer of 1934 many Witnesses were acquitted by the courts. The Gestapo of Hanover complained several times that, because of the many acquittals, the Witnesses used this to plead in new cases brought against them and were confirmed in their view that the prohibition of their activities was against the law. But this soon changed. Many more arrests took place in different parts of Germany. In September 1936 there was another wave with a thousand arrests, of whole groups in Berlin, Bremen, Leipzig and Munich, including the majority of the district leaders. In Hamburg 29 accused were sentenced to imprisonment of three to four years. At the end of 1936 the Munich Gestapo stated that, although every attempt at activity was punished, 'in spite of that the illegal doings of the sect increase from month to month'. This was dramatically proved on 12 December when more than 3000 Witnesses at a given time systematically distributed a

Resolution passed by a congress held at Lucerne and printed in Switzer-land condemning the measures of persecution: 'We protest sharply against the cruel treatment of Jehovah's Witnesses by the Roman Cath-olic hierarchy and its German allies and in all other continents.' Thou-sands of copies wre put into letterboxes, put down at frontdoors and sent by post. The Gestapo considered it an open attack on the Hitler government.[6] It was a propaganda coup which none of the other under-ground groups could have matched.

In 1937–38 persecution became much more severe and there was a new facet. In 1937 the Ministry of Justice instructed all subordinate authorities to inform the Gestapo one month before the expiration of a sentence, so that it could immediately transfer the released prisoner to a concentration camp, and this became standard practice. In the same year a newly married couple were arrested because they refused to give the Hitler salute in the registry office. In 1939 a musician was sent to a concentration camp because he did not respond to the Hitler salute of the conductor. After mass arrests the society's leadership was reorganized; there were again 13 districts, divided into subdistricts and these into main groups and subgroups. The lowest unit was a cell with a few cell servants, all as a safeguard against destruction. At the head stood a Reich Servant who was replaced after each arrest.[7] It was a complete hierarchical structure, difficult to penetrate for the Gestapo, in spite of great efforts.

The conflict was exacerbated by the introduction of general conscrip-tion in the spring of 1935 because the Witnesses were strict pacifists and refused any form of military service. Soon special courts sentenced young Witnesses for refusal to serve. In June 1937 a conference was held in the Ministry of Justice at which a very senior official, Dr Wilhelm Crohne, pronounced:

> They have become an association highly dangerous to the state and are in part directed from abroad. They have written on their banner among other words not only the refusal of military service, but also the refusal to work in any enterprise working for the *Wehrmacht*.

They even declined to work at the railways or the post offices in case of war. He claimed that Communism was penetrating 'with force' into the association which, according to his reckoning, had one to two million members.[8] It was a gross overstatement, probably so as to stress the vast importance of the issue and the dangers threatening Germany from the society so that its persecution could be stepped up.

About the same time an 'Open Letter to the German people believing in the Bible and loving Christ' was distributed in the Rhineland, in Aachen, Bochum, Dortmund, Düsseldorf, Gelsenkirchen, Hamm,

Krefeld: in spite of 'sadistic physical maltreatment perpetrated also on women and children of tender age' with horsewhips and truncheons it proved impossible 'to extirpate Jehovah's Witnesses in four years', for they would not be intimidated and would continue 'to obey God more than people, as Christ's apostles also did when they were forbidden to preach the Gospel'. The results, the Open Letter continued, were prison sentences of up to five years and after that incarceration in a concentration camp, and in some places, such as Bavaria, the Ruhr and East Prussia, 'abuses which are no different from the tortures of the Inquisition'. Eighteen Witnesses had been murdered while in custody. In a cellar in Dortmund the Gestapo found 30,000 copies of the Open Letter. In its report for 1938 the Gestapo Headquarters stated that, of all the forbidden sects, only the Witnesses were still active, but the import of their literature across the French and Swiss frontiers had been more or less stopped. During 1938 about 800 Witnesses were arrested, among them many who refused to vote in the 'election' of April (after the occupation of Austria) and many who disobeyed the order of mobilization and did not fulfil their military duties.[9]

The waves of arrests and the mass trials of the years 1937–38 severely damaged the society's organizational structure so that for some time there was no coordinated resistance in Germany as a whole. In Mannheim, 48 Witnesses were tried and sentenced at the end of 1937; six died while in custody. In Leipzig, 186 men and women were tried and sentenced by a special court. Between 1936 and 1939 the Munich special court sentenced 274 Witnesses for 'malicious slander'. In Austria, after the German occupation, the Witnesses were very active – until many were arrested in 1939. In Germany it took some time before communications between the different groups were rebuilt and an organizational net was re-established. But the members' loyalty was by no means broken. They strongly criticized the 'lukewarm' and 'fearful' among their own ranks who might contemplate doing military service without weapons (which in any case was not permitted by the army). What was crucial in the eyes of the intrepid was: not to serve the organization of Satan, not to conclude any compromise with those in power.[10]

During the war the majority of the Witnesses continued their entirely uncompromising attitude. This extended to precautions against air raids. As their *Mitteilungsblatt* put it in 1942: 'A Christian will not take part in an organization for air defence because such an organization is more or less linked to military institutions and because he would thus silently admit that he expected salvation and safety from it.' People's only protection was Jehovah. In the same journal a trenchant comparison between Nazi Germany and Soviet Russia appeared. The Nazi press, it said, always criticized Bolshevist Russia for traits it considered typical and characteristic of it; but in certain matters Soviet Russia and Nazi Germany were as similar as two eggs: 'Russia has a cruel dictator, we have the same. There bloody terror rules, with us too. Russia has the GPU and we have the Gestapo. There Siberia and GPU prisons, here concentration camps and Gestapo cellars.'[11] It was a true comparison, an early attempt to see the similarities of totalitarianism.

In 1939 one of the district servants, the roofer Julius Engelhard, went underground to bear witness to the faith and then organized a new network in the south-west and west of Germany. In 1940 he took his illegal quarters in Oberhausen in the Ruhr where an active group of Witnesses existed and the society's literature was duplicated. In the years 1941–43 27 editions of the *Wachtturm* were produced there in small editions of 240 to 360 copies and distributed over a wide area, reaching Mannheim and Munich in the south, Saxony in the east and Schleswig in the north, in spite of wartime conditions – until the small group in Oberhausen was discovered and arrested in 1943. The 'People's Court' in Berlin pronounced eight death sentences. But this did not mean the end of activity. Witnesses imprisoned in the concentration camp of Wevelsburg under relatively lax conditions organized the printing of the *Wachtturm* for northwest Germany and it was distributed by women members of the association outside. During three months of 1943 it was also printed on an allotment in Berlin and later in Magdeburg.[12] In spite of all arrests, the activities never stopped and many contacts were renewed.

For the Witnesses who were called up and refused to serve, the *Reichskriegsgericht* (Supreme Court Martial) in Berlin, presided over by Admiral Max Bastian, had to pronounce sentence. Whoever did not obey the military summons after 26 August 1939 had to reckon with a death sentence for 'disintegration' of the *Wehrmacht*. During the first year of the war (until September 1940), 117 death sentences for 'disintegration' were pronounced by this court; all but five of them concerned Jehovah's Witnesses. Later the same court sat at Torgau in Saxony. Among the men tried there on the same grounds, the large majority were Witnesses. Some then repented and were sentenced to prison terms: that made it possible to transfer them immediately to a punitive military unit with its very high rate of casualties, 'to prove themselves at the front'. But the large majority refused to recant and were sentenced to death. We do not know how many were thus sentenced but the estimate is 250 to 300.[13]

More death sentences were pronounced by the 'People's Court' in Berlin and other courts. When Helene Gotthold was sentenced in August 1944 her daughter was told that no announcement of it was permitted. According to a summary drawn up by the society in 1974 of the punishments meted out, 233 Witnesses were sentenced to death (but this cannot have included the Court Martial sentences) of whom 203 were executed; 635 died while imprisoned and 6019 suffered imprisonment[14] – nearly one quarter of the membership. In the concentration camps a substantial percentage of the prisoners belonged to the society, in Buchenwald in May 1938 as many as 12 per cent of the prisoners, in Mauthausen in December 1939 5.2 per cent, and in the central concentration camp for women, Lichtenburg, about 20 per cent: more than of any leftwing group. It has been estimated that about 2000 Witnesses were sent to concentration camps. Even there they were active, held religious services, tried to influence others by their 'missions', and maintained contact with the outside. Underground literature was smuggled in, for example baked in a cake or hidden in an artificial leg. Earlier estimates that about 2000 Witnesses were killed or that every fourth of them lost his or her life cannot be maintained, but the figures are awful enough.[15]

Characteristically Witnesses helped Jews who tried to hide in Berlin during the war. As one Jewish woman remembered, she and her mother were first helped by Witnesses, the owners of a small laundry who secretly washed for Jews. They invited the persecuted women, 'their willingness knew no bounds'. A large percentage of the Witnesses came from the lower classes. In Hamburg, for example, 55.6 per cent were working-class, 15 per cent domestic servants, 11 per cent old-age pensioners and 12.6 per cent white-collar workers – together the vast majority of the members. In the Ruhr and Rhenish towns the social composition seems to have been similar.[16]

In general the Witnesses provided an unrivalled example of courage and steadfastness, equalling that of many other martyrs to the faith. In percentages they had more victims than the Communists and their secret organization was much superior to that of the KPD. They refused any compromise and they showed what could be done in Nazi Germany – and they suffered for it on a vast scale.

Notes

1. Detlef Garbe, *Zwischen Widerstand und Martyrium. Die Zeugen Jehovas im 'Dritten Reich'*, Munich, 1993, pp. 41f., 56ff., 78; Michael Kater, 'Die Ernsten Bibelforscher im Dritten Reich', *Vierteljahrshefte für Zeitgeschichte*, xvii 1969, p. 187.
2. Garbe, *Zwischen Widerstand*, pp. 84ff., 99; Kater, 'Ernste Bibelforscher', p. 187.
3. Garbe, *Zwischen Widerstand*, pp. 86ff., 96, 104, 106f.

4. Ibid., pp. 109f., 121ff., 150f.
5. Kater, 'Ernste Bibelforscher', p. 196; Garbe, *Zwischen Widerstand*, pp. 223, 226f.
6. Mlynek, *Gestapo Hannover*, pp. 188, 213; Garbe, *Zwischen Widerstand*, pp. 226f., 231, 240f., 245f.; Schadt, *Verfolgung*, p. 246; Marssolek and Ott, *Bremen*, pp. 306f.; Kater, 'Ernste Bibelforscher', p. 198.
7. Ibid., p. 206; Garbe, *Zwischen Widerstand*, pp. 153f.; 243f.; Rossaint and Zimmermann, *Widerstand*, p. 66.
8. Garbe, *Zwischen Widerstand*, pp. 289f.
9. Dohms, *Flugschriften in Gestapo-Akten*, p. 433; Högl and Steinmetz, *Widerstand*, p. 262; Heinz Boberach (ed.), *Meldungen aus dem Reich*, ii, Herrsching, 1984, p. 52: quoted as Boberach, *Meldungen.*
10. Garbe, *Zwischen Widerstand*, pp. 259, 315, 317, 326; Schadt, *Verfolgung*, pp. 113f.; Kater 'Ernste Bibelforscher', p. 198; Hüttenberger, 'Heimtücke-fälle', *Bayern in der NS-Zeit*, iv, p. 447.
11. Quotations from Garbe, *Zwischen Widerstand*, pp. 157, 325.
12. Beuys, *Vergesst uns nicht*, pp. 529f.; Matthias and Weber, *Widerstand*, pp. 422f.
13. Garbe, *Zwischen Widerstand*, pp. 357ff., 365ff., 382; files of the *Reichs-kriegsgericht* in the Czech State Archives where I looked through them.
14. Garbe, *Zwischen Widerstand*, p. 481; Högl and Steinmetz, *Widerstand*, p. 263; Rossaint and Zimmermann, *Widerstand*, p. 66.
15. Garbe, *Zwischen Widerstand*, pp. 394f., 486; Kater, 'Ernste Bibelforscher', pp. 213f.
16. Wiener Library London, Zeugenberichte, no. 192; Garbe, *Zwischen Widerstand*, p. 496. The resistance of the Jehovah's Witnesses is a very much neglected subject, now partly remedied by Dr Garbe's monograph, but requiring much more local research.

CHAPTER EIGHT

The Hitler–Stalin Pact and after

On 24 August 1939 the world – and the Germans – were surprised by the news that the German Foreign Minister, Joachim von Ribbentrop, had signed a pact of neutrality with Stalin which guaranteed to Hitler that there would be no second front in the coming war: the attack on Poland could start. Germany and the Soviet Union could divide that unfortunate country between them; it was its fourth partition. About the same time the Central Committee of the KPD called on its adherents in Germany to organise 'mass meetings at the stations and fraternization with the mobilised soldiers in the streets'. If the anti-war mood was favourable they should hold 'short demonstrations in the streets for peace' and shout 'We want peace! Down with Hitler!' Courageous action by individuals could be decisive and carry along others. When war broke out in September the Central Committee declared that, in contrast with other currents of the German opposition, the opinion of the KPD had always been 'that the deliverance of our people from the fascist dictatorship could not come from outside (war) but would be the result of the fight of the masses for the overthrow of the dictatorship'. Now, however, the Social-Democratic leaders 'proclaimed their alliance with the reaction in England and France and with the German bourgeoisie to suppress the German people's revolution', for in reality they did not wage war on Nazi Germany but on the German people with the aim 'to eliminate the German working class from the building of the new Germany'.[1] All ideas of a united front were buried, the bitter fight against the Social Democrats was resumed, the old party line prevailed once more.

On 3 September, the day Britain and France declared war on Nazi Germany, the Secretariat of the Central Committee stated:

> The criminal attitude of some former SPD leaders has facilitated Hitler's preparations for war and prevented a union of the opposition in the emigration. Therefore today no common platform of the opposition exists for the overthrow of Hitler. The KPD is the only power in Germany which – linked to the masses – has proclaimed clearly its intentions, has entered the path leading to a people's revolution without wavering.

In the *Kommunistische Internationale* Wilhelm Florin took up the cudgels against the Social Democrats, completely identifying the 'war criminals' in Berlin with those in London and Paris: the SPD was supporting the latter because it feared social revolutions and was 'only prevented by special circumstances' from openly supporting the imperialist German war party. 'They [the SPD leaders] have sunk deeper even than in 1914 and work as agents in the pay of English and French imperialism'. A leaflet distributed in Germany emphasized that all conditions for cooperation with the SPD were destroyed; its members would have to embrace Marxism-Leninism and become 'comrades in arms of the Communists'. Early in 1940 a leaflet distributed in Bremen classified the SPD as traitors and allies of the Imperialists. It was a clear return to the 'united front from below' against the SPD and it was based on total ignorance of the conditions prevailing in Germany where Hitler's victories produced widespread enthusiasm.[2]

From Berlin the exiled SPD leaders were informed that many former trade unionists saw the Pact as a confirmation of their negative attitude to the Communists: 'We have always known that one day the brothers will get together.' Outbreaks of fury against the Communist wirepullers had occurred, 'and whoever in the factory defends the German–Russian Pact is completely rejected by the older workers, whether he intends to provoke or is an honest convinced Communist'. From the Rhineland it was reported that the Communists felt 'deceived and they often clearly say in conversations that the agreement Hitler–Stalin for them means a terrible disappointment'. In Upper Silesia the Pact had a depressing effect; among former Communists there was only one opinion: 'Moscow has committed the most monstrous treason against the working-class movement'. When it was a question of preserving their power the dictators were capable of committing any treason – now it was proved that no difference existed between Hitler and Stalin. At one mine a large chalk inscription appeared: 'Down with Stalin and Hitler – Long live the free republic!' From Berlin, on the other hand, it was said that even critical Communists did not reject everything coming from Moscow. Apparently some were 'very pensive and searching for a new way', but others still hoped that 'in Germany the workers under Communist leadership and ... with Russia's help would rise against the Nazis'.[3]

There were also many voices expressing approval of Hitler's war policy. In the Saar many workers thought the Nazis had turned to the left. One of them declared:

> Now we must stand behind the *Führer*, a revolution would be treason. If Germany loses the war we will have to accommodate ourselves to the new situation. But it would contain the germ of a new war if Germany would be dismembered as in the Peace of Westphalia.

In Berlin, another report stated, many wanted Hitler to go, but at the same time they 'have a panic fear of the consequences of defeat'. They would rather keep Hitler than face what might came after him and feared complete chaos, robbing and murder. This attitude, prevalent among the middle classes, 'automatically excludes every thought but that of victory'. That this attitude was by no means confined to the middle classes emerged from a postwar interview with a Communist deputy from Württemberg who was then incarcerated at Dachau:

> When the war broke out and Hitler celebrated one victory after the other there were of course some among our comrades who . . . said resignedly: 'Hitler will triumph, the world belongs to him and no one will be able to remove him and his hand'.

But the majority of the prisoners thought differently: 'We will live longer than Hitler, and not the other way round.'[4] That was the attitude of the loyal Communists.

The Hitler–Stalin Pact certainly had a very negative effect on KPD activities in Germany. The number of underground leaflets recorded sank from 277 in December 1939 to only 82 in April 1940. In the year 1939 there were 15,922 of them, in 1940 only 1277. There was even a rumour 'in Marxist circles' that after 1 December 1939 the KPD would again become a legal party. It may have been this growing passivity which induced the exiled KPD leaders in Moscow to decide at the end of 1939 to form a central operative leadership in Berlin as it had existed in the early years of the Nazi regime, to coordinate and control the activities of the isolated party groups. But several instructors sent to Germany were soon arrested, and attempts to infiltrate leading party officials from Sweden or another neutral country failed and were given up.[5] Given the resources available to the Gestapo it would almost certainly have led to another disaster.

Yet there was Communist activity in Germany, although not under a centralized leadership. In October 1939 leaflets were posted in Berlin-Charlottenburg:

> The working class will see to it that at the end of the Second World War a large number of the European nations will break the shackles of bourgeois class rule and do away with the exploitation of people by people. Thereafter the air in Europe will be purer.

A leaflet written by a Communist teacher, who organized underground groups among his colleagues, warned the Berliners in 1940:

> The real war is still to come – destruction of our cities, hundreds of thousands under the ruins – do you want that this terrible war should destroy our homeland? Raise your voices for Peace! Stop the war which only helps the rich and makes the poor suffer . . .

In June 1940 the party's central organ, *Rote Fahne*, claimed that 'the pernicious policy of the rulers of England and France and their Social-Democratic lackeys has led to the mass battles in which the peoples [suffer] for imperialist war aims'. In November another Communist leaflet proclaimed boldly:

> The English capitalists do not want to give up their domination over a large part of the world, and the German capitalists want to gain world domination. Thus the war on both sides is an imperialist war – an unjust war. This war only aids the rich. The capitalists chase our fathers and sons on to the battlefield for new markets, for more profits. The peoples on both sides did not want this war.[6]

Exiled German Communists in Britain equally insisted that it was an imperialist war which deserved no support from their side.[7] That remained the party line until June 1941.

In Berlin Robert Uhrig in 1939 established a KPD group with cells in five city districts and meetings organized in the woods. In central Germany a larger organization came into being in 1940 with cells in the leading factories of Halle and Merseburg. In Hamburg several leading Communists released from concentration camps re-established contacts and a functioning district organization with several hundred members. In Mannheim another released Communist leader, Georg Lechleiter, founded a KPD group. The Communists of Dortmund established contact to Berlin and Amsterdam. But in Bavaria, where the older groups had been wiped out by the Gestapo, no attempt was made to restart underground activities.[8] All the attempts mentioned were made by old KPD officials after their release from a concentration camp; they knew they had to reckon with the death penalty if caught.

Shortly after the outbreak of war with the Soviet Union the Gestapo listed the main topics of Communist propaganda. In the first instance these were questions of daily life, such as shortages of food and articles of consumption, price rises combined with lower quality; questions of work, such as unfavourable working conditions, lower piece and premium rates, excessive working speed; then social issues, deductions from wages, in particular for unemployment insurance (when there was no unemployment), comparison of the old unions with the DAF, which was considered 'an expensive club', and above all the *Vertrauensräte* who did not defend the workers' interests and depended on the employers.[9] It was a large list of grievances which gave the Communists plenty of openings. The real question, however, was how effective Communist propaganda was at a time of great German victories and a quasi-alliance of Nazi Germany with Soviet Russia. Even after the German attack of June 1941 the chain of German victories continued for some time.

If the activities of the KPD up to June 1941 were on a low scale, those of the SPD were even lower, for hardly any organized socialist groups were left. In March 1940 the Gestapo recorded it had received reports from several parts of Germany about 'brisk' activity of the 'Marxists'. Their followers met once more in the old party pubs and arrests were carried out in Berlin, Chemnitz, Darmstadt, Karlsruhe, Lüneburg and in Tilsit in the east. In Wiesbaden SPD followers were arrested when they celebrated MayDay in a wood. At the Borsig works in Berlin a small cell existed, the members of which refused any contact with the KPD because they feared the spies in its ranks. All this was on a small scale. But that the SPD in Berlin was by no means dead emerged in the autumn of 1942 when more than a thousand assembled spontaneously at the funeral of Franz Künstler, the former SPD chairman, who had suffered badly from repeated imprisonment.[10]

The exception was Bavaria, especially Augsburg. There the Gestapo in the spring of 1940 discovered an underground group which provided reports for a party official in Switzerland, and 21 people were arrested. Augsburg was also the centre of socialist groups organized by Waldemar von Knoeringen from abroad. When he moved to Paris in 1938 he entrusted the accountant Hermann Frieb with liaison work between Augsburg and Munich and the sending of reports through a courier. For work during the war, instructions filling eight pages were sent by courier in the form of a microfilm hidden in a key. They should eschew any action and only act if a revolutionary situation were to develop, 'according to the often discussed principles of revolutionary socialism'.[11] The Bavarian groups were all that was left of *Neu Beginnen* in Germany after the arrests in Berlin in 1938. It was a very exceptional case, based on cautious conspirative methods.

Twelve months before the German invasion of Russia the Security Service of the SS recorded with pride that the great German victories deprived

> hostile groups everywhere of the soil in which they could grow. All look, full of confidence and thanks, to the *Führer* and his... *Wehrmacht*. Oppositional endeavours meet everywhere with sharp rejection ... Among the old Communist and Marxist circles there can no longer be any question of organized hostile activity. Here the successes of the war have had a clearly crippling effect.

There still appeared, however, quite unimportant critical remarks, slogans painted on walls, colportage of foreign radio news, and in sporadic cases distribution of 'hate' writings and leaflets. This was an overdrawn picture, but – as far as the leftwing 'enemies' were concerned – it was not entirely fanciful. That the regime feared them nevertheless was

shown by the preventive arrest of hundreds of leftwingers in the early
months of the war.[12]

Also recorded were individual acts of courageous opposition. Early
in 1940 coal wagons at Ruhr mines bore the inscriptions: 'Work must
only last eight hours', 'Down with Hitler' and 'Send the *Bonzen* to the
front'. In December more inscription were reported: 'The director gets
2500 marks, the trammer gets 2.50 marks'. When the Christmas
bonuses were cut it was written: 'Soon we'll be in different hands, then
there will again be bonuses'. In August 1940 the Gestapo reported
growing dissatisfaction among the miners about their treatment by the
managers. In the Leuna chemical works near Halle the inscriptions ran
more simply: 'Down with Hitler' and 'Red Front'. In Würzburg in
Bavaria, according to the Gestapo, 'unrest' existed among the working
class early in 1941; 'there the word "swindle" can again be heard: these
people will have nothing to laugh about if we win the war . . . Some
are getting fat while others starve.' Yet in Hof, also in Bavaria, the
police recorded 'the impeccably patriotic attitude' of Communists and
Social Democrats, many of whom allegedly were keen on being called
up. From Düsseldorf it was mentioned that the critics of the regime
were trying to create unrest by their nagging: 'as a result of their
political training they understand superbly well how to adapt themselves
to other people and so to foster their designs in a cautious and hidden
way.' At their Skat games they had ample opportunity to talk in that
vein and to give and receive information.[13]

In Berlin, an illegal journal, *Das Freie Wort*, appeared in 1940 which
declared:

> Even if Germany defeats England and America the costs of this
> war are already so high (not counting the enormous blood
> sacrifices) that after the end of the war we will have to pay exactly
> like our enemies. And to whom must we pay? To the industrial
> barons who win every war! German people, change your minds in
> the twelfth hour. Overthrow the Nazi plutocracy . . .

Other issues stated that the German people 'must sacrifice, sacrifice and
sacrifice again', and for whom: 'Solely for the megalomaniac plans of
world dominion of our plutocratic clique of leaders!' As to the aims
of the unknown group:

> We desire freedom of opinion and of the faith. We want freedom
> of labour. We want the prevention of future wars by the nationaliz-
> ation of the armament industry and the confiscation of war profits!
> We want the creation of a true representation of the people![14]

In the summer of 1941 popular opinion in Münster was aroused by
the courageous sermon of Bishop Clemens August Count Galen
against the killing of innocent people (the euthanasia murders of the

mentally ill by the Nazis): a killing of innocents, the bishop declared, was only permitted in a just war or in self-defence. The sermon circulated in many hundreds of clandestine copies and caused enormous excitement in a country which had become aware of the sudden deaths of so many ill people. Measures to be taken against the bishop were discussed but he was not arrested. Goebbels had to admit that nothing effective could be done 'at the moment'. He feared that, if something was done against Galen, 'the population of Münster would have to be written off during the war', and to this 'the whole of Westphalia could be added'. One workman responded to the Hitler salute of his foreman in Münster by shouting 'What, the murderer!' He was arrested and still steadfastly maintained that Hitler was a murderer. A local armaments factory informed the Gestapo that the sermon was the subject of heated discussions 'which clearly do not contribute to the intended unity of our people but lead to a schism'. In the midst of war this was a worrying prospect. In Würzburg in 1940 a working-class woman was jailed for two months for saying the Jews should be left in peace, Germany should make peace, the bloody Italians got the coal, not the Germans.[15]

Short strikes or refusals to do certain work did occur, but there were few of them and they had no political motive. In May 1940 the miners of a mine near Bitterfeld refused to work at Whitsun, but under pressure they agreed to do certain tasks which could under no circumstances be postponed. At some Ruhr mines the miners categorically refused night-work or to make good a shift lost because of an air raid alarm, and the management considered this, after tumultuous scenes, 'similar to a strike'. At Penzberg in Bavaria the managers demanded two hours of additional work because of a stoppage caused by technical difficulties, and 134 miners refused. Interestingly enough, it was the former chairman of the factory council who stated the reasons in detail; as all workers were needed there was no punishment. In the area of the Kassel court of appeal 43 people were arrested in 1940 because of refusal to work, and 113 in 1941.[16] This also indicates that such refusals were not very widespread.

There was the all-pervading fear of the Gestapo and the concentration camps. In Augsburg an outspoken district leader of the NSDAP sharply criticized its practices in 1940, especially that 'since the beginning of the war people sit in klink on account of trifling affairs and in most cases are exposed to arbitrary treatment' in a concentration camp: this surely was not the way to strengthen 'the people's community' or to further National Socialist education. He would admit that in certain cases resistance had to be broken by force but he considered it 'an impossibility' that 'fathers are put into a concentration camp while their sons are fighting the enemy'. In his opinion, the Gestapo sometimes adopted methods which 'have to be classified as directly damaging the people's interests'. He may also have thought of the Gestapo practice to arrest 'recalcitrant workers' from midday on Saturday to Sunday evening – and that was one of the mildest forms of punishment.[17]

At the beginning of the war, on 4 September 1939, a decree on the economy in wartime abolished all bonuses for overtime, work on Sunday, holidays or at night, all leave was cancelled and working hours beyond the still legal eight-hour day were sanctioned. This in practice meant a ten-hour day, and even longer working hours were permitted, as already practised widely in the armament industry. The legal limitations for work of women and juveniles were considerably loosened. The *Treuhänder* were empowered to fix minimum wages and working conditions in industry. Two months later an emergency meeting of the authorities concerned, the Ministries of Labour, Economics and the Interior, was held to discuss the effect of these measures. In the discussion it was stated that in fact the majority of workers in the armament industry stayed away on Sundays, that there was an increase of absenteeism at night work, that up to 80 per cent of the building workers were absent on Saturdays after payday on Friday, that the workers demanded wage rises on a large scale because their wages were insufficient to buy the food they were entitled to according to the rationing system. It was also said that 'the average worker ... has reached the limits of his physical endurance, for many years he has had to sustain too hot a pace', as proved by the sickness statistics which in some places showed rises of up to 50 per cent. The result of the discussion was that important provisions of the decree of 4 September were gradually withdrawn. In November the bonus rates for work at night, on Sundays and holidays were restored and the pre-war regulations for leave were reintroduced. In December all work above ten hours was made subject to overtime payment of time-and-a-quarter; in September 1940 the pre-war overtime rates which related to the eight-hour day were restored. It was a piecemeal retreat, and as a result the workers' income was rising.[18]

In the autumn of 1939 the DAF organized an enquiry into the causes of absenteeism in the district of Berlin because the measures taken so far had been unsuccessful. In the first week of October 3.7 per cent of working hours were lost by absenteeism, a percentage which would increase if those who were really ill were added. In the most glaring cases the workers had been imprisoned for two days without any result, and in general their example only induced others to follow suit. In most cases the workers' replies were: 'Who has nothing to eat cannot work.' 'When my family is hungry my good nature comes to an end.' 'I cannot work if I get dry potatoes at home.' In the most serious cases the culprits were dismissed, but the labour offices merely sent them to another factory where the same was repeated. In some factories delivery dates were missed on account of absenteeism. In a conference held in the Ministry of Economics in November 1939 it was stated that, on account of the decree of 4 September, 'true developments of sabotage' occurred in certain factories. In October the central office of the Gestapo noted that building workers 'were leaving the sites for most trifling reasons and can hardly be induced to resume work'. The economic reasons should be investigated first, and then 'draconic' measures must be taken; the workers must be told about 'the deeds and their consequences'.[19]

In August to September 1939 up to 20 per cent of the workforce were absent in Berlin armament factories on the day after payday and the numbers reporting sick increased sharply. The workers desired their wages to remain under the tax-free allowance of 234 marks because otherwise too little remained and there was too little to buy in the shops; they were not impressed by the fines which the manager could impose. At the Ruhr mines the *Treuhänder*, in the first seven months of 1940, pronounced 2136 warnings on account of absenteeism and in 261 cases proposed the imposition of 'protective custody'. For the whole economic area of Westphalia – Lower Rhine the figures in the same period were 8877 warnings and 767 proposals of 'protective custody'. During the war years 5426 workers of the Krupp steel factory at Essen were reported to the Gestapo for absenteeism, not counting mere warnings and threats which must have been much more numerous. In a single factory in Bremen 36,000 working hours were missed in 1940. At the Vulkan dockyard 300 workers were missing every Saturday because they worked on their allotments. In Leipzig the Gestapo in 1940 registered 2000 cases of absenteeism and work refusal among the German workers.[20]

The employers reacted to the problem with growing harshness but little success: with public reprobation, deductions from wages and leave, fines, cancellation of special food and tobacco allowances for 'heavy' and 'very heavy' workers, threats of imprisonment and call-up for the army. But skilled workers were so badly needed that threats with calling in the Gestapo did not always materialize. And there certainly was another valid reason for absenteeism: overwork and fatigue. For the Saar district the Armaments Inspectorate reported early in 1940 that the output had not increased. In most factories the men were working ten hours, the march to and from work took them about two more hours; 'in many cases manifestations of fatigue' appeared. The demand for Sunday work produced negative results. In June and July 1941 63 and 43 per cent respectively of the Saar miners were absent, in the Ruhr district in some cases over 50 per cent of the workforce. The *Treuhänder's* request to work on Sundays to compensate for certain holidays met with little response. Or the miners, if they worked on Sunday, took another day off. When the management refused to accept excuses for absence on Sunday, more workers were absent on other days.[21]

There were also signs of passive resistance. At one Ruhr mine the miners in May 1940 finished work exactly as prior to the extension of their working hours. If the labour exchange refused to sanction a change of job, miners committed misdemeanours or insulted their superiors in order to extract permission. Some simply left and broke their contract. The labour offices recorded a growing amount of requests to change jobs. When at one Ruhr mine a prolonging of working hours was decreed in July 1940, miners tore the announcement off the wall. In view of their solidarity no arrests were carried out. When two compulsory workdays were announced at another mine in May 1941 61 and 399 men respectively did not turn up.[22]

The courts had to intervene in many cases. In 1940 there were 1676 cases of 'breach of work discipline' in which sentence was pronounced, in 1941 2364. In the latter year it was announced that in cases of particularly obstinate absenteeism the culprits would be sent to a Work Education Camp 'so as to make it crystal clear to them that in wartime everybody has to work very hard'. The labour office of Wesermünde built a special camp for 'recalcitrant' men which in June 1940 held 70 prisoners. A young deportee from Luxemburg recounted that he was sent to a labour camp near Trier where many Saar miners were confined to 'labour education' for a maximum of eight weeks on account of absenteeism or a row with the foreman; there was heavy work and bad food.[23] These were not concentration camps, the treatment was somewhat better and the period of imprisonment was limited. But the Dachau concentration camp also had a special unit – separate from the other prisoners – for 'recalcitrant' and 'notorious' absentees.

Special problems were presented by working women, especially unmarried ones who were conscripted for labour and resented it. During the first year of the war the number of employed women declined by 6.4 per cent because the wives of soldiers received comparatively high allowances and many 'hasty' marriages took place, as the Plenipotentiary for the Economy stated early in 1940. Repeated appeals to perform 'service of honour' for the fatherland met with little response. In 1939–40 monotonous complaints were made by the armament inspectorates about the work of women and their low morale. Many women married to soldiers gave up their jobs, others stayed at home 'ill' or after Christmas (first getting the special bonus). In many armament factories 20 to 25 per cent of the women were missing, and in some cases the figures were still higher; large numbers were absent on Saturdays. In September 1940 the administrative head of Upper Franconia reported that the women's willingness to work declined more and more. Those with husbands in the forces 'try by all possible methods to stop work'; those who left when their husband was conscripted 'can only in the rarest instances be induced to restart work'.[24]

But working women had to face serious difficulties. They had no time to queue for food and if they came late there was little left. The crèches and kindergartens were overcrowded and places were difficult to find. In addition to long working hours they had to do their household chores. No wonder that armament factories with a high percentage of female labour only fulfilled their production targets to about 75 per cent. Absentee women were usually warned and not punished severely, but in specially 'hard' cases short prison sentences were imposed. What aroused the ire of working women was that ladies of the better classes were not assigned to war work but had plenty of time to play about. In the autumn of 1939 the labour offices were inundated with protest letters because young women advertised in the press to find 'ladies of equal views' for playing chess or a musical instrument. This theme was to occur time and again in the war years; it was a great grievance and an issue of social class. In Würzburg, it was reported early in 1941, it was widely believed that the wives of senior officials and officers 'continue to lead a comfortable life of idleness', while working-class women were conscripted for labour.[25]

Exactly as at the time of the Munich crisis, there seems to have been much apprehension but little enthusiasm for the war. At the outset, as an opposition group found, there was 'a little consternation' in a Cologne factory but no indignation; the mass of the people reacted apathetically. Many seemed to be disappointed because they had apparently trusted the ever repeated professions of peace by the Nazis, but 'they put up with it'. In November 1939 the SPD reports from the Rhineland noticed that there was much grumbling about long working hours, no rights, little to eat, but 'Hitler stands outside all discussion. Before the people criticize him things must get much worse'. A few weeks later it was reported from the same area that there were 'hurrah patriots' but few among the workers. The writer noticed several times that among the visitors to a pub someone came, grumbled, argued and then quickly disappeared on a bicycle, 'a kind of grumbler troup'. In Berlin there was 'no enthusiasm but no active anti-war mood . . . A large section feel primarily as Germans and do not want to be proscribed as traitors'. Early in 1940 the mood in a small industrial town of West

Germany was: 'The unripe youths are as in 1914 enthusiastic, but the war is not popular.' The people feared for the future and asked how many sacrifices the war would demand. The report ended: 'We have got time, and also the confidence that our time will come.' From Westphalia too the answer came: 'We are biding our time.' The majority were resigned, apathetic, even indifferent, concerned about expected shortages and living conditions. There was no anti-war feeling.[26]

Considerable criticism was reported from Augsburg by the district leader of the NSDAP who described the general mood as depressed and nervous. What the people demanded above all was complete fairness in the allocation of goods and food. They could not understand that poultry was available at very high prices and was not rationed which meant 'intentional preference' for the well-to-do. In November 1940 the same man specifically criticized the housing conditions, in particular of families with many children, which made the propaganda about the English slums look 'ridiculous'. By the 'enumeration of poor wages, bad housing and such like, and luxury on the other side', comparison with the conditions in Germany was provoked, people could notice similarities with the bigwigs who had risen through the Nazi party; their 'feudal' lifestyle called forth unfavourable comments. The Security Service of the SS also noticed criticism of Nazi propaganda efforts. Why was it announced that some English towns were bombarded several times when the same town was described as 'a dead city' and as 'completely destroyed' after the first attack? How could the Londoners buy food with the constant air raid warnings because, according to the German reports, they were hardly ever able to leave their cellars? Either the German reports were incorrect, or most inhabitants had left London, or they were unconcerned and continued their daily routine in spite of alerts. Clearly, Nazi propaganda overreached itself and caused widespread doubts.[27]

Serious food shortages developed in the autumn of 1940. Meat and fats were only available with serious delays and the quality of sausages deteriorated more and more. The housewives complained, but advertisements appeared offering chickens, ducks and geese at high prices. Fruit and vegetables were scarce nearly everywhere, and indignant complaints arose about preferential distribution. When fruit reappeared in the spring of 1941 it was too expensive for most workers. From Würzburg it was reported that the workers' children

> must look on when the children of the rich eat it. Nor could he [the worker] afford a quarter of wine which now costs at least 50 pfennigs, and the foreign wines exhibited in the delicatessen shops at 3 to 5 marks a bottle could only have been imported for the German plutocrats.

In Franconia a bricklayer simply declared in 1941: 'They promised to help the workers but they aimed too high and hit the throat.' Cases such as this were 'not exceptional'. The Security Service of Würzburg even saw the makings of 'a new illegal party' the members of which were united by enmity to National Socialism and judged the internal situation from that point of view. They openly expressed their dislike of new laws, of the government's building projects, the plans of new social legislation, etc. They pointed to the limitations of personal freedom, the 'threat to Christian beliefs', the doings of the Gestapo, the corruption of the party bigwigs 'and thus carried dissatisfaction and doubt into ever wider circles'.[28]

In Bremen the workers' mood differed strongly from factory to dockyard. Early in 1941 the Gestapo found it 'very good and confident' in the aircraft factories, but 'not only not good but partly precarious' at the Weser dockyard. There the workers complained about insufficient deliveries of clothes and shoes; when Great Admiral Erich Raeder spoke there in February the workers listened in stony silence. Four months later Rudolf Hess flew to Scotland and this caused 'enormous excitement', 'paralysing alarm', a 'most serious breakdown' of the public mood, as government reports from Bavaria put it in June 1941. The Hess case produced 'a true shock' among people with a positive attitude to the state, and 'spiteful satisfaction' among those with negative views. Some said Hess could not possibly be ill as he flew from Augsburg to Scotland and found the place where he wanted to land. The Messerschmitt workers of Augsburg believed that the cause was 'a severe crisis of leadership of the regime', a foreman reported.[29] Yet even if they were sceptical and disliked many features of the regime the majority continued to work for the war effort. They groused and grumbled but they worked; there was no unrest.

Absenteeism among the young workers in particular was the cause of constant complaints. The manager of the *Glanzstoff* chemical works stated early in 1940 that the youngsters refused Sunday work because they claimed Sunday for themselves. Six months later it was noted at a factory conference of the same concern that 'with good will' they could produce more but did not yet possess the 'seriousness required for intensive work'. In 1941 a zinc factory in the Ruhr declared that 15 young workers between them had missed 1400 hours during the first seven months of the year. Their behaviour towards older workers and their superiors was full of 'cynical impertinence' and the firm requested 'more severe methods of punishment' to teach the youngsters 'some discipline'. It could hardly be expected that they worked with enthusiasm if they earned a mere 33 to 44 pfennigs an hour, as the DAF district leader of Freiburg noted in May 1941.[30] It must also be assumed that foremen and older workers often took out their frustration on the youngsters.

Early in 1940 the Gestapo reported they had discovered a network of the dissolved *Bündische Jugend* in the Cologne–Bonn area. Their illegal groups 'formed a reservoir for all youngsters who for one reason or another adopt a negative attitude to the new state'. Everywhere these illegal *bündisch* groups performed outrages against HJ members, robberies of HJ homes and deeds of violence, but violence was also committed by the HJ patrol service. When a small group of boys on a hiking trip left the train at Oberbarmen in the Rhineland, as one of them remembered, members of the patrol service fell upon them with their leather belts, took away their clothes and equipment, drove them into a cellar, shaved their heads and beat them until blood was flowing. When the HJ later organized a 'week of action' in Wuppertal their adversaries created disturbances by laughing, shouting, running alarm clocks and starting fires. They also acquired blank forms of the local HJ unit and used them to obtain free rail tickets and official vouchers, with the help of a typewriter supplied by a local clergyman. They combined with other similar groups to disturb Nazi meetings and to attack homes of the HJ. They adopted a special kind of youth culture in opposition to Nazi society and its values, spreading from one town to another – not really political but driven into open opposition by the persecution they had to suffer.[31]

Their longing was for the freedom which the Nazis and the HJ denied them. Among many non-political songs they sang a changed version of a song popular in the HJ: 'On Rhine and Ruhr we march, for our freedom we fight, the patrol service, tear them asunder, *Edelweiss* marches, clear the streets.' And: 'We are criminals in your state, we take pride in our crimes. We are the youth of treason, on us serfdom will founder.' They were romantics, and they were not afraid.[32]

It has to be remembered, however, that even in the Rhenish towns where they were relatively strong the 'Edelweiss Pirates' were only a small minority among the working-class youths, isolated by their special garments and habits. Many more youngsters belonged to the HJ, if without any enthusiasm because service was now obligatory. Yet the Pirates succeeded in denying the HJ members the use of some streets. In certain working-class quarters uniformed HJ members could not venture out after dark. All the efforts of the special patrol service did not alter this state of affairs.

The years 1939 to 1941 present a confused spectacle. The activities of the KPD were on a low burner, and those of the SPD even more so. The large majority of the German workers, while not opposed to the Nazi regime, did not support the war effort with any enthusiasm.

Absenteeism was as prevalent, if not more so, than before the outbreak of war, and there was much opposition to longer working hours and to work on Sundays and holidays. The women and the young workers were particularly difficult, and even the terror could not change this. The great military victories of 1939–40 overshadowed events on the home front. As the Security Service claimed, they 'had a markedly crippling effect' on oppositional activities, but they did not change the basic attitudes of the German workers. They worked but they did not put themselves out.

Notes

1. Dahlem, *Am Vorabend*, ii, p. 336; Duhnke, *KPD*, pp. 337f. Both documents were then published in the party's official organ, *Rundschau*, the successor to *Inprekorr*.
2. Dahlem, *Am Vorabend*, ii, p. 419; Duhnke, *KPD*, pp. 340f., 359; Beatrix Herlemann, *Auf verlorenem Posten*, Bonn, 1986, p. 23.
3. *Deutschland-Berichte*, vi, 1939, no. 8, pp. 986ff., vii, 1940, no. 1, p. 25.
4. Ibid., vii, 1940, no. 4, pp. 221, 223; Bettina Wenke, *Interviews mit Überlebenden*, Stuttgart, 1980, p. 55.
5. Mann, *Protest und Kontrolle*, p. 206; Pikarski and Übel, *KPD lebt*, p. 107; Arnold Sywottek, *Deutsche Volksdemokratie*, Düsseldorf, 1971, p. 108; Weber, 'Kommunistischer Widerstand', p. 97; Boberach, *Meldungen*, ii, p. 422.
6. Ibid, p. 400; van Dick, *Oppositionelles Lehrerverhalten*, pp. 501f.; Pikarski and Übel, *KPD lebt*, pp. 197, 199.
7. Personal recollection about heated discussion with interned German Communists in the summer of 1940.
8. Wolfgang Schumann and Gerhart Hass, *Deutschland im Zweiten Weltkrieg*, i, Berlin, 1974, p. 280; Duhnke, *KPD*, pp. 460, 463; Hochmuth and Meyer, *Streiflichter*, pp. 341ff.; Matthias and Weber, *Widerstand*, p. 323; Högl and Steinmetz, *Widerstand*, p. 114; Mehringer, 'KPD in Bayern', p. 281.
9. Pikarski and Warning, *Gestapo-Berichte*, ii, Berlin, 1989, p. 33.
10. Boberach, *Meldungen*, iii, pp. 828f.; Schumann and Hass, *Deutschland*, i, p. 298; Hans-Rainer Sandvoss, *Widerstand 1933–1945. Berlin-Wedding*, Berlin, 1983, p. 37.
11. Boberach, *Meldungen*, iv, p. 1047; Hetzer, *Industriestadt Augsburg*, p. 200; Mehringer, 'Bayerische Sozialdemokratie', p. 404.
12. Boberach, *Meldungen*, iv, p. 1305; Domarus, *Nationalsozialismus, Krieg und Bevölkerung*, p. 74.
13. *Deutschland-Berichte*, vii, 1940, no. 2, p. 120; Schumann and Hass, *Deutschland*, i, p. 591; Steinert, *Hitler's War*, p. 64; Kershaw, *Public Opinion*, pp. 303f.; Mann, *Protest und Kontrolle*, p. 217.
14. Quoted by Beuys, *Vergesst uns nicht*, p. 429. This clearly was a group which was neither Communist nor Social Democrat.
15. Kuropka, *Meldungen aus Münster*, pp. 540–43; Gellately, *Gestapo*, p. 207; Ernst Klee, 'Euthanasie' im NS-Staat, Frankfurt, 1983, p. 335.

16. Werner, '*Bleib übrig*', pp. 152, 158f.; Tenfelde, in *Bayern in der NS-Zeit*, iv, p. 333; Fischer-Defoy, *Arbeiterwiderstand*, p. 194.

17. Domarus, *Nationalsozialismus, Krieg und Bevölkerung*, p. 91; Winkler, *Frauenarbeit*, p. 98.

18. Mason, 'Labour in the Third Reich', pp. 140f.; Schumann and Hass, *Deutschland*, i, pp. 200f.; Rüther, *Arbeiterschaft in Köln*, pp. 290, 297; Mason, *Arbeiterklasse und Volksgemeinschaft*, pp. 1183ff.

19. Ibid., pp. 1167f., 1174ff., 1184.

20. Mason, 'Arbeiteropposition', p. 305; Werner, '*Bleib übrig*', p. 73; Detlev Peukert, 'Arbeitslager und Jugend-KZ', in idem and Reulecke, *Die Reihen fast geschlossen*, p. 425; idem, *Volksgenossen*, p. 254; Marssolek and Ott, *Bremen*, p. 363; Schumann and Hass, *Deutschland*, i, p. 593.

21. Mai, 'Warum steht der deutsche Arbeiter', p. 224; Hachtmann, *Industriearbeit*, p. 300; Mallmann and Paul, *Herrschaft und Alltag*, p. 60; Werner, '*Bleib übrig*' pp. 152f., 398; Wisotzky, *Ruhrbergbau*, p. 260.

22. Ibid., p. 260; Werner, '*Bleib übrig*', pp. 62f., 100; Rossaint and Zimmermann, *Widerstand*, p. 155; Dorn and Zimmermann, *Bewährungsprobe*, p. 289.

23. Werner, '*Bleib übrig*', pp. 176, 178; Mason, *Sozialpolitik*, p. 322; Bettina Wenge, *Interviews mit Überlebenden*, Stuttgart, 1980, p. 220f.

24. Werner, '*Bleib übrig*', pp. 74, 76; Schumann and Hass, *Deutschland*, i, p. 201; Schefer, *Wo Unterdrückung ist*, p. 289; Mason, *Arbeiterklasse und Volksgemeinschaft*, p. 864; Eiber, 'Frauen in der Kriegsindustrie', *Bayern in der NS-Zeit*, iii, p. 602.

25. Winkler, *Frauenarbeit*, pp. 91, 93, 95–98; Kershaw, *Public Opinion*, p. 303.

26. Rüther, *Arbeiterschaft in Köln*, p. 291; *Deutschland-Berichte*, vi, 1939, no. 11, p. 1039, vii 1940, no. 1, pp. 17, 21, 25, no. 3, pp. 164f.; Schumann and Hass, *Deutschland*, i, p. 212.

27. Domarus, *Nationalsozialismus, Krieg und Bevölkerung*, pp. 85ff.; Boberach, *Meldungen*, vi, p. 1809.

28. Maser, *Das Regime*, pp. 284ff.; Elke Fröhlich, 'Stimmung und Verhalten der Bevölkerung', *Bayern in der NS-Zeit*, i, pp. 613, 619f.; Steinert, *Hitler's War*, p. 121.

29. Marssolek and Ott, *Bremen*, p. 363; Domarus, *Nationalsozialismus, Krieg und Bevölkerung*, pp. 132f.

30. Wicht, *Glanzstoff*, pp. 174, 176; Detlev Peukert, 'Protest und Widerstand von Jugendlichen' in Löwenthal and zur Mülen (eds.), *Widerstand und Verweigerung*, p. 181; Steinert, *Hitler's War*, p. 94.

31. von Hellfeld, *Bündische Jugend*, pp. 136f.; Buscher, *Stigma*, pp. 150, 178, 249, 263, 314.

32. Songs of the Edelweiss Pirates kindly supplied by Paulus Buscher and Wilhelm Scheping. See also idem, 'Oppositionelles Singen Jugendlicher im Dritten Reich', *Resistance to National Socialism*, Nottingham, 1993, pp. 89–109.

CHAPTER NINE

War with the Soviet Union

The German attack on the Soviet Union in June 1941 did not mark an immediate turning point in the war, nor did it appear to most Germans as the dreaded war on two fronts, as the war in North Africa was not considered a major theatre of war. But it did mean almost from the outset a tangible worsening of the food situation – the expectations of getting large supplies from the conquered Ukraine were never fulfilled – and ever growing shortages of many articles of consumption. As early as September 1941 the Security Service of the SS (SD) recorded that many people 'spoiled by the quick course of the previous campaigns . . . and under the influence of more noticeable scarcities in the food supply, looked with a certain apprehension at the campaign in the east which in their opinion was taking too long.' In the autumn there was a crisis in the provision of potatoes in Cologne and elsewhere. While in the previous winter 75 per cent of the inhabitants had the supply for the whole winter in their cellars, by mid-November 1941 only 22 per cent were provided for and even that not for the whole winter. The general mood was described as 'extremely critical'. In December the Armaments Inspectorate noted 'indignation' among the people queuing for food and remarks such as 'that the alleged [!] successes in the east were less important than the need to get enough to eat'. In working-class districts 'turbulent scenes' occurred in front of the shops so that the police had to intervene repeatedly. Even in agricultural East Prussia many rationed items of food – milk, butter, cheese, eggs – were not obtainable in the permitted quantities in October and for a time there was a local bread shortage; so the public prosecutor reported from Königsberg, without any explanation how such a state of affairs could have arisen.[1]

In 1942 things got much worse. In March agents of the SD reported that

> the feeling not to have enough to eat . . . depresses above all the working people from whom high performances are demanded in the enterprises. It also depresses the housewives . . . who every day have to queue in the markets and shops – often in vain – to get a few potatoes of poor quality or a few turnips.

Later in the same month the SD stated that, according to reports from all parts of the Reich, the announcement of a considerable cut in the food rations (even those for very heavy workers) caused 'serious

disquiet, especially in workers' circles'. For a large part of the population it was 'virtually crushing', like no other wartime measure. The
workers of the big cities and industrial areas considered the previous
ration 'barely enough'; now many did not show any understanding for
the new measures and the mood reached a point lower than at any
earlier time. Some even expressed their feelings by clear hints about a
decline of their output, their inability to work all that hard. For the
housewives it was 'virtually impossible to feed their families adequately
in view of the lack of potatoes and vegetables', and the workers were
strongly embittered that the better-offs could get, apart from their
rations, goods in short supply on account of their connections and
their money. At the end of March the SD reported 'very disagreeable
scenes' from large factories, especially in Dresden and Frankfurt and
also the Sudetenland. The many appeals to work harder were considered
'a mockery': the cut in the rations would result in a cut of their output.
The managers and the *Vertrauensräte* had their hands full to quieten
the workers, especially women, many of whom reacted with sharp
utterances of disgust.[2]

Where the women queued for food remarks were heard that the cuts
had not yet reached their lowest point and that more disagreeable
surprises were in the offing, even if the harvest were reasonably good.
But a bad harvest would jeopardize even a barely sufficient food supply,
it was recorded in April 1942. In working-class circles there were
frequent remarks that it need not have come to this if sharp measures
had been taken in time against illicit barter, panic food purchases and
excessive prices. In the towns of the Rhenish–Westphalian industrial
area strong complaints were made about the shortages. From Dortmund
it was reported that children came to school without any breakfast or
missed school on account of the shortages. Many workers and white-
collar workers declared that it was impossible to keep up their output
much longer without serious damage to their health. Many looked at
the military situation and the outcome of the war from the point of
view of the food shortage and reached the conclusion 'that Germany
had certain limits with regard to the length and conduct of the war'.
In June it was lack of bread which caused many to remark: 'If we do
not have enough to eat now what will it be like in the coming winter?'
Women went to the economic offices with their children whose hunger
they could no longer satisfy. At that time the official bread ration for
'normal' consumers was two kilos per week if it was obtainable. In the
large towns people discussed the military situation less than the lack of
potatoes and of leather for shoes, the insufficient supplies of coal and
medicines.[3]

If during the winter the lack of heating material was a constant source of complaints, in the spring it was the lack of vegetables. In April 1942 it was reported from East Prussia that women often queued for hours at the greengrocers and that prices had risen sharply, yet only a very small number could get any vegetables. In June it was added that cuts in the rations caused a great demand for fish, fruit and vegetables and long queues at the shops. A side effect of the scarcities was the occurrence of boils and gum troubles. There was insufficient fat and the bread ration was too small for large families; the cuts were a 'heavy burden'. And that from a province with rich agriculture and a long coastline. In the same month the SD reported the vegetable shortage caused serious outbursts of bad temper against leading personalities and better-placed people who, through their personal connections, had to suffer far less from the restrictions than ordinary men and women.[4]

By July 1942 the SD reports from the Rhineland showed a deterioration of the situation. In Bochum, Dortmund, Hagen the queues at the greengrocers began at 5 or 6 a.m., in some cases even earlier. Expressions such as 'We will not suffer this any longer', 'We'll create a commotion' could be heard every day. In Bochum tumultuous scenes occurred in front of a greengrocer when some women were seen to be served preferentially. A working-class woman shouted: 'We will not permit this any more, we stand here for five hours and have nothing to eat at home!' In Herne the delivery vans could not unload because of the risk of being stormed by angry women. People were threatening the greengrocers. Masses migrated to the country to get vegetables from the producers so that many did not appear for work. In other large industrial towns the situation was no better. In Dessau in central Germany long queues formed in the markets before the market women arrived. Clashes and brawls occurred daily and the police had to intervene. As a result the SD found that the 'offensive spirit' of earlier campaigns had disappeared. Workers drastically declared that, if the food situation did not improve, they could no longer do the work demanded of them. The housewives were in 'despair' and looked to the coming winter 'with the greatest worries'. If fruit and vegetables finally became available the workers complained they could not afford the high prices with their fixed wages.[5]

With the growing shortages, not only of food but of all articles of consumption, barter trade became much more frequent although the authorities considered it a criminal offence. In its defence a lawyer declared in court that it surely was not a crime 'if someone in view of the prevailing food rations used illicit means to get the food essential for his life'. In Munich another lawyer exclaimed to the judges: 'Bear in mind that the people have hunger, hunger!' In Augsburg, it was recorded at the end of 1942, it was generally suspected that businessmen and others through barter or connections knew how to get more food and luxuries than they were entitled to. By the end of 1943 the forbidden trade was quite regularized and people talked openly about the 'black market' where goods could be obtained which others hardly ever saw. Tobacco was the 'new money' for which much could be got in the country and also in the towns, so the SD reported. In rural areas near Hamburg barter trade functioned on the basis of peacetime prices, for example three bottles of cognac for one goose, or near Danzig ten cigarettes for 50 grams of meat. With regard to fruit people thought that 'self-help' was the only way to get anything at all. Large numbers no longer felt that to 'organize' something was punishable; this was one of the most important reasons for the growth of the barter trade. Shopkeepers in Cologne would only part with their wares if offered some 'real value' in return, and so the black market flourished.[6] Conditions were approximating those which existed in Germany in the last years of the First World War.

The greatest problem, however, was the severe shortage of potatoes which continued unabated. To compensate for it people ate more bread, but bread too was in short supply and the ration insufficient. In November 1943 the women's greatest worry was the 'potato emergency' and the lack of vegetables. Many mothers had sleepless nights, for 'they did not know what to serve' to their children. Shopping often became like 'running the gauntlet', and the shopkeepers no longer showed the smallest measure of politeness to their customers. In the same month the SD also noticed that many shops had not been able to distribute potatoes for more than four weeks. Among the working population there was 'great depression and often embitterment', and in the whole of Germany memories of the 'turnip winter' of 1916–17 revived. In the spring of 1944 the potato shortage was getting worse, with 'unfavourable' effects.[7]

Women, even those without children, were not keen on starting warwork. In the summer of 1941 a large armament factory in Cologne tried to persuade the wives of its workers to start industrial work. Of the 120 wives invited in small groups (all without children) only 13 accepted; the others excused themselves on the grounds of bad health, looking after old relatives, etc. Those who did work often absented themselves. A factory in the Ruhr which employed 150 women complained that at least 30 were missing regularly, not just for days but for weeks or months. When the firm requested them by registered letter to resume work they did not react or declined to accept the letter. Invitations to appear at a meeting of the *Vertrauensrat* were equally ignored. In August 1941 the SD noted a general lack of discipline among working-class women which in many places caused a shortfall of production of about 20 to 25 per cent. According to the SD, many women took up work for the Red Cross or a welfare association to escape industrial labour, or they got married and pregnant, or were able to produce a medical certificate exempting them from heavy work. In January 1943 the Plenipotentiary for Labour, Fritz Sauckel, issued a decree obliging all non-employed men and women to register for 'tasks of defence'. But the estimated three million women concerned shrank to the 1,260,000 who registered, and the figure of women employed only increased by about 370,000. According to German statistics, only 46 per cent of employable women actually worked in 1943 (in Britain the figure was over 60 per cent). Women who had to look after small children were exempt.[8]

The principal grievance of working women was the idleness of the 'ladies' of the better classes, the wives of officers, entrepreneurs, bigwigs and the well-to-do. In 1942 the SD quoted the letter of a frontline soldier:

> I do not allow my wife to be chicaned when I am at the front. I have forbidden her to work as long as rich women and girls are not conscripted for labour . . . If sacrifices are demanded all must bring them without a difference of the purse. The wife of a worker is as valuable to the state as the wife of a factory manager. The production of children these ladies leave in any case to our wives.

When DAF officials were asked why not all women were equally directed they found themselves in a very difficult situation. At factory assemblies shouts were heard: 'Where are the others? That's all we want to hear.' These outbreaks were a recent development indicating that the bad mood was spreading. If the officials did not react the workers concluded that the NSDAP itself did not want a change. If they tried to hush up things they had to defend something 'contrary to the workers' sense of social justice'. Many DAF officials felt cornered and uncertain and then used arguments which were not credible, such as 'that the women now idle would not receive any share in the fruits of the war'. Such remarks, the SD found, were not conducive to calming the atmosphere but led to more irritation, 'because they would of course not be believed'. Young women in ski clothes and with suntanned faces had a provocative effect on the workers who did not understand why the state did not enforce. a 'solidary lifestyle' on all Germans. From Augsburg the mayor in 1944 reported a widespread opinion that many women of the so-called better classes were shirking the duty to work and in certain cases were even permitted to have domestic servants.[9] If people expected social justice from the regime they were disappointed.

On account of the increasingly heavy air raids many women and children were evacuated to 'safe' areas and this caused new problems. Those sent to rural East Prussia in 1943 often disliked the lack of amenities they were accustomed to and did not want to share the labours of their unwilling hosts. It was also noted that the women from Berlin groused and grumbled much more than the staid East Prussians and looked at the latter's 'political discipline' as a sign of stupidity and of limited views. In spite of all dangers many returned to Berlin – and after all, danger was also approaching East Prussia. In the Rhenish industrial towns women who returned from evacuation found that the food offices would not give them ration cards. In Witten 300 women demonstrated publicly against this ruling and the police was called by the bureaucrats. But, rather surprisingly, the policemen refused to act because they believed the women to be in the right and the refusal to be illegal. Similar scenes occurred in Bochum, Hamm and Lünen where excited crowds demanded their ration cards. Miners refused to work unless the cards were issued. Many 'leading persons' were publicly reviled including the *Gauleiter*. The women simply declared they would suffer the air attacks rather than return to their evacuation quarters and one of them pronounced: 'My children stay here and if I have nothing to eat then I will perish together with them.'[10] The German working-class women were far from silent and acquiescent; they knew what they wanted and, more courageous than their menfolk, were not afraid to take on the authorities.

Especially in the west of Germany the almost constant air raids caused widespread despondency. As the SD notice early in 1943, the women were 'almost in despair' about the size of the attacks and the prospects for the future they entailed. There were rumours that the anti-aircraft defences had recently been curtailed in favour of Milan and Turin, and many similar rumours were current in the west. A few months later the SD reported that 'isolated enemies' used the attacks to make 'remarks against state, party and leadership', that some tried to 'incite and egg on' those who had suffered damage. 'Negative utterances' were ascribed to people who allegedly lost their nerve, for example in Düsseldorf: 'For this we have to thank our *Führer*' – and that in the presence of an SS man. In Barmen a woman who lost her son, daughter-in-law and grandson was found crying by two SA men who tried to comfort her but she shouted: 'The brown cadets are responsible for the war. You should be at the front and have seen to it that the English cannot penetrate here.' Few people were still using the Hitler salute, most said rather ostentatiously 'Good morning'. In Düsseldorf a tale was going round of the erection of a gallows with a picture of Hitler. In the industrial districts a poem was quoted: 'Dear Tommy, keep on flying, here we all are miners, fly on to Berlin, there they have all cried "yes".' The constant alarms and attacks caused a gradual weakening; the continuous fear for life and goods affected the nerves and in the end led 'to a fatalism bound to influence the attitude'; people asked how long they could sustain this burden.[11]

Women again took a prominent part. In August 1943 a 'typical' event was recorded from Brunswick. In the market two women conversed loudly about the air attacks: nothing had been heard of the announced revenge, the means for it apparently lacking. Some railway workers added: 'There is a means, our government must go, we need a new government.' The mayor of Göttingen who entered a railway carriage showing his golden NSDAP badge was jostled and told that he was one of those with whom accounts would have to be settled. A woman put her sleeve under his nose: he could be certain that the day of reckoning was coming. Another woman who had suffered bomb damage remarked in 1943 all setbacks could have been avoided if the 'brown bigwigs' were not at home but at the front and fulfilling their duty like the Russian Red Commissars. The woman was arrested but the public prosecutor said it would be unjust to prosecute this one woman, as such a remark occurred in something like a quarter of all criminal cases brought for different reasons; remarks comparing the fat *Bonzen* with the Red Commissars who did their duty were only too common. In Dortmund a captain stopped a soldier for not saluting properly in April 1943 but found that the soldier was a deserter. Quickly a crowd of 300–400 collected, mainly consisting of women, and adopted such a threatening attitude that the officer was forced to escape on a passing tram. Shouts were heard: 'Give us back our boys, our men!' and 'There will be a revolution!'[12]

That not all Nazi propaganda about the 'terror attacks' was believed was shown by a report from Augsburg in 1942 that according to all accounts the British pilots were looked at with admiration: as soldiers they aimed their bombs accurately at targets which were important for the war effort and hit them precisely. From Würzburg the police recounted that after air attacks the NSDAP officials found it 'particularly difficult to fulfil their duty'; their brown uniforms had the same effect as a red rag on a bull, they were seen as 'the culprits'. From Berlin the SD reported 'negative utterances', especially made in air raid shelters, often without any contradiction by those present. A woman declared: 'If the Nazis had not taken over we would not have been through this.' But a worker argued: 'What would have happened otherwise? Do you believe that the Russians with their strong armaments would have left us in peace?' A soldier on leave, on the other hand, found that after a heavy attack people in their excitement made remarks such as '*Führer* command, we have to suffer it'. In February 1944, after a particularly heavy air raid on Berlin, the SD noted more 'attacks on leading personalities who were held responsible for the war'; among the women the opinion was widely held that they had enough of the war, 'this pointless destruction' must be stopped.[13]

But there were also examples to the contrary. In Nuremberg, according to the SD, a woman who commented on a Hitler speech in 1943 that she missed an announcement as to when the war would end, there 'surely had been enough of it', was almost beaten by other women present. When Hitler spoke on 8 November (the 20th anniversary of his Munich Putsch), some people indeed criticized certain points, but they were quite unimportant in comparison with many approving and enthusiastic comments. Even those who were inclined to criticize were positively influenced, the SD found. The large majority of the workers returned after heavy air raids. After the devastating attack on Hamburg in 1943 many returned and resumed work. But after four heavy attacks on Cologne in the summer of 1944 about a thousand men and women did not return to the Ford factory. The others came back after an interval, in spite of all destruction and suffering. Large numbers still believed in a final German victory – and feared the consequences of defeat.[14]

If their machines could be repaired after raids, workers continued to work in the open air until the halls were repaired. After an attack on Bochum in November 1944 which wrought heavy destruction in working-class quarters, soldiers were detailed to help with the clearance. When a man pointed out to them that there was no point in this and that the war was lost, a worker beat him to death amid the acclamations of the onlookers. After several heavy raids on Nuremberg in August 1943, on the other hand, many workers did not reappear for days on end and tried to move to less endangered places. In Berlin too, after a heavy raid, many workers only appeared in the factory for a few hours and left soon on account of the transport difficulties. Many women workers sought quarters outside Berlin without informing the management.[15]

With regard to the war in Russia a good deal of scepticism was recorded almost from the outset, and not all the bombastic German victory announcements were believed. As early as September 1941 it was widely held that, in spite of the Red Army's enormous losses in men and material, there was no 'noticeable slackening of Bolshevist resistance': it was claimed too often that 'the major part of the Bolshevist core units was annihilated', that the 'Russian leadership had lost control of the situation'. Many Germans, according to the SD, thought that the campaign was lasting too long and looked at its course 'with some disquiet'; the opinion was gaining ground that progress was 'very slow'. By November many were anxiously asking how the war in Russia could be terminated. People acknowledged that no peace or armistice with Stalin was possible, but to occupy the whole of Russia was surely impossible because there were not enough German troops for this. People simply could not understand why the German armies did not advance more quickly because (according to the announcements) 260 well-equipped Soviet divisions had been annihilated and what remained were poorly equipped and poorly trained units. In wide circles it was feared that the end of the war was still far away and this caused a 'certain indifference', especially among women and workers, with regard to the battles in the east. In December the population learned from soldiers' letters of 'the unbroken fighting strength of the Bolshevist forces' which attacked everywhere on the eastern front 'with unbelievable force' and caused heavy German losses. Their use of massed tanks, artillery and aeroplanes disproved the German propaganda claims that Bolshevism had been decisively defeated. Letters from the front complained of lack of food and winter clothing. Soldiers even asked for parcels with bread as they had been without food for days. The contents of these letters quickly spread among the families of fighting soldiers.[16] Indeed, winter clothing was so short that vast collections of warm clothes were organized, for the army had made no proper preparations for a winter campaign.

At the beginning of 1942 rumours about a retreat of the German units on all sectors of the eastern front were circulating. From the Bavarian district of Mittenwald the gendarmerie reported that the people were 'tired of war'. The mood was compared to that of 1917: the morale was poor and people did not believe in an early end of the war. They suspected, in view of the ever repeated mass attacks of the Red Army, that the Soviets had 'enormous reserves of material from formidable armament factories in the Urals'. In March fears were expressed in many towns that in the long run the German eastern front would not be able to hold out; certain units must be so weakened that they could not be used in a spring offensive. The Russian resources clearly were not exhausted and there was much speculation as to whether American deliveries were taking place and about the enormous capacity of Soviet industries. In June 1942 open fears were expressed about the military situation, that 'time worked against us'. Comparisons were made with the First World War which Germany lost, in spite of all victories, on account of the length of the war.

In July the SD registered a 'fervent longing for an early end of the war'; especially the hard-pressed inhabitants of the big cities were 'slowly' getting tired of the war on account of the air raids. By the end of 1942 many believed that Soviet Russia still had 'unlimited reserves' as shown by the many tanks knocked out according to German claims. Articles in the German press such as 'Heaviest Soviet losses' or 'The Soviet economy mortally hit' encountered 'the greatest scepsis', for the Red Army attacked again and again. Fears were also expressed about Rommel's retreat in North Africa where the initiative seemed to have passed to the enemy.[17]

In January 1943 the head of the Bavarian district of Swabia wrote that there was despondency on account of the many soldiers killed; it was generally believed that a large German army was surrounded at Stalingrad. By the end of the month the fate of the army was considered 'sealed', Russia's power of resistance had clearly been underestimated very badly. For the first time an unfavourable end to the war was considered possible. Some thought it would only be 'half so bad', but according to the SD the overwhelming majority thought it would mean the end. Many believed that Stalingrad meant 'the beginning of the end'. The public mood in Bavaria reached 'a low point hitherto unknown', the administration recorded; there was a general longing for peace. The situation was increasingly compared with that of 1918: after all the German victories, came 'the great setbacks'; then, too, the USA were in the background and only started when Germany was already exhausted. Leftwing workers remarked that they always had to work hard and from Bolshevism they expected nothing worse than much work and low wages. The sacrifices at Stalingrad and elsewhere were like those in the First World War: from Dresden alone 3000 men were missing at Stalingrad, from one village in Swabia 25. From the front soldiers wrote of 'panic flight', all heavy weapons and material were left behind, they could save nothing but their 'naked lives'.[18]

In July 1943 the SD registered a significant change. Since Stalingrad the spreading of low jokes, even about the *Führer*, had much increased, and in pubs and factories people were telling each other the 'newest' political jokes. At the front they sang: 'Everything passes, retreat in December, offensive in May', but at home the version was: 'First goes the *Führer*, and then the party'. A sign of the deterioration of attitudes also was that large numbers 'in an ill-disciplined way' showed their fears about the outcome of the war. Without considering the effect, people 'blew into the horn of *Miesmacherei*' (carping criticism). Many members of the NSDAP no longer wore the party insignia, the use of the Hitler salute had 'noticeably declined'. People were convinced that Germany had lost the military superiority and began to picture in detail what the defeat would bring. Hostile remarks were no longer countered with any conviction. A party member was accosted on a train how he could still wear 'such a thing' as the party badge. A soldier wrote to his wife she should get rid of his SA uniform because a new time was coming. Remarks could be heard to the effect that under the Social Democrats things had been better and war would not have happened. Indoors and outdoors all conversations, often with totally unknown persons, were dominated by the question what the future would bring. Among the workers the opinion was widespread that Bolshevism was no threat to ordinary people who had nothing to lose – only the 'bigwigs' would suffer. German propaganda, the SD noted, found it increasingly difficult to counter this argument.[19]

German propaganda was also criticized when it spoke of Churchill as 'Roosevelt's adjutant' or 'Churchill receiving orders from Roosevelt'. People remembered earlier 'orders' which led to the loss of North Africa and Hitler's conferences with numerous European politicians: it was not ridiculous if the responsible leaders of the other side conferred with each other and it was all the same whether Churchill went to Roosevelt or Roosevelt to Churchill. In September 1943 the official announcements were criticized that the German armies were dictating 'the law of action' to the advancing Red Army, as well as that giving up large spaces to the enemy was of no importance, for earlier the conquest of such spaces was 'characterized as a decisive gain for our war potential'. At the end of 1942 a *Landrat* in Franconia described 'fatigue, indifference, depression . . . distrust of the truth and completeness of the press and radio news' as the most important traits of the general mood. He thought it was 'pointless' to demand ever greater performances, to extend the working hours further and further.[20]

Meanwhile the Soviet offensives continued unabated; the Red Army first crossed the Dnieper and then the Dniester and the German retreat continued. In October 1943, according to the SD, even 'the greatest optimists' began to 'scratch behind their ears' and people doubted openly whether 'we can stop the Bolshevists' who, in spite of heavy losses and the difficulties caused by destruction, conducted their mass offensives. This time it was the Germans who waited for 'generals rain and mud' to slow the enemy's advance. In November the SD found that those who wanted peace at any price were comparatively few but many wanted a compromise peace. The former considered the war lost: people from all social groups and especially workers and peasants who were badly off or very religious, as well as intellectuals and economic circles; in their opinion it was 'high time to finish to avoid further useless bloodshed'. These 'elements' believed that a lost war was far better than it was claimed. From Franconia it was reported in May 1943 that there was much criticism of the *Führer* and the measures taken by him – he always acted according to his own opinions, did not accept any advice and thus caused serious conflicts between his closest collaborators. Even the measures taken against the Jews were criticized, for the goods destroyed in 1938 were now badly needed. At another place in Franconia a saying of the *Führer* was quoted: 'In 1933 he had declared that in ten years' time Germany would look different' – that was the only prophecy of his which had come true. The informant claimed that this joke was circulated by women evacuated from Düsseldorf: in any case it was widely recounted.[21]

All reports show how sceptical large numbers of Germans had become with regard to the propaganda churned out by the regime and how critical of official claims. Even the sacrosanct person of Hitler was criticized. People were no longer afraid to speak their minds quite openly. A worker of the MAN at Augsburg declared in a train: 'Nothing decent to eat, only rubbish to buy, nothing to smoke – now they can only let us kick the bucket!' No one objected. A worker in Schweinfurt remarked: 'We workers have the feeling that we have been placed outside the law.' In September 1943 the mood in a small town in Franconia was described by the SD as 'impotent fury against the leadership', which would rather let the whole nation perish than give in. 'They already discuss publicly which prominent people would "hang" after the war.' As to the opinion in the Franconian countryside, the SD simply stated after the overthrow of Mussolini: 'As the mood was already at point zero a further deterioration was hardly possible.'[22]

The air raids and increasing difficulties of public transport made the old problem of absenteeism more acute. In the autumn of 1942 the SD registered a whole list of 'derelictions of duty', such as reporting sick without reason, breach of contract, unpunctuality, constant attempts to change jobs, avoidance of certain kinds of labour, requests for leave on insufficient grounds, opposition, painting of slogans. Some reports mentioned 'punishable passivity which was difficult to prove' and more and more frequently dereliction of duty. In some cases German workers even asked Russian prisoners of war to slow down their efforts, so as not to show their own reserves of strength. The decline of working morale was made clear by the mounting number of sickness reports. Women and youths were especially prominent in their lack of willingness. During the first six months of 1943 more than 14,000 Germans were sentenced for lack of 'work discipline'. In cooperation with the relevant ministries and the Gestapo the DAF introduced a scale of punishments for absenteeism and bad performance – as a 'means of education' before more drastic punishment.[23]

The Sunday shifts introduced for the miners were particularly unpopular. In 1943 the miners complained that they hardly got any free time, and that such shifts were not demanded in any other trade. In the Aachen coal district the large majority were so against special shifts over Easter that a compromise was reached: fathers whose children took holy communion would be exempt if they produced a certificate signed by a competent parson. Thereupon the large majority showed such certificates, whether they had children taking communion or not: at one mine 70–80 per cent, of which perhaps 5–8 per cent were justified. Remarks were made: 'For ten years they have pushed the parson to the wall, now they bring him back again' and 'We will never capitulate'. In 1942 two miners were arrested in Saarbrücken because they refused to work additional Sunday shifts and were sent to a concentration camp. In June 1941 only 67 per cent of the Saar miners did the compulsory Sunday shift, and in July only 43 per cent. At some Ruhr mines more than half the miners were absent in certain cases.[24]

Yet in other industries the working hours did not increase significantly. The male working hours remained fairly constant around 51 hours a week from 1941 to 1944, and those of women even declined somewhat. In an iron foundry of the north-west the discipline declined sharply after the evacuation of the men's wives and children. The men declined to work on Sunday because they had household chores and wanted to visit their families. The management refused to accept any excuse and suspected a kind of 'strike'. The Gestapo arrested two workers who were released after three days – and Sunday work was resumed. In the towns hit by repeated air raids and suffering from growing shortages it became of primary importance to 'organize' food and other goods, to keep warm and to have a roof over one's head, while wages ceased to be of vital importance because there was so little to buy. In any case the additional shifts were worked by the Aachen and Ruhr miners but with a reduced output.[25]

The pogroms of 1938 aroused widespread indignation and active sympathy with the persecuted, but during the war interest in the Jewish question flagged and the mass deportations did not arouse much comment, as most people were increasingly busy with their own problems. A Communist leaflet written by Berta Fuchs, 'a German working-class woman', protested against the deportations from Düsseldorf from where 'a thousand elderly, infirm, war invalids, long baptized people and many who did not even know they were of Jewish descent' were deported. 'Scenes of infinite suffering' took place at the Gestapo and one named official was pilloried as 'the greatest sadist of humanity': 'must we not be ashamed to be Germans?' After the discovery of the mass graves of Polish officers at Katyn in 1943 the SD noted that people were saying: the Germans had no right to accuse the Soviets of mass murder because Poles and Jews had been killed by the Germans in much larger numbers.[26]

Many rumours were circulating and this could hardly be prevented in view of what so many soldiers could observe in the east. A Communist accused of treason in Frankfurt stated in his trial in 1944: in Russia the Jewish transports were moved to sidetracks, doused with petrol and set on fire, small children were seized by their legs by SS men and thrown with their heads against a tree. Although the details were not correct the man had obviously heard what was happening in the east. Jews also received active help when they went into hiding. Many were sheltered in the Swedish church in Berlin. There one day they saw to their horror two uniformed policemen approaching. But it turned out they were old Prussian officials and Social Democrats. They considered the Nazi methods illegal, hated Goebbels, knew of the hidden Jews and warned them of visits by the Gestapo: proper policemen would certainly not arrest people in the middle of the night without a warrant. Two Jewish women were hidden in a workers' settlement in the north of Berlin by a former trade union secretary – until neighbours became curious and enquired about the 'visitors' and they had to leave: 'It's no longer possible, I am afraid.' Another Jewish woman travelled to Weimar with two small children where she talked to a man she met in a small café. He asked whether she could not find a room; he only had a small flat and family but she could come to him. When she told him she was Jewish he replied now he would help her even more willingly. He was the last surviving Social Democrat of Weimar and he found a refuge for the children with his cousin who also wanted to help. In Berlin-Wittenau employees of the Alfred Teves factory looked after hidden Jews and provided food for them. As food was rationed this was one great difficulty, but a greater one was presented by the air raids as the hidden people could not go to the shelters.[27]

Another Jew was hidden by a family in Luckenwalde to the south of Berlin. There he found in 1943 a small resistance group 'For Peace and Reconstruction' which hid Jews, collected money and distributed leaflets. But in 1944 the members of the group were arrested and several killed in a concentration camp. Another small group formed by the physicist Dr Robert Havemann, 'European Union', in 1942 eschewed all open propaganda, helped many Jews and provided documents for them. They were arrested in 1943 with the help of a police agent and several were sentenced to death. In Hamburg, the so-called KdF group saw as one of its main tasks the hiding of persecuted people. It hid Jewish children, provided foreign workers with food and cooperated with prisoners of war in preparation of the end of the Nazi regime. Its members too were arrested and many executed. In Mannheim, a group around the physicist Dr Carl Hermann provided support and false papers for Jews. In 1943 five members were arrested and sentenced to several years in a penitentiary. In Stuttgart, a small group helped Jews to escape to Switzerland – until they too were arrested. In East Prussia it was the lone employee of the administration of moors, Hermann Kurras, who hid 13 escaped Jews on his isolated farm, until he made critical remarks in a pub in 1944. The police went to investigate, the Jews were discovered, and Kurras and his wife were executed.[28]

These attempts ended in tragedy, but they show that there were Germans willing to help at the risk of their lives – surrounded by a sea of indifference and often tacit support for the measures of persecution. Large numbers knew what was happening in the concentration camps and heard rumours about the gruesome events in the east but they remained silent. All the more courageous were the few men and women who helped.

The reports quoted show how many were sceptical of the official announcements and suspicious of Nazi propaganda. The dramatic events of the war against Soviet Russia and the devastating air raids provided great opportunities for bitter criticism and oppositional remarks. For many Stalingrad marked the turning point of the war – and for that catastrophe Hitler himself was responsible, even if this was not generally known. By 1943 it was clear that Germany could not possibly win the war, and the massive air raids contributed to the feeling of despondency and depression which spread in the large towns. Many retired into a private circle of family and work, many were exhausted by heavy labour and the search for food, many despaired of the future – and others moved into active opposition. There were cracks in the façade but the regime remained firmly in control.

Notes

1. Boberach, *Meldungen*, viii, p. 2724; Rüther, *Arbeiterschaft in Köln*, pp. 307f.; Tilitzki, *Alltag in Ostpreussen*, p. 160.
2. Maser, *Regime*, p. 284; *Bayern in der NS-Zeit*, i, p. 306; Boberach, *Meldungen*, ix, pp. 3504f., x, pp. 3543, 3613.
3. Ibid., x, pp. 3595, 3639, 3772; Maser, *Regime*, p. 284.
4. Tilitzki, *Alltag in Ostpreussen*, pp. 191f., 201f.; Boberach, *Meldungen*, x p. 3873.
5. Ibid., pp. 3918f., 3934ff.; Rüther, *Arbeiterschaft in Köln, p. 366.*
6. Boberach, *Meldungen*, xi, p. 3999, xvi, pp. 6261f.; Domarus, *Nationalsozialismus, Krieg und Bevölkerung*, p. 88; Rüther, *Arbeiterschaft in Köln*, p. 316.
7. Boberach, *Meldungen*, x, p. 3936, xv, pp. 6026, 6063f., xvi, p. 6469.
8. Rüther, *Arbeiterschaft in Köln*, p. 337; Schumann and Hass, *Deutschland*, iii, 1982, pp. 213, 216f.; Boberach, *Meldungen*, vii, p. 2640.
9. Ibid., ix, pp. 3388f., 3450, xi, p. 4103; Domarus, *Nationalsozialismus, Krieg und Bevölkerung*, p. 103.
10. Tilitzki, *Alltag in Ostpreussen*, p. 262; Boberach, *Meldungen*, xv, pp. 6030ff., and many similar reports.

11. Ibid., xii, p. 4652, xiii, pp. 4924, 5217, xiv, pp. 5356f.
12. Ibid., xiv, pp. 5446f., 5620f.
13. Ibid., x, p. 3641, xv, p. 6188, xvi, p. 6379; Fröhlich, in *Bayern in der NS-Zeit*, i, p. 647.
14. Boberach, *Meldungen*, xv, pp. 5770, 5989; Werner, '*Bleib übrig*', p. 261.
15. Seebold, *Stahlkonzern*, p. 272; *Bayern in der NS-Zeit*, i, p. 315; Boberach, *Meldungen*, xvi, p. 6379.
16. Ibid., viii, pp. 2712, 2724, 2948, 2995, 3070.
17. Kershaw, *Public Opinion*, p. 319; Boberach, *Meldungen*, viii, p. 3122, ix, pp. 3409, 3449, 3523, x, p. 3803, xi, p. 4016, xii, pp. 4490, 4576, 4601.
18. Ibid., xii, pp. 4720, 4751, 4800, 4821f.; Domarus, *Nationalsozialismus, Krieg und Bevölkerung*, p. 136.
19. Peukert, 'Arbeiterwiderstand', pp. 317f.; Boberach, *Meldungen*, xiii, p. 5064, xiv, pp. 5398f., 5447, 5461, 5532, 5562, 5675.
20. Ibid., xiii, pp. 5289f., xv, p. 5824; Beuys, *Vergesst uns nicht*, p. 500.
21. Boberach, *Meldungen*, xv, pp. 5824, 5937f., 6050; Fröhlich, in *Bayern in der NS-Zeit*, i, pp. 640, 651.
22. Ibid., pp. 638, 642, 651.
23. Boberach, *Meldungen*, xi, pp. 4301f.; Schumann and Hass, *Deutschland*, iii, pp. 239, 243.
24. Werner, '*Bleib übrig*', pp. 245, 398; Boberach, *Meldungen*, xiii, pp. 5282f.; Mallmann and Paul, *Herrschaft und Alltag*, p. 358.
25. Hachtmann, *Industriearbeit*, p. 51; Werner, '*Bleib übrig*', pp. 271, 398; Rüther, 'Lage und Abstimmungsverhalten', p. 258, and *Arbeiterschaft in Köln*, pp. 424f.
26. Herlemann, *Auf verlorenem Posten*, p. 292; Kershaw, *Public Opinion*, p. 366.
27. Keval, *Widerstand und Selbstbehauptung*, p. 215; Leonhard Gross, *Versteckt*, Reinbek near Hamburg, 1983, pp. 225f.; Inge Deutschkron, *Ich trug den Gelben Stern*, Cologne, 1983, pp. 133f.; Wiener Library London, Zeugenberichte, nos. 192, 459, 886.
28. Thomas Franz and Jan Merk, 'Jugendwiderstand im Nationalsozialismus', *Internationale Korrespondenz zur Geschichte der deutschen Arbeiterbewegung*, xxviii 1992, p. 415; Weisenborn, *Lautloser Aufstand*, p. 169; Hochmuth and Meyer, *Streiflichter*, pp. 453ff., 460ff.; Matthias and Weber, *Widerstand*, pp. 459f.; Müller, *Stuttgart*, p. 507; Tilitzki, *Alltag in Ostpreussen*, p. 62.

CHAPTER TEN

Revival of the opposition

Opposition in the Third Reich took many different forms, from simple refusal to obey orders and protests in the food markets and shops about the shortages, to active political opposition which was considered treason and during the war punishable by death. A widespread form of opposition was listening to the BBC or Moscow Radio – out of distrust of German propaganda – which during the war was a criminal offence. Spreading the foreign news or listening in a group would be equivalent to treason. The BBC's German service was certainly listened to by many thousands, and so was Moscow Radio.

In January 1943, at the time of Stalingrad, the Security Service (SD) 'surmised' that foreign stations were listened to more frequently. When Moscow announced that two named soldiers from Breslau were Russian prisoners of war their families received respectively more than 20 and 40 anonymous letters to inform them. Previously the number of letters received in such a case had been much smaller. A family in Siegburg received 18 letters that their son was alive. In a similar case in Danzig the soldier's family was visited by four unknown men and got five letters that their son had broadcast from Moscow. As Moscow used German soldiers in its programmes, giving names and addresses, many listeners wrote to the families in question giving them the good news, or people copied leaflets with the names and posted them to the families, as the Gestapo noted in April 1943. In Dresden the Social-Democratic owner of a radio shop converted German radios unsuitable to receive foreign stations so that they could be listened to and supplied Poles in Poznań with the parts they needed for the same purpose. During the first six months of 1943 1314 Germans were arrested for listening to foreign stations. Some Germans declared quite openly that these brought 'less propaganda and polemics and more concrete news' than the German stations and satisfied the 'hunger for news' of the people.[1]

To spread the news broadcast by foreign stations was much more dangerous. In 1943 a German milker was sentenced to death for listening to foreign news together with Polish prisoners of war, and a German watchman in Bremen suffered the same fate. Early in 1944 a Saar miner was sentenced for listening in the dormitory of a mine together with others who were 'completely indifferent', recounting political jokes and not using the Hitler salute. In Lusatia six workers were arrested for listening to foreign 'hate' stations together with foreigners. More serious was the case of two workers from Saarbrücken who wrote down the news broadcast by foreign stations, duplicated them and put them up on walls. One of them died in captivity. The longer the war lasted the less people considered it an offence to listen to the BBC or Radio Moscow and denunciations became less frequent.[2] The programmes with German prisoners of war speaking to their compatriots were particularly popular.

By 1943 the obligatory Hitler salute was used less and less. In the spring the *Landrat* of Füssen in Bavaria reported that it had become rare, one could almost speak of a '*Grüss Gott*' movement. From Catholic Eichstätt the same was reported; only religious motives were now used in the local death announcements. In April 1944 the mayor of Brebach in the Saar wrote that there the Hitler salute had been in general use but now the habit was changing. In Berlin factories speakers of the Nazi women's organization who addressed the workers were shouted and whistled down in 1942. They could not answer the ever repeated question why women of the better social classes were not conscripted for work like the others. The slogan of the 'People's Community' was turned against them by leftwing workers and old members of the NSDAP who were equally opposed to this social discrimination. Small signs of solidarity were shown to released political prisoners. A young woman from Wiesbaden who was freed in May 1942 found a bunch of flowers on her office table and was welcomed in the canteen by her colleagues – and warned to take care what she said to certain people. The chef of personnel pressed her hand: 'One day you will be proud to have been imprisoned', and the manager invited her to dinner.[3] This may have been an exceptional case in a small firm, but it showed which way the wind was blowing: at a time when the outcome of the war was by no means certain.

Examples of active resistance became more frequent. In April 1943 leaflets were scattered in the streets and squares of Munich: 'Down with Hitler! We want peace!' In Berlin-Charlottenburg, after a heavy air raid, pictures of Hitler were thrown into burning houses and the *Führer* was verbally abused. In the Mansfeld area of central Germany the version after the overthrow of Mussolini in July 1943 was: 'Finis Italiae! Benito went to hell, Adolf must go to the devil.' A leaflet of the 'Europen Union' founded in Berlin by Robert Havemann and others, proclaimed in 1942: 'Freedom of speech and faith, freedom of meeting and organization, equality before the law and equal law for everybody.' Although Hitler had succeeded in destroying the old political organizations, the leaflet continued, one thing he had not accomplished: 'He could not eradicate the old and eternal liberal ideas born in Europe in the great revolutions.' Socialism did not mean extermination of the bourgeosie, the abolition of private property and 'the establishment of a bloody dictatorship of dogmatic Marxists', but it did mean 'the removal of private interests from politics and economics by the transfer of the means of production to the ownership of society'. Socialist economics alone would allow social justice and the development of European culture.[4] The 'European Union' not only helped Jews but established systematic contacts to foreign workers.

In February 1943 the Westphalian *Gau* of the NSDAP reported that in trains Hitler was called 'the mass murderer of Stalingrad'; those who said so were neither arrested nor beaten up. Soon afterwards the chief of the German police, Heinrich Himmler, was informed that in a munitions factory in Brandenburg a very bad mood existed among the workers, and he suggested arrests and death sentences for the 'worst agitators' as a warning. This was carried out. In Essen a miner was denounced by two Nazis in 1943 because he remarked in a hospital that when Hitler spoke there he had left because he did not want to see Hitler's 'mug' and listen to his rubbish; the SS were murderers and the army was trained to commit crimes; the soldiers were fed up with the war and so many were deserting that one company was reduced to 30 men. The miner and his wife were sentenced to death by the 'People's Court' and executed. So was Albrecht Ege in Frankfurt, although no treason could be proved against him. Ege used to meet other former Social Democrats in a pub where they always sat at a round table and were observed by a Gestapo agent. In that pub the Hitler salute was not given, the German news service was derided as 'rubbish' and the military communiqués declared as untrue by the men sitting at the round table. Ege informed the others in a more or less hidden form what he had learnt from the foreign broadcasts and – particularly reprehensible – had friendly relations with Jewish women. When one of them was to be deported he ordered a travel bag for her, another one gave him her typewriter before her 'evacuation'. Although the court had to admit that not only former Marxists but also others who were 'beyond reproach' sat at the round table it found that Ege had formed 'a loose organization' (which was quite obviously not the case) and in November 1942 it passed a death sentence, which was carried out.[5]

In 1944 three Frankfurt workers were sentenced to between three and seven years in a penitentiary: one of them, who had no party affiliation, because he refused to work on Sundays and encouraged his colleagues to do the same. When women were conscripted for labour in 1943 he remarked that would not apply to the wives of millionaires, it was just 'talk'. He derided the engineer who was head of his section and dissuaded his colleagues from consulting him. The engineer, he said, was just one of those who did no work and sported the NSDAP badge on his breast, and he also attacked a worker who was a member of the SA. The second accused, a former Communist, called members of the NSDAP 'blacklegs with that emblem on the breast'; nothing had changed, he claimed, the workers carried the burden, everything was 'swindle', the *Vertrauensräte* were corrupt and did nothing for the workers. He received the heaviest sentence, like the other two for 'impairing the German will of resistance'. A worker from Dudweiler in the Saar was arrested and prosecuted for saying that previously it had been 'Wilhelm by the grace of God' and now it was 'I arsehole from Berchtesgaden' (Hitler's mountain retreat). In the first six months of 1943 982 Germans were sentenced for treason and 948 death sentences were carried out. During the same period 8850 people were arrested for leftwing activities, 8727 for 'resistance activity', and as many as 11,075 for 'opposition' (meaning a less severe crime).[6] Another 10,773 were arrested for illegal contacts with prisoners of war and foreign slave labourers. Together with those sentenced for listening to foreign broadcasts the figures indicate how many Germans were involved in forbidden activities.

During the war years some of the small socialist groups mentioned earlier were still active although they did not engage in open propaganda. What was left of the ISK after the heavy arrests of the late 1930s consisted of loose circles, especially in Berlin, Bochum, Bremen, Göttingen and Hamburg, who listened to the BBC. Their leaders in London tried to establish contact and in 1943 Änne Kappius appeared in Bremen, sent from London to assess the situation. Another woman member of the ISK was killed when crossing the German frontier. In 1944 Jupp Kappius parachuted into Germany with British help, reached Bochum and then made his way to Bremen where the ISK had a small group of members released from imprisonment. They were not discovered by the Gestapo. The same was true of the Bremen contacts of the SAP which were maintained at great risk by Swedish sailors. The SAP also had some contacts in other towns. It aimed to cooperate with other leftwing groups in Germany and the emigration, and to survive until the end of the regime.[7] After its end the ISK as well as the SAP merged with the refounded SPD in which some of their members played a very prominent part.

The small *Neu Beginnen* groups in Bavaria did not survive the war. When the German advance on Moscow came to a halt in the winter of 1941–42 their leader, Bebo Wager in Augsburg (Hermann Frieb had been called up), thought the time had come to act as Germany's defeat seemed imminent to him. He adopted a policy of expansion so as to be prepared 'in case of a lost war . . . to take over the leadership in the event of a revolutionary situation'. In a phase of hectic activity the old cautious tactics and the rules of conspiracy were cast aside. Some members were given iron filings to sabotage the railway line. to the Brenner (supply line to Italy and the Africa Corps), but some members objected. Among the new recruits were old comrades – and a Gestapo agent. In 1942 the Gestapo first liquidated an associated Austrian group in Salzburg and then the groups in Munich and Augsburg. In the interrogations Wager declared the organization was created 'to avoid chaos after the war and to recreate order'. He and Frieb were sentenced to death and executed in August 1943; many others had to serve long terms of imprisonment, but the sentences on Nerdinger and another man were suspended because the Messerschmitt firm claimed them as skilled workmen. Frieb and Wager succeeded in building illegal groups which continued to function over many years without suffering substantial loss, but the faulty assessment of Germany's military situation proved their undoing.[8] The original *Neu Beginnen* group in Berlin only became active again after the end of the war, as part of the refounded SPD.

Pride of place among the active underground organizations belonged to the KPD. Its aim remained the creation of a centralized organization with an all-German leadership: an aim that was impossible to achieve under the conditions of the Third Reich and the war. The KPD was active in most parts of Germany; wherever earlier networks had been destroyed they were rebuilt – often under the guidance of old party functionaries who were released from a concentration camp and faced a certain death sentence when apprehended. They also relied on instructors sent from abroad, often parachuted from Soviet aeroplanes – another source of grave danger. Propaganda was carried on as before by leaflets and underground papers, quite often printed, to mobilize the 'masses', without conspicuous success.

At the beginning of 1942 Wilhelm Knöchel, who was trained in Moscow, a former leader of the underground miners' union, returned to Germany disguised as a silver cleaner in a dining car coming from Amsterdam. He was the first of the party leaders to work in Germany for many years, and he maintained contact with Moscow by radio via Amsterdam. He organized a network of instructors in the Rhine–Ruhr area, supervised the creation of new party cells and the publication of papers, especially the *Friedenskämpfer* (Fighter for Peace), with the principal slogan 'Peace – Freedom – Progress'. In 1942 nine issues appeared. The paper appealed to the workers to work more slowly, to refuse overtime, to demand more food, to create illegal factory committees 'in preparation for mass strikes and mass demonstrations to end the war and to overthrow Hitler'. It appealed to the soldiers to end 'the infamous war', to get rid of the officers and to desert to the Red Army with their weapons: they should form 'illegal soldiers' committees' in all the units. 'Comradeship and friendship with the foreign slave workers (is) in our own interest. If they work more slowly and produce waste, then we do it even more so.' 'Every decent German' would help the foreign workers wherever he could. There was a lesson to be drawn from the revolution of 1918:

> The coming people's revolution . . . will not only overthrow the brown watchdogs of the plutocrats. It must also annihilate them, the monopolists, bank-kings and large property owners so that they cannot, perhaps after another twenty years, engulf our people in a Third World War. A 1918 which led to Hitler must not be repeated.

The German working class had the responsibility to carry out a 'people's revolution': a 'great responsibility but a proud task'.[9]

Another underground paper, the *Ruhr-Echo*, went further in propagating illusory slogans. In August 1942 it summoned the workers to establish 'illegal fighting organs', to prepare and conduct 'political mass strikes and mass demonstrations with the slogan: for Peace!' Everywhere the workers were to form self-defence units and to arm themselves against the Nazi terror. An underground conference of the KPD of the Lower Rhine–Ruhr area (actually attended by Knöchel and three others) expressly repudiated the opinion held by some 'party members' who opposed any activity because the time was not yet ripe, for 'the fight of the party over the years has proved that something can be done'. But wisely it did not say what could be done under the conditions of ever increasing terror. The papers published under Knöchel's guidance also brought reports about the real damage caused by the air raids and used this to call for an end to the war in order to avoid the complete destruction of the towns. At least one old KPD official, when asked to form a factory cell and to see to the distribution of the papers, declined, for this would mean a catastrophe for all members and he was not prepared to be responsible. A small group of young Communists also rejected the old methods which would lead to great losses; any anti-war activity would cause arrests, even more quickly than in 1933. Yet when Moscow in the autumn transmitted instructions to form everywhere workers' and soldiers' councils (a reminder of 1918), Knöchel was alarmed and told his secretary in Amsterdam: 'What political slogan is that? It does not correspond to the political conditions of Hitler's Germany. Do the Muscovites live on the moon?' When the Gestapo pounced early in 1943 mass arrests, of more than 500 men and women, were carried out and continued into the summer in many Rhenish towns. Knöchel himself was arrested in Berlin, tried and executed. Many others shared his fate.[10]

A Communist leaflet distributed in Hamburg to the workers building fortifications called on them to refuse all military drill in their camps, to work slowly and badly, to sabotage the war effort, to see to decent treatment of the prisoners of war, and ended: 'Long live the victory of the working class!' A leaflet written by Dr Theodor Neubauer in 1943 contained a sharp attack on the German bourgeoisie which allegedly was prepared 'to save its existence as exploiters, to sell the whole of Germany to the Anglo-American imperialists and to accept a peace ten times worse than Versailles'. Germany would become 'a colony of the capitalist exploiters and would not have the possibility of modern industrial development and therewith of modern culture. That would mean a decline into barbarism!' What must be obtained was an alliance with the Soviet Union 'in the framework of a union of socialist republics'. More realistically a leaflet issued in Leipzig about the same time encouraged the workers in case of air raids to leave the factories and look after their families. Then they should not return to work and excuse themselves with the clearing of debris or bad transport conditions. 'To work more slowly leads to a quicker end of the war.' The KPD group in Leipzig had cells in 17 factories and was aided by several doctors who issued sickness certificates and falsified medical reports to prevent a call-up; a factory manager helped to get exemptions from military service. Neubauer's group was centred on Thuringia and had cells in many local factories, a specially large one in the Zeiss works at Jena. In September 1943 Neubauer used a printing works for his leaflet 'Hitler's war is lost! Only infantiles still dream of victory!' His organization lasted until July 1944 and was then 'liquidated' – it survived much longer than most others.[11]

In the summer of 1943 Neubauer contacted a large Communist group in Leipzig, led by the former Reichstag deputy Georg Schumann, and soon after a group in Berlin led by Franz Jacob, Anton Saefkow and Bernhard Bästlein. Their aim was to form an organization for Berlin and all central Germany with a centralized leadership: an extremely hazardous undertaking. In Leipzig the Schumann group had cells in 15 factories and a youth group of about 120. There Schumann and Otto Engert formulated 'Guiding Ideas' for the 'Liquidation of the imperialist war and Nazi rule' which were revised several times. Similar to Neubauer's statement, it accused the German bourgeoisie of the intention 'to capitulate before the Anglo-American imperialists, to hand over to them the whole of Germany as a basis to render armed assistance in their coming conflict with the Soviet Union'. Germany would become 'a colony of foreign exploiters', to the certain ruin of its people. 'Only in the closest cooperation with the Soviet Union which harbours no plans of conquest ... can the German people secure their national and social freedom.' They must overthrow the old powers and destroy the capitalists' might: a policy the working class could only realize under the leadership of the Communist Party, with the active participation of all. During many months this platform was sharply criticized by the members because allegedly it did not conform to the instructions broadcast from Moscow which did not envisage the immediate establishment of a socialist Germany and power to be taken by the KPD but favoured the development of a broader movement: in Germany the preconditions for the establishment of a proletarian dictatorship did not exist and a democratic republic would have to come first. The KPD leaders in Moscow favoured the adoption of democratic slogans, for peace and democracy, in cooperation with all enemies of the Nazis.[12] In Russia this policy led to the foundation of the 'National Committee for a Free Germany' by the KPD leaders and German prisoners of war. Its paper appealed to the Germans to follow the example of the Freiherr vom Stein and General von Yorck who had cooperated with Russia in the fight against Napoleon.

After some visits by Neubauer, Anto Saefkow came from Berlin to Leipzig to coordinate their activities and to discuss the tasks of the party with those in Leipzig. They were now willing to accept the instructions from Moscow and the policy of the National Committee founded there, and adopted its name for Leipzig. A new paper against war and Nazi rule early in 1944 called for an alliance of all Antifascists. They were also told of the plans of Carl Goerdeler, the conservative former mayor of Leipzig, to overthrow Hitler and were willing to cooperate to achieve this aim; they were prepared to 'ally themselves with the devil'. As a survivor put it later, they saw in Goerdeler something like a 'Kerenski figure'. But it turned out that he was against the release of all political prisoners and was strongly anti-Communist. In any case, all plans were aborted by mass arrests in Leipzig which began in July 1944. The court passed 13 death sentences. Schumann, Engert and eight others were executed early in 1945.[13] That the mass arrests in Berlin, Magdeburg, Leipzig and Thuringia all started at the same time indicates that the contacts between the different groups were carefully observed by the Gestapo – or were due to its agents – and that the attempt to form a central leadership proved fatal to all of them. The losses were 'irreplaceable'.

In Berlin, mass arrests of Communists took place early in 1942 which extended to other towns. A Gestapo agent was a member of the leading group. Many of the contacts were compromised by pairs of parachutists who came down in East Prussia with instructions to go to Berlin or Hamburg. The Gestapo had detailed information about them – their false papers, their ration cards, their bank notes – and two of them were quickly arrested. In spite of all handicaps Jacob, Saefkow and Bästlein succeeded in building yet another large underground group, with cells in about 30 large factories, organized according to the cadre principle. As the Gestapo concluded, the identical methods used by the factory cells made it clear 'that the underground work was directed from a central post': a fact it believed important for further enquiries. Loyal to the instructions received from Moscow the material destined for the cadres stated in September 1943 that certain steps would lead to the establishment of working-class power: the first was the fight to end the war and to overthrow fascism. As long as this was not done, 'we Communists are prepared, postponing all further reaching demands, to go part [!] of the way together with all those patriotic forces which like us want to overthrow the Hitler regime'.[14]

Only a few weeks later a paper entitled 'Strategy and Tactics of the Proletarian Class Struggle' put it rather differently.

> When the political crisis of German Fascism has fully developed into the crisis of the German bourgeoisie the proletariat has the possibility . . . under our leadership to conquer power and to establish the dictatorship of the proletariat.

This was not the time to observe 'the democratic sides of our party's constitution. As long as Himmler rules in Germany the party must be centralized'. And 'The German proletariat cannot be victorious without an independent Communist Party and its strict discipline'. The paper also contained the old illusions about the 'masses': 'The German workers positively await that we – the revolutionary avant-garde – give back to them the consciousness of their own power'; provided that they were led by 'a truly Bolshevist party', they would fulfil their 'historical mission'.[15] No one could say that the leaders of the underground KPD were not quite open about their ultimate goals, but this was only meant for the party cadres. In July 1944 the leaders – like those in Leipzig, Thuringia and elsewhere – were arrested, some after two meetings with prominent Social Democrats which were shadowed by the Gestapo.

It seems that only a few acts of sabotage were committed by German Communists or their sympathizers. In 1942 workers cooperating with a Communist instructor destroyed machines at a Düsseldorf armament factory by putting mud or iron filings into them. In November there was an attempt to blow up a railway bridge over the river Sieg. In December six workers of a powder factory at Ingolstadt in Bavaria were arrested because they caused several explosions and a fall in production. In Düsseldorf a skilled worker was arrested because he damaged a machine for the production of hand-grenades so that a cogwheel broke. In a fuel factory at Lützgendorf Communists, together with Polish workers, organized sabotage and fires. In Leipzig, German and Polish workers together sabotaged the production of weapons and damaged mines.[16] This is not a very impressive list. Many more acts of sabotage seem to have been committed by foreign workers.

But there is ample evidence that many German workers, especially women, helped and fed Soviet slave workers and other foreigners. The large majority of Germans were indifferent or vented their spleen on the foreigners. They could now feel superior to them, often had to instruct and supervise them or were foremen in command of a group of foreign workers. In September 1942 the SD reported that especially the women were inclined to feel sorry for the Russian workers who were insufficiently fed and had to do very heavy labour. It was said that a Russian woman whose foot was badly hurt by a piece of iron falling on it had to limp, badly bleeding, without shoes or socks, back to the camp: this the German women could not stomach. In contrast with their attitude a German worker stated on a train: 'The main thing is that we win the war even if the Russians have to kick the bucket.' Many agreed but two women shook their heads in disapproval. According to the report, the treatment of the Soviet men and women was the subject of many discussions in which German armament workers did not side with the Russians.[17]

The chemical works at Holten in the Ruhr employed 6000 'Eastern workers' who were badly clad, often hungry and without shoes. When they were led to work German women threw bread and clothes to them: their treatment was 'a shame for all of us'. The German guards objected but the women persevered. Later they undertook to give their men additional supplies of bread and butter to take to the Russians whom the women looked after. Similar events occurred at some of the Ruhr mines. Women brought things along when the shift was due to start; the start-time was then changed, but the women soon found out. When the guards intervened the women declared they should be ashamed to let people run about in such a condition. In a Berlin tram in 1944 an Italian declined to give up his place to an elderly woman, remarking he had also paid for his ticket. Thereupon some women took his side: it was essential to remain human, for 'we have accumulated enough guilt by our treatment of the Jews and Poles for which we would have to pay'.[18]

In Oberhausen in the Ruhr, miners organized help for Russian prisoners of war with food and clothes. Other miners gave bread to their foreign underlings or exchanged the toys they made for food. Some even gave them quantities of salt to produce stomach pains and nausea so that they would be unable to work. One machinist recounted that he had seen to it in the canteen that the 'Eastern workers' got food and some bread. At Christmas and Easter he took some of them home to have a meal and took them around to see the town. Other workers from the Ruhr confirmed that they had clandestinely given bread and butter to their Russian co-workers or had dropped it so that the Russians could pick it up. In Breslau two workers were arrested for actions of solidarity with prisoners of war. The mayor of Augsburg reported in February 1944 that 'numerous German housewives and even soldiers on leave' supplied Russian women workers with bread, bread coupons and cards 'in fair quantities'. If some Germans objected, the answer was that these poor chaps had to eat. Daily contacts with the Russian workers showed that they were not the 'subhumans' of Nazi propaganda but were intelligent, good workers (if only reasonably well treated) and personally likeable. One minor former trade union official even hid escaped Russian prisoners of war whom he found in a wood of the Saar, provided them with food in the winter of 1944 and brought them news of the military situation. He was to be arrested but nothing could be proved.[19] Especially men and women of the Ruhr showed human decency, often without any political motive.

There was also some political cooperation of German Communists with Soviet workers or prisoners of war. In July 1944 the Gestapo stated that former Communists who were believed to have stopped all activities were again illegally active, that instances of cooperation with 'Eastern workers' had occurred. In Leipzig, for example, they cooperated with German Communists and produced leaflets in German and Russian in the flat of a German Communist. Five Germans and 39 Russians were arrested. In Chemnitz, Germans established contact with Eastern workers with the aim of occupying the most important factories in case of a revolution, and the Eastern workers formed groups similar to the German factory cells, which were discovered in six local factories. They planned common actions and sabotage as well as the elimination of 'leading personalities in state and party'. Forty-three Germans and 13 Russians were arrested. In the autumn of 1944 a German deserter was parachuted into East Prussia. Although the drop was noted by the police he found an obliging gendarme to show him the way, succeeded in reaching Bremen and contacted the Communists there. He was not discovered, and radioed news about the Bremen armament factories to Moscow, but his hostess saw from the cyrillic labels in his clothes where he had come from.[20]

Many reports complained about the low working morale of juvenile workers. In the *Treuhänder* reports about breaches of contract young workers figured prominently in certain towns with 50, 60 or 80 per cent. Complaints that the youngsters were loafing never ceased. In a police razzia of March 1943 in the Berlin district of Schöneberg 153 of them were apprehended, including a clique with the name of the 'Club of the Sinisters'. They aimed at taking revenge for the restrictions on their freedom of movement by attacking uniformed members of the HJ. Sixteen boys and four girls were arrested but the majority were released with a warning. In Königsberg in East Prussia about 50 to 60 youngsters were arrested in 1943 who had organized assaults on members of the HJ patrol service and burglaries – allegedly without any political motive. Definitely political were the *Schreckensteiner* in Brunswick who provoked clashes with HJ members and beat them up. They also maintained contacts with foreign workers and were even supported by local people with food and money, as the public prosecutor reported in September 1943.[21] Apparently such cliques hostile to the HJ existed in many German towns, some more political than others.

In 1943 the public prosecutor of Frankfurt stated that political tendencies among the 'asocial youths' could not be established, that their principal motive was an 'untamed longing for freedom': a remarkable admission. In Hamburg a 'Deathhead Band' of about 30 to 40 in 1942 organized systematic attacks on uniformed HJ members. They roamed along certain streets or sent out scouts on bicycles to spy out the HJ and in particular the patrol service, who were ambushed. In the working-class quarters of Halle there existed *Proletengefolgschaften* (Proletarian Retinues). In 1944 Heinrich Himmler issued a circular about the cliques and the fight against them. It distinguished three different kinds: those with 'criminal-asocial associations', those with 'political-oppositional' leanings and those with 'liberal-individualist' inclinations, a preference for English clothes, jazz, Swing and hot music. The cliques were often based on a common place of work, a school or a neighbourhood. Initially they were inoffensive, but later 'threatening developments' could occur, often caused by one boy with 'asocial and criminal leanings' who would exploit the youths' longing for adventure.[22] That was the picture Himmler drew of the rebellious youngsters in the Third Reich where, as the Gestapo stated in 1943, even hiking in independent groups was prohibited.

All the groups mentioned were limited to one town, but the 'Edelweiss Pirates' flourished in the whole area of the Lower Rhine. Originally quite unpolitical, they were politicized by the attentions of the Gestapo, as one of them remembered. It was even suggested to them that they could sing their songs in the HJ: a prospect they heartily disliked. 'In course of time a more or less passive opposition to the Nazis developed into political thinking and acting.' In Mülheim near Cologne they met at the Rhine bridge: boys and girls sang and played music. In Dortmund many came from socialist families or the 'Red Falcons' (the SPD children's groups). On a bridge they noticed a Nazi-painted slogan

'Wheels roll for victory' and they added 'Nazi heads roll after war'. In Essen they wrote anti-Nazi slogans and gave money stolen from HJ homes to families of political prisoners. In Wanne-Eickel near Bochum they collected leaflets dropped from RAF planes and put them into letterboxes. In Germersheim near Düsseldorf they wrote in 1943 'Down with Hitler!' 'Down with the Nazi bandits!' and 'The High Command lies!' These were uncoordinated spontaneous actions; they showed that by this time the different groups were motivated by a strong anti-Nazi spirit.[23]

In Wuppertal Edelweiss distributed a leaflet addressed 'To the enslaved German Youth': Nazi Germany wanted to put them into the Hitler Youth where they would be 'trained militarily in marching, shooting, map-reading and technical matters', to make them

> cannon fodder for Hitler's lust for power. German youth, rise to fight for the freedom and the rights of your children and grand-children, for if Hitler wins the war Europe will be in chaos, the world will be enslaved for ever. End the slavery before it is too late. Lord, make us free!

In the same area they attacked with combined forces a great celebration of the HJ district of western Westphalia for the tenth anniversary of the 'seizure of power', with slogans such as 'German workers want peace and bread! We will only be victorious if we get enough to eat!' They hid German deserters, provided food and false papers for them and helped Dutch forced labourers to reach the frontier, as one of them remembered. But their favourite targets were the HJ homes and the HJ patrol service. As a judge in Cologne put it in 1943, 'these boys accept anything but not coercion. And if coercion was exercised by other youngsters they became personal enemies.'[24]

In Düsseldorf the Edelweiss Pirates made contact with an instructor of the KPD, distributed its leaflets and sticky labels which they fixed on notice-boards and telephone kiosks. The instructor and Knöchel met the Pirates' leader, Werner Heydn, a young turner, and told him how important it was to strengthen anti-war feelings, especially among the young. In his turn Knöchel, in true KPD fashion, wanted the Pirates to join the HJ to stir up the members against their leaders and to organize protests, but this they rejected. In any case, Knöchel and the instructor were soon arrested and at the end of 1942 the Gestapo took action against the Pirates. 28 groups in Düsseldorf, Duisburg, Essen and Wuppertal were dissolved and about 130 members arrested. The dissolved groups had about 740 members, most of them in Düsseldorf and Duisburg. According to the Gestapo, they merely wanted to escape HJ service and to appear different. The young leader from Düsseldorf with his KPD contacts escaped with a sentence of two years of imprisonment; with him 50 others were tried.[25]

In September 1943 seven boys from Wuppertal aged between 15 and 18 were tried by the Juvenile court for participating in activities of the forbidden *bündisch* youth movement, wearing *bündisch* outfits and singing its songs, for forming cliques hostile to the HJ and attacking its members. In the opinion of the court this was an attempt 'to undermine the home front and thus to contribute to the downfall of the Third Reich'. But in view of the age of the accused the punishments were mild, consisting of youth arrest or short prison sentences.[26] If the Third Reich was really threatened by the clashes with the HJ and the other activities, it seems to have been built on rather shaky foundations.

With the fortunes of war turning against Nazi Germany, opposition to the war became stronger in many parts of Germany, and non-political opposition became more political. Many listened to foreign stations and were less afraid to speak their minds although the Gestapo and the courts remained as dangerous as ever. In the opposition women again took a prominent part. The KPD in vain attempted to re-establish a leading group for Germany as a whole; the attempts made in Berlin, Saxony and central Germany ended in catastrophe. Perhaps the most remarkable phenomenon on the opposition side was the Edelweiss movement which proved that youth could not be regimented for ever, that working-class youths in particular rebelled against coercion and formed their own loose associations which could not be entirely suppressed and, the longer the war lasted, became clearly anti-Nazi. It was a pointer to the future and a hopeful sign, at a time when everything seemed black and the population of the industrial areas were suffering very badly. Another hopeful sign were the small acts of solidarity with the foreign slave workers. The repression of the KPD groups in July 1944 coincided with that of the plot of 20 July, and was on a vast scale: a loss the party was unable to make good.

Notes

1. Boberach, *Meldungen*, xii, p. 4699, xiii, pp. 4924, 4944, 6149; Pikarski and Warning, *Gestapo-Berichte*, ii, p. 370; Schumann and Hass, *Deutschland*, i, p. 293, iii, p. 241.
2. Mammach, 'Zum gemeinsamen Kampf deutscher und polnischer Antifaschisten während des Zweiten Weltkrieges', *Beiträge zur Geschichte der Arbeiterbewegung*, xii 1970, p. 120; Mallmann and Paul, *Herrschaft und Alltag*, pp. 351, 410; Steinert, *Hitler's War*, p. 208; Pikarski and Warning, *Gestapo-Berichte*, ii, p. 385.

3. Domarus, *Nationalsozialismus, Krieg und Bevölkerung*, p. 173; Eva Kleinöder, 'Verfolgung und Widerstand der Katholischen Jugendvereine', *Bayern in der NS-Zeit*, ii, p. 233; Mallmann and Paul, *Herrschaft und Alltag*, p. 410; Winkler, *Frauenarbeit*, p. 113; Bembenek and Schumacher, *Nicht alle sind tot*, p. 96.

4. *Bayern in der NS-Zeit*, i, p. 314; Boberach, *Meldungen*, xv, p. 6168; Schumann and Hass, *Deutschland*, iii, p. 272; Klaus-Peter Schulz, *Proletarier, Klassenkämpfer, Staatsbürger*, Munich, 1963, pp. 166f.

5. Steinert, *Hitler's War*, pp. 191, 249, n. 2; Ernst Schmidt, *Lichter in der Finsternis*, Frankfurt, 1980, pp. 329–33; Wippermann, *Leben in Frankfurt*, iv, pp. 106–11

6. Keval, *Widerstand und Selbstbehauptung*, pp. 210–17; Mallmann and Paul, *Herrschaft und Alltag*, p. 345; Schumann and Hass, *Deutschland*, iii, pp. 241ff.

7. Hochmuth and Meyer, *Streiflichter*, pp. 151f.; Marssolek and Ott, *Bremen*, pp. 230, 233, 384, 386f.; Brandt, *Erinnerungen*, p. 135.

8. Mehringer, 'Bayerische Sozialdemokratie', pp. 404f., 408ff., and *Waldemar von Knoeringen*, pp. 231ff.; Hetzer, *Industriestadt Augsburg*, pp. 20ff., 205.

9. Herlemann, *Auf verlorenem Posten*, pp. 44ff., 182, 189, 213, 235, 261; Bludau, *Gestapo*, pp. 167f.

10. Peukert, *Ruhrarbeiter*, p. 299; Herlemann, *Auf verlorenem Posten*, pp. 68, 85, 92, 94, 101; Beuys, *Vergesst uns nicht*, p. 516.

11. Ibid., pp. 519ff.; Pikarski and Übel, *KPD lebt*, p. 219; Schumann and Hass, *Deutschland*, iv, pp. 546ff.; Weber, 'KPD in der Illegalität', p. 99.

12. Ibid., p. 98; idem, *Der deutsche Kommunismus. Dokumente*, Cologne, 1963, pp. 418ff.; Erich Köhn, 'Der Weg zur Gründung des Nationalkomitees "Freies Deutschland"' in Leipzig, *Zeitschrift für Geschichtswissenschaft*, xiii 1965, pp. 24, 26ff., 35.

13. Ibid., pp. 30–35; Schumann and Hass, *Deutschland*, v, 1984, p. 315.

14. Beuys, *Vergesst uns nicht*, pp. 464ff.; Heinz Höhne, *Kennwort Direktor*, Frankfurt 1972, pp. 183f.; Duhnke, *KPD*, p. 486; Pikarski and Warning, *Gestapo-Berichte*, iii, p. 113; Schumann and Hass, *Deutschland*, iv, p. 531.

15. George Kennan and Herman Weber, 'Aus dem Kadermaterial der illegalen KPD 1943', *Vierteljahrshefte für Zeitgeschichte*, xx 1972, pp. 434ff., 445.

16. Peukert, *KPD im Widerstand*, pp. 360f.; Pikarski and Warning, *Gestapo-Berichte*, ii, p. 314; Mammach, 'Zum gemeinsamen Kampf', p. 121.

17. Boberach, *Meldungen*, xi, p. 4236.

18. Peukert, *Ruhrarbeiter*, pp. 286f.; Rossaint and Zimmermann, *Widerstand*, p. 175; Hans Dietrich Schäfer, *Berlin im Zweiten Weltkrieg*, Munich, 1985, pp. 247f.

19. Herlemann, *Auf verlorenem Posten*, p. 97; Dorn and Zimmermann, *Bewährungsprobe*, p. 322; von Plato, *Verlierer*, pp. 30ff.; Schumann and Hass, *Deutschland*, iii, p. 285; Domarus, *Nationalsozialismus, Krieg und Bevölkerung*, p. 105; Mallmann and Paul, *Herrschaft und Alltag*, p. 397.

20. Pikarski and Warning, *Gestapo-Berichte*, iii, pp. 83ff., 138f.; Marssolek and Ott, *Bremen*, p. 386.

21. Boberach, *Meldungen*, xi, pp. 4302, 4562; Schäfer, *Berlin*, pp. 193f.; Tilitzki, *Alltag in Osptreussen*, pp. 234f.; Bein, *Widerstand*, p. 133.

22. Heinrich Muth, 'Jugendopposition im Dritten Reich', *Vierteljahrshefte für*

Zeitgeschichte, xxx 1982, p. 408; Peukert, *Edelweisspiraten*, pp. 187, 213; von Hellfeld and Klönne, *Verlorene Generation*, pp. 318, 333f.

23. Schabrod, *Widerstand*, p. 175; Arno Klönne, 'Jugendprotest und Jugendopposition', *Bayern in der NS-Zeit*, iv, p. 611; Högl and Steinmetz, *Widerstand und Verfolgung*, p. 205; Kenkmann 'Navajos', p. 151; Peukert, *KPD im Widerstand*, p. 392.

24. Schabrod, *Widerstand*, p. 175; Peukert, *Edelweisspiraten*, p 81; Buscher, *Stigma*, pp. 376f.; idem, 'Aus der Erfahrung des Jugendwiderstandes', in Hinrich Siefken and Hidegard Vieregg (eds), *Resistance to national Socialism*, Nottingham, 1993, pp. 140ff.; Muth, 'Jugendopposition', pp. 377, 414.

25. Schabrod, *Widerstand*, pp. 176, 193, 199; Peukert, *KPD im Widerstand*, p. 392; Herlemann, *Auf verlorenem Posten*, p. 89; von Hellfeld and Klönne, *Betrogene Generation*, p. 290.

26. Buscher, *Stigma*, p. 267.

CHAPTER ELEVEN

The last year of Nazi rule

In the last year of the war the majority of the workers continued to do their jobs as best they could, in spite of heavy air raids and the shrinking size of the Greater German Reich. There was no sign of revolution or open anti-war activity. A neutral observer who went around Berlin on 3 February 1945 after a particularly heavy raid noted:

> No indications of unrest, no shouting or screaming, no tears. Complete apathy. No one has the strength to instigate a riot against Hitler and the totalitarian state, not to mention against the war.

A woman with close connections to the conservative opposition found it 'incredible' that the workers were still persevering: 'Why is there no uprising of the masses which coming from their side would be easier?[1] But it was not easier, with the SS, army, police and Gestapo arraigned against them, and no functioning party or other organization preparing an uprising or issuing a summons. In 1918 at the time of the German collapse, workers' and soldiers' councils had sprung up spontaneously everywhere to take over power, and that is what the British authorities expected might happen again.[2] But the soldiers were fighting or in captivity and the workers remained passive and quiet.

Early in 1944 the SD informed the Party Chancery that 'the number of pessimists and sceptics had increased more and more', most Germans could 'not imagine how things could change once more'; the danger was that the 'frightening ideas of the pessimists would establish themselves firmly in large sections of the population'. The news of the start of the Russian winter offensive of 1944 awoke renewed fears of the 'inexhaustible human and material resources of the Soviets and of the often-quoted Russian superiority in winter warfare'; already the term 'Russian winter offensive' created widespread anxiety. People asked how far the German army command intended to retreat and whether it still had the possibility of deciding on this. Many were 'half in despair' about the course of events and were awaiting further 'blows of fate'. The enemy was far superior in numbers and material and the Germans had their hands full in defending themselves 'at all corners'. By March 1944 people were talking about the 'inexorable approach of the Bolshevists'. The fear of more devastating air raids, the sacrifices so many families had to bear, the opinion that Germany – as in the

First World War – had to fight against 'a row of superior enemies' caused people to doubt 'the sense of the whole affair'. In April the SD reported from Augsburg that the last 'terror attack' increased the general unrest. In the towns people talked in a veiled way, and in the country side openly that a good outcome of the war was out of the question. The large majority wanted 'peace at any price'. In contrast with the official bulletins, soldiers on leave from the front spoke of a 'regular flight'.[3]

In March 1944 Albert Speer, the Minister for Armaments, increased the working time in the aircraft industry from 60 to 72 hours, for women and juveniles to 60 hours a week, and in the armament industry in general to 60 hours. He also demanded increased working on Sundays. In July all limitations of working time were cancelled. On account of the severe disruptions of the whole transport system, however, the hoped-for increase of production was not achieved. Workers were saying, the SD recorded, that working more than from early morning to late at night was impossible, and they had nothing to lose anyhow – an extension of the working time to 72 hours could not be maintained with the existing rations. The women in particular complained because they could not feed their men adequately when so much was demanded from them. A 'fatalistic resignation' was spreading. People drifted without any firm picture and repeated what they had heard, whether it was negative or optimistic. In May workers complained bitterly about the call-up for anti-aircraft duties: 'men who stand all day in the factory and do heavy work and often are not healthy' were called up, while their betters 'can always shirk everything'. Later in the year it was the call-up of all men between 16 and 60 for the *Volkssturm*, as military service was imposed on everybody, which was criticized. As the gendarmerie of Feldkirchen in Bavaria reported, the men said: 'We don't want to fight, we rather want peace. With us the war cannot be won.' In Stuttgart workers were asking whether members of the propertied classes would do their duty, and there were endless negative comments.[4] No wonder, because the equipment and weapons for the units were totally inadequate.

In the summer the Second Front was finally established in France, and on the German side the V1 and V2 were launched as 'weapons of revenge'. But already at the end of June the SD recorded that many people had expected the V1 to eliminate resistance in England with one blow, but now the lack of any visible effect, the heavy fighting in Normandy and a new Soviet offensive caused 'a general deterioration of the mood'. 'Enthusiasm, expectation of victory and confidence in German military power' almost vanished and serious doubts were expressed 'about the devastating effect of the revenge weapon'. In July the general mood was influenced by the developments on the invasion front and the quick surrender of Cherbourg, by annoyance with the earlier German propaganda about the great strength of the 'Atlantic wall'. Simple people felt 'tricked' and general pessimism prevailed, especially in southern Germany. Königsberg and Danzig were threatened by the Russian advance and rumours circulated that East Prussia was being evacuated. The tempo of the Red Army's advance was compared to the earlier German 'Blitz' victories. Many feared a new catastrophe on the eastern front. Later in July the SD found that the fighting in France and Italy and the 'revenge weapons' were discussed much less than the events in the east.

> The fact that the Soviets stand at the gates of the Reich over-shadows everything, and all sections of the people, especially women with children, show a deep depression coupled with anxiety for the future.

The mood of the broadest circles reached 'freezing point'.[5]

Yet in spite of all the pessimism the German workers continued to do their duty – probably from a mixture of motives: innate discipline, native patriotism, anger about the air raids, fear of the future, anxiety to preserve their working places, a spirit of perseverance and dogged-ness. From Halle in central Germany it was reported in December 1944 that the workers were more confident than other social groups. At a factory meeting in Dresden the workers remarked they really must 'get going to make good the imbalance in the west' where such quantities of weapons and material were lost. In February 1945 a report based on opinion polls found that opinions such as 'Everything is lost anyhow, why work' and 'In three months' time the war is lost' were current among the middle classes; but the workers of the big factories 'fulfilled their duties in an exemplary fashion'. There was hardly any grumbling and Communist propaganda was rejected. What was criticized was the example given by 'many leading personalities' who, against orders, sent their families to more western areas. In many places the workers con-tinued to work until the last day of the war, or at least until the raw materials gave out or the factory was destroyed.[6] Fear of the Gestapo may have played a part in this but cannot have been the only reason.

Yet, especially after severe air raids, there was much 'abuse and attacks on leading personalities who were made responsible for the war', it was recorded in Berlin in February 1944; many women were 'fed up' with the war and wanted 'this pointless destruction' to end. In January 1945 the Bavarian police reported that, after the last 'terror attack' on Munich, people made 'very radical remarks about party officials in uniform' and even talked of violence, and party circles spoke quite openly about it.[7] The NSDAP and its officials – called 'gold pheasants' after the colour of their uniforms – were blamed for the attacks and the war in general. Nazi propaganda designed to stir up hatred was falling flat.

In September 1944 German one-mark notes were found in the streets of Augsburg with the imprint 'Every day that Hitler lives thousands of soldiers, women and children must bleed to death' and 'Germany perishes, that is the work of the Nazis'. In a small town in Bavaria, the gendarmerie recorded, swastikas were torn down and swastika monuments blown up. The mood was 'depressed and despondent, and partly very irritable' and there was a lot of passive resistance. At the end of 1944, the most senior judge of Baden reported, a woman entering a well-known butchers in Karlsruhe greeted with 'Heil Hitler!' Thereupon a man seized her hair and shouted: 'This scoundrel and war criminal must be hanged and you with him, they should be hung from a beam and a fire started below so that you roast slowly.' No one in the shop said anything or signalled any wish to help her. At the official notice board of a small Bavarian community a notice was posted addressed to the soldiers and armament workers:

> The German peace movement calls you! Every German is called upon to sabotage this pointless struggle demanded by Hitler and Himmler by all the means at his disposal! . . . The day to fight openly against Nazi tyranny is approaching![8]

The appeal was signed 'National Peace Movement', but there is no indication who was behind it.

In the ruins of the destroyed Rhenish towns a kind of countersociety came into being, consisting of deserters from the armed forces, underground political workers and escapees, foreign slave workers, black marketeers and criminals. The economy was that of the black market where anything could be bought: cigarettes, spirits, butter and fats – and weapons. According to the Gestapo, in Cologne alone 20 such underground groups existed, each with 3 to 20 members. Twenty-nine people were killed by them, among them the head of the local Gestapo and two other Gestapo officers, six policemen, five NSDAP officials, five soldiers and one member each of the SA and HJ. The main target of the largest 'band' were the officials of the Gestapo and the Nazi party. The band was closely connected with the Edelweiss Pirates of Cologne-Ehrenfeld, a working-class quarter with a strong anti-Nazi tradition. The Pirates' parents or close relatives had belonged to the SPD or KPD and many had suffered persecution. In April 1944, as a birthday present to Hitler, they derailed an army train at Ehrenfeld station, and they planned to blow up the Gestapo headquarters and the courtroom. They aimed at preventing the local Nazi leaders and Gestapo men from fleeing; they wanted to hand them over to the approaching Americans. They hated a regime which persecuted so many people they knew. In the autumn of 1944 they were arrested and their leaders were publicly hanged. They were strongly anti-Nazi but without any clear political conception.[9]

The Ehrenfeld Pirates had close contacts with similar groups in other parts of Cologne with whom they planned common actions and the distribution of underground papers. As the Cologne public prosecutor stated in January 1945, their activities led to 'serious concern' among the HJ, especially in Cologne, Bonn and Düsseldorf. After darkness uniformed members of the HJ could not cross the streets 'without fear of being accosted by Edelweiss Pirates or being pounced upon'. In Wuppertal too, the Pirates cooperated with military deserters, hid them, provided food for them and had contacts with Russian prisoners of war and slave labourers. They wanted to sabotage German military transport and to cooperate with the Americans.[10]

Very different in character and more in line with traditional leftwing activity was the 'National Committee for a Free Germany' founded in Cologne in 1944, clearly inspired by the National Committee founded in Russia by the KPD leaders. It had about 200 members among whom there were non-Communists, but the leadership was firmly in Communist hands. Its leaflets and posters urged desertion from the forces, sabotage of production, a slow working pace, and damage to the machines to hasten the end of the war. It had close contact with foreign workers whom it supplied with food and clothes. Its political aim, in accordance with the official policy of the KPD, was the establishment of a state that was antifascist and democratic. It aimed at cooperation with the Allies but wanted to confront them with its own ideas about the revival of trade unions, a free press, a health service, a new municipal administration, and to that end formed subcommittees to work out plans for the future. The committee established cautious contacts with Social Democrats and liberals to put forward names suitable to fill the local posts, which were to be given to antifascists of all parties. Some Communists were very critical of these plans but the leaders persevered. It was an example of the old 'popular front' tactics revived for the postwar period.[11]

In November 1944, however, the leaders and many members of the committee were arrested. The leaders were tortured to death by the Gestapo; many more were to be executed but saved at the last moment by the arrival of the Americans. In 1944 a similar National Committee was founded in Stuttgart by an art historian. It was much smaller and had links to resistance groups in Alsace. In June 26 of them were arrested. In Hamburg, a larger group with the name *Kampf dem Faschismus* (Fight against Fascism) at the end of 1944 began preparations for the time of the Nazi collapse, to prevent the blowing up of bridges and other installations, in cooperation with foreign workers of many nationalities. Many of them were arrested in 1945 and many killed. In Bremen, the KPD formulated a programme of a 'united front from General Sedlitz to Pieck', in line with the instructions coming from Moscow. In Hanover, former trade unionists began to look for people to take over leading positions in the town and to prevent Nazi sabotage; they discussed what had to be done 'when the Nazi have gone'.[12] They were not arrested.

The exhortations of the exiled KPD leaders in Moscow to form committees corresponding to the National Committee for a Free Germany seem to have met with a rather limited echo in Germany. Probably the cadres in Berlin and central Germany were destroyed to such an extent by mass arrests that there was little response. They awaited the arrival of the Red Army and in its wake came the exiled leaders with Ulbricht at their head. All the attempts listed above occurred in West Germany, in areas not affected by the arrests of July 1944.

When the Americans and British advanced into Germany early in 1945 another Nazi propaganda lie was disproved. As an SS officer wrote to his superiors, the inhabitants of a Saar village who awaited the Americans had 'the highest opinion' of them and refused to be evacuated. When an army major wanted to force 30 women to leave their village 'for military reasons' they not only refused but began to shout insults: they had been well treated by the Americans and even given soap and chocolate when they had occupied the place. The women considered a German victory 'out of the question' and, if forcibly removed, would make propaganda for the Americans. By the end of March 1945, according to another SS report, no one in Stuttgart believed in a change in the fortunes of war. If someone said as an exception that new weapons would be ready within a few weeks to defeat the enemy, the answer was 'a pitiful smile', for where would they be produced and where should the materials come from? There was no transport for the separate parts which would have to be made in different factories. Yet in early April the administration of Upper Bavaria reported that the workers 'completely and steadfastly' did their duty 'under most difficult conditions'.[13] They can hardly have believed that the war could still be won.

In mid-April a small leaflet was distributed in Berlin by a resistance group:

Whoever still carries out the orders of the Nazis is an idiot or a

> scoundrel . . . Is Berlin to suffer the fate of Aachen, Cologne and
> Königsberg? NO! Write everywhere your NO! Form resistance cells
> in barracks, factories, air raid shelters!

The 'No' was painted at night on many walls of the devastated city. In
the same month a leaflet appeared in Hamburg not to allow the SS to
build nests of last resistance; the town must be surrendered without a
fight! Another leaflet declared that to defend Hamburg was 'lunacy':

> Show the world that we have nothing in common with the
> swastika . . . We march for an immediate end to the war. The last
> living and working places are not to be laid in ruins . . . Hamburg
> must not be defended if Hamburg is to live.

In Bremen a local antifascist committee established contact to a group
of officers opposed to a continuation of the war so as to obtain weapons
for reliable dockers who were to arrest the local Nazi leaders. After the
end of the war this group played an important part in initiating new
political developments,[14] as did similar groups elsewhere.

In many places, however, people who wanted to surrender to the
advancing Allied armies met fierce opposition from the last-ditch
defenders of the regime, especially the SS. In Düsseldorf four men
were shot, in Mülheim another four, from different political parties. In
Solingen, a small group used to discuss the situation by listening to the
BBC; towards the end of the war it decided to act. On 15 April,
when the Americans were approaching, they went to the town hall and
demanded that the police officer in charge should order white flags to
be put out. When he refused they disarmed him and removed him from
office. A police sergeant who was willing was appointed to replace him
and white flags were hoisted. But on the next day an SS patrol
appeared and opened fire, and then retreated. A citizens' committee
was formed, tank traps were removed, and the Americans marched in
without finding any obstacle.[15]

In Bavaria, where German resistance continued, more people were
killed at the very end of the war. In Windsheim to the west of Nuremberg a large crowd demonstrated in front of the town hall to persuade
the officer in charge to withdraw his units from the town. Women
entered his commandpost and he could only save himself from them
by calling in help from the air force. On the next day the Gestapo
appeared, asked for the ringleaders and shot one woman in front of
her husband. In late April army officers for a short time occupied
Munich's radio station, calling for freedom and an end to the war, but
they were overpowered on the orders of the local *Gauleiter*. Taking
their cue from the officers a resistance group at Wasserburg on the Inn
appealed to the inhabitants not to render any further resistance. A

court-martial appointed by the *Gauleiter* condemned them to death, but they escaped execution.[16]

Less fortunate were the Social Democrats and Communists of the 'red' mining town of Penzberg in Upper Bavaria. There the former mayor, Hans Rummer, on 28 April went to the mine where work was stopped; adherents of both parties then marched to the town hall. Rummer expelled the Nazi mayor from office and pledged the municipal officials to follow his instructions. They discussed further measures and requested the inmates of the nearby camps to preserve order. But then a captain appeared, reported to his superiors and was ordered to arrest the rebels. Troops occupied the town hall, arrested seven men, and the *Gauleiter* ordered their execution, without any trial. He also sent a unit of Nazi diehards to Penzberg to restore 'order' and they hanged another 16 people. The unit withdrew on 29 April and on the 30th the Americans marched in.[17] That was the tragedy of a small community in which the two leftwing parties had always had a large majority.

When the war was virtually over the Hitler regime still found its ardent defenders, not only from the SS but also from the army. Hundreds of deserters and oppositionists were still killed by Nazi hangmen; in its deaththroes the regime was as vicious as it had always been. The Hitler Youth used to sing that Europe would stand in flames when the *Germanen* went under. Much of Europe did stand in flames when Hitler's rule ended, yet a new Europe and a new Germany were to arise from the ashes. For the time being Germany was divided, and in the east the Communists were to wield power for 44 years, but they were put in power by the Red Army.

Notes

1. Theo Findahl, *Undergang Berlin*, Oslo, 1945, p. 91, quoted by Schäfer, *Berlin*, p. 279; Ursula von Kardorff, *Berliner Aufzeichnungen*, Munich, 1962, p. 151.
2. Personal recollection.
3. Boberach, *Meldungen*, xvi, pp. 6204, 6231f., 6312, 6362, 6455; *Bayern in der NS-Zeit*, i, p. 661.
4. Werner, *'Bleib übrig'*, p. 255; Winkler, *Frauenarbeit*, pp. 161f.; Boberach, *Meldungen*, xvi, p. 6499, xvii, pp. 6556, 6565; *Bayern in der NS-Zeit*, i, p. 675; Steinert, *Hitler's War*, p. 281.
5. Boberach, *Meldungen*, xvii, pp. 6614, 6633, 6638, 6647, 6652.
6. Steinert, *Hitler's War*, p. 290; Klaus-Jörg Ruhl, *Deutschland 1945. Alltag zwischen Krieg und Frieden*, Darmstadt, 1984, pp. 52f.; Herbert, *Arbeiterschaft im 'Dritten Reich'*, p. 357.
7. Boberach, *Meldungen*, xvi, p. 6379; *Bayern in der NS-Zeit*, i, p. 679.
8. Domarus, *Nationalsozialismus, Krieg und Bevölkerung*, p. 166; Maser,

Regime, pp. 344f.; Ruhl, *Deutschland 1945*, pp. 17f.; *Bayern in der NS-Zeit*, i, p. 679.

9. Viebahn and Kuchta, 'Widerstand in Köln', p. 340; Bernd-A. Rusinek, *Gesellschaft in der Katastrophe. Terror, Illegalität, Widerstand*, Essen, 1989, p. 439; Matthias von Hellfeld, *Edelweisspiraten in Köln*, Cologne, 1981, pp. 9–13, 31, 40, 56, 58, 87f.

10. Ibid., pp. 40, 68; Buscher, 'Aus der Erfahrung des Jugendwiderstandes' pp. 142f.

11. Rusinek, *Gesellschaft in der Katastrophe*, p. 393; Peukert, *KPD im Widerstand*, pp. 407, 415; Brunn, 'Verfolgung und Widerstand in Köln', pp. 31f.; Viebahn and Kuchta, 'Widerstand in Köln', p. 343.

12. Brunn, 'Verfolgung und Widerstand', p. 32; Müller, *Stuttgart*, p. 508; Schumann and Hass, *Deutschland*, vi, p. 315; Zorn, *Widerstand in Hannover*, pp. 220ff.; Marssolek and Ott, *Bremen*, p. 387.

13. Ruhl, *Deutschland 1945*, pp. 84, 94; Werner, '*Bleib übrig*', p. 352.

14. Ruth Andreas-Friedrich, *Schauplatz Berlin*, Munich, 1962, p. 162; Hochmuth and Meyer, *Streiflichter*, pp. 381, 560f.; Marssolek and Ott, *Bremen*, p. 387.

15. Beuys, *Vergesst uns nicht*, p. 567; Sbosny and Schabrod, *Widerstand*, pp. 120f.

16. *Bayern in der NS-Zeit*, i, pp. 685f.

17. Tenfelde, 'Proletarische Provinz', ibid., iv, pp. 377–80.

CHAPTER TWELVE

Conclusion

The kaleidoscope of working-class attitudes to the Nazis reaches from support to total opposition, and the two extreme attitudes were those of minorities. As we have seen, already in the 1920s and early 1930s the NSDAP enjoyed considerable working-class support, although to what extent is still controversial. Nazi propaganda was particularly successful among certain sections of the working class: the young, the unemployed, those not unionized, artisans and agricultural workers, promising them the end of a 'system' of misery and often near-starvation. When Hitler came to power there was one cardinal fact weighting in his favour: the gradual disappearance of unemployment – job security, even if the wages were very low and the workers lost their rights and were no longer free to change their jobs. Between 1936 and 1938 Hitler's striking successes in the field of foreign policy and the renunciation of the Treaty of Versailles were approved by most Germans. As a Communist writer put it some years ago:

> The overwhelming majority of the Germans followed the Nazis, partly enthusiastically, partly expectantly and with a certain scepsis, but not without some sympathy with a 'new order' which increased with the consolidation of the regime; apparently it brought work for all and internal peace, it promised social security and Germany's 'rebirth'.[1]

The demoralization of the German working class by almost permanent unemployment and miserable 'welfare' support should not be underestimated. Those still employed were separated from the unemployed and solidarity suffered. It remains true, on the other hand, that before 1933 many more workers voted for the two working-class parties than for the NSDAP and that their combined strength remained fairly constant in spite of the slump, while the NSBO remained very weak.

The 'seizure of power' was accomplished without any resistance from the left, the proud German working-class movement caved in to Nazi thugs, and this further contributed to the demoralization on the left. For years the two leftwing parties had been busy fighting each other, the gulf separating them was another factor that considerably helped the Nazis. After 1933, the majority of the workers made their peace with the regime, became apathetic and resigned 'as nothing could be done anyhow', but they distrusted the new 'bigwigs' of the DAF, and the

NSDAP and Nazi propaganda efforts.[2] Many missed their trade unions and regretted their lost rights. In the factories many consulted the old union officials rather than the appointees of the DAF whom they did not trust.

A sizeable minority of Social Democrats and Communists were not willing to knuckle under and to accept passively whatever the new regime might order them to do. The widespread terror accompanying the 'seizure of power' and the mass arrests of the early months told them enough. Large numbers responded by forming underground groups, producing and distributing underground leaflets and papers and disturbing Nazi propaganda as best they could. In 1933 and 1934 hundreds of clandestine groups sprang up all over Germany – and quite often they were equally quickly liquidated by the Gestapo. By their almost open methods of agitation and often clumsy tactics the adherents of SPD and KPD facilitated its work, and in particular the KPD only slowly gave up propaganda among the 'masses' and its attacks on Social Democracy as 'the main enemy'. The 'united front from below' aimed at undermining the loyalty of Social Democrats to their party, and even when the tactics changed after 1935 a united front never came into being. The old Communist centralist party structures were rebuilt time and again with terrible losses. It has been reliably estimated that the KPD between 1933 and 1935 lost about 75,000 members through imprisonment and that several thousands of them were killed. That means that about a quarter of the members registered in 1932 were lost.[3]

In the early years of the Nazi regime the Social Democrats too suffered very severe losses through carelessness and faulty methods of underground work, but they learnt more quickly that all broad propaganda methods were unrealistic under the conditions of the Third Reich. Both parties suffered badly from infiltration by Gestapo agents who were often old comrades 'turned round'. In the case of the Communists, they were men disillusioned about the possibilities of resistance or completely unsettled by the suddenness and completeness of the Nazi victory, eager to rehabilitate themselves in the eyes of the new authorities. Others were won over after their arrest by promises of freedom and financial rewards. Those released should have been distrusted but this was not always the case. It has been claimed recently that in this way working-class opposition was usually 'liquidated from within',[4] but as a general claim this seems rather farfetched and does not include the majority of the Social-Democratic groups. What remained of them in the end were the countless clubs, co-ops, choirs and small associations for different purposes from chess to music, the *Stammtische* in many pubs which could not all be suppressed. They bore witness to the loyalty of the German working-class movement.

In the workers' settlements of many large towns and mines loyalty also survived, a tradition of proletarian life and common experience – which was not that of the Nazis. These traditions also showed themselves in the help given to the miserable Eastern workers with food and clothes, especially by women, in the Second World War, as well as in the ever repeated loud protest against the exemption of better-class 'ladies' from factory labour. A new form of protest appeared in many towns in the form of cliques of youngsters against regimentation and compulsory membership in the Hitler Youth, in opposition to a regime which prohibited even hiking in groups. The 'Edelweiss Pirates' were above all inspired by an elementary longing for freedom and opposition to compulsion. This brought them into head-on conflict with the HJ and soon also with the Nazi state which was built on coercion. But their political ideas were hazy. The most efficient and long-lasting underground organization was built by the Witnesses of Jehovah who were inspired by their faith to suffer any persecution.

In the Third Reich there were many forms of opposition, from saying '*Grüss Gott*' instead of '*Heil Hitler*' and telling a political joke, to painting 'Down with Hitler!' on house walls and distributing underground literature. Historians have debated what deserved the name of resistance or opposition and what did not. What about the many readers of the *Sozialistische Aktion*? and what about the many Social Democrats who sat at a *Stammtisch* and discussed political events? They were certainly oppositional in their attitude but hardly deserve the name of resisters. Between 1933 and 1939 more than 5000 men and women were tried by just one 'special court', that of Munich, for *Heimtücke* (malicious remarks) but they may just have made one oppositional remark or have fallen foul of a Nazi bigwig. Even the term 'unorganized disobedience' which has been suggested for them may be too strong.[5] In any case, the multitude of such cases and the widepsread disbelief in Nazi propaganda show that Nazi ideology was not as powerful as has sometimes been stated, that very large numbers kept their distance and judged for themselves. The fact that during the war listening to foreign stations became a criminal offence shows that the Nazi authorities recognized the weakness of their own arguments. The SD reports and the many sentences prove how many Germans disregarded the prohibition, in spite of the risk. The military communiqués on the progress of the war were from the outset met with a good deal of scepsis which from 1943 onwards turned to outright disbelief.

Those who resisted or opposed the regime in one form or another were numerous but only a minority. The large majority obeyed more or less willingly. It is clear from the reports that the majority of the German workers did their duty and worked reasonably well while the war lasted, and that fear of the Gestapo was not the only reason for doing so. They feared the consequences of defeat and a Soviet victory. They were moved by hatred of the air attacks, by loyalty to their firm, pride in their work, recognition of their importance by the regime and an innate sense of discipline. In particular the skilled armament and building workers had been able to improve their position substantially in spite of the official wage stop. Sabotage of production did not occur on any significant scale and Communist propaganda did not succeed. It was too unrealistic and too far removed from the ordinary worker's political horizon. Even if it had been more realistic it would have failed.

Even if the majority of the workers had made their peace with the Nazi regime it also remains true that of those who were imprisoned for political reasons the large majority belonged to the working class. Of 21,823 Germans imprisoned at the *Steinwache* in Dortmund for political offences, the overwhelming majority were workers. Of 629 people from Solingen who were involved in political opposition, over 70 per cent were workers and presumably many of the 49 housewives listed also belonged to the working class. In Oberhausen in the Ruhr the number was close to 90 per cent.[6] For less industrialized areas the figures would no doubt be lower, but the German working class certainly provided the bulk of those who suffered for their political convictions. In the years 1933 to 1944 2162 people were arrested in Essen for leftwing political activity and 1721 in Düsseldorf, among them 297 women. In the penitentiary of Brandenburg 1807 people were executed for political reasons during the war and 775 of them were workers or artisans.[7] It was a proud record. They could not overthrow the regime, but that was an impossible task. When it was attempted in 1944 by military and conservative circles they failed equally. It was only after a lost war that the regime finally succumbed and even in its downfall it engulfed many of its opponents. For the dictatorship the disjointed opposition was only an irritant but – like other minorities – it was persecuted without mercy.

Notes

1.   Mammach, *Widerstand 1933–1939*, p. 161.
2.   Peukert, *KPD*, p. 316, and 'Der deutsche Arbeiterwiderstand', p. 654.
3.   Hermann Weber, 'Die Ambivalenz der kommunistischen Widerstandsstrate-

gie', in Schmädeke and Steinbach (eds), *Widerstand gegen den Nationalsozialismus*, p. 79.

4. Klaus-Michael Mallmann and Gerhard Paul, 'Allwissend, allgegenwärtig, allmächtig? Gestapo, Gesellschaft und Widerstand', *Zeitschrift für Geschichtswissenschaft*, xli November 1993, pp. 994ff.
5. Hüttenberger, 'Heimtückefälle', *Bayern in der NS-Zeit*, i, pp. 446f., 523.
6. Ian Kershaw, *The Nazi Dictatorship*, London–New York, 1993, p. 172; Sbosny and Schabrod, *Widerstand in Solingen*, p. 131; Rossaint and Zimmermann, *Widerstand*, p. 208.
7. Weisenborn, *Lautloser Aufstand*, p. 258; Christl Wickert, 'Frauenwiderstand?', in Anselm Faust (ed.), *Verfolgung und Widerstand im Rheinland und in Westfalen*, Cologne, 1992, p. 108.

Bibliography

Sources

Allen, William Sheridan (ed.), *The Infancy of Nazism. The Memoirs of Ex-Gauleiter Albert Krebs, 1923–1933*, New York–London, 1976.

Bludau, Kuno (ed.), *Gestapo – Geheim! Widerstand und Verfolgung in Duisburg 1933–1945*. Bonn–Bad Godesberg, 1975.

Boberach, Heinz (ed.), *Meldungen aus dem Reich. Die geheimen Lageberichte des Sicherheitsdienstes der SS, 1938–1945*, 16 vols, Herrsching, 1984.

Bohn, Willi (ed.), *Stuttgart: Geheim! Widerstand und Verfolgung, 1933–1945*, Frankfurt, 1978.

Deutschland-Berichte der Sozialdemokratischen Partei Deutschlands (Sopade), 7 vols reprint, Salzhausen-Frankfurt, 1980.

Dohms, Peter (ed.), *Flugschriften in Gestapo-Akten. Nachweis und Analyse der Flugschriften in den Gestapo-Akten des Hauptstaatsarchivs Düsseldorf*, Siegburg, 1977.

Fröhlich, Elke (ed.), *Die Tagebücher von Joseph Goebbels. Sämtliche Fragmente*, ii, Munich, 1987.

Heyen, Franz Josef (ed.), *Nationalsozialismus im Alltag. Quellen zur Geschichte des Nationalsozialismus vornehmlich im Raum Mainz-Koblenz-Trier*, Boppard, 1967.

Kennan, George, and Weber, Hermann (eds), 'Aus dem Kadermaterial der illegalen KPD 1943', *Vierteljahrshefte für Zeitgeschichte*, xx 1972, pp. 422–46.

Klein, Thomas (ed.), *Die Lageberichte der Geheimen Staatspolizei über die Provinz Hessen Nassau, 1933–1936*, Cologne, 1986.

Kuropka, Joachim (ed.), *Meldungen aus Münster 1924–1944. Geheime und vertrauliche Berichte von Polizei, Gestapo, NSDAP und ihren Gliederungen, staatliche Verwaltung, Gerichtsbarkeit und Wehrmacht über die gesellschaftliche und politische Situation in Münster*, Münster, 1992.

Mammach, Klaus (ed.), 'Die KPD und das Münchener Abkommen 1938', *Zeitschrift für Geschichtswissenschaft*, xvi 1968, pp. 1034–48.

Mammach, Klaus (ed.), *Die Berner Konferenz der KPD (30. Januar–1. Februar 1939)*, Frankfurt, 1974.

Mason, Timothy W. (ed.), *Arbeiterklasse und Volksgemeinschaft. Doku-*

mente und Materialien zur deutschen Arbeiterpolitik, 1936–1939, Opladen, 1975.

Matthias, Erich (ed.), *Mit dem Gesicht nach Deutschland. Eine Dokumentation über die sozialdemokratische Emigration. Aus dem Nachlass von Friedrich Stampfer,* Düsseldorf, 1968.

Mlynek, Klaus (ed.), *Gestapo Hannover meldet . . . Polizei- und Regierungsberichte für das mittlere und südliche Niedersachsen, 1933–1937,* Hildesheim, 1986.

Neu beginnen! Faschismus oder Sozialismus. Als Diskussionsgrundlage der Sozialisten Deutschlands von Miles, Karlsbad, s.a. (1933).

Nitzsche, Gerhard (ed.), 'Deutsche Arbeiter im Kampf gegen faschistische Unterdrückung und Ausbeutung. Gestapomeldungen aus den Jahren 1935 bis 1937', *Beiträge zur Geschichte der deutschen Arbeiterbewegung,* i 1959, pp. 138–49.

————and Übel, Günter (eds), 'Die KPD – führende Kraft im antifaschistischen Widerstand. Aus der Tätigkeit illegalar Leitungen der KPD im Lande', *Beiträge zur Geschichte der Arbeiterbewegung,* xx 1978, pp. 691–702.

Pikarski, Margot, and Übel, Günter (eds), *Die KPD lebt! Flugblätter aus dem antifaschistischen Widerstandskampf der KPD, 1933–1945,* Berlin, 1980.

————and Warning, Elke (eds), 'Über den antifaschistischen Widerstandskampf der KPD. Aus Gestapo-Akten', *Beiträge zur Geschichte der Arbeiterbewegung,* xxv 1983, pp. 67–87, 398–410, 548–60, 704–10, xxvi 1984, pp. 55–62, 338–46.

————*Gestapo-Berichte Über den antifaschistischen Widerstandskampf der KPD, 1933 bis 1945,* 3 vols, Berlin, 1989–90.

Plum, Günter (ed.), 'Die KPD in der Illegalität. Rechenschaftsbericht einer Bezirksleitung aus dem Jahre 1934', *Vierteljahrshefte für Zeitgeschichte,* xxiii 1975, pp. 228–35.

Ruhl, Klaus-Jörg (ed.), *Deutschland 1945. Alltag zwischen Krieg und Frieden in Berichten, Dokumenten und Bildern,* Darmstadt, 1984.

Schadt, Jörg (ed.), *Verfolgung und Widerstand unter dem Nationalsozialismus in Baden. Die Lageberichte der Gestapo und des Generalstaatsanwalts, 1933–1940,* Stuttgart 1976.

Schramm, Percy Ernst (ed.), *Hitlers Tischgespräche im Führerhauptquartier 1941–1942,* Stuttgart, 1963.

Sozialdemokratische Partei Deutschlands, *Revolution gegen Hitler! Die historische Aufgabe der deutschen Sozialdemokratie,* Karlsbad, s.a. (1933).

Stoop, Paul (ed.), *Geheimberichte aus dem Dritten Reich. Der Journalist H.J. Noordewier als politischer Beobachter,* Berlin, 1990.

Thévoz, Robert, Branig, Hans and Lowenthal-Hensel, Cécile (eds),

Pommern 1934/35 im Spiegel von Gestapo-Lageberichten und Sachakten, Cologne, 1974.

Tilitzki, Christian (ed.), *Alltag in Osptpreussen, 1940–1945. Die geheimen Lageberichte der Königsberger Justiz 1940–1945*, Leer, 1991.

Vollmer, Bernhard (ed.), *Volksopposition im Polizeistaat. Gestapo- und Regierungsberichte, 1934–1936*, Stuttgart, 1957.

Weber, Hermann (ed.), *Der deutsche Kommunismus. Dokumente*, Cologne, 1963.

Wichers, Hermann (ed.), 'Zur Anleitung des Widerstands der KPD: ein Rundschreiben des ZK-Sekretariats an die Abschnittsleitungen vom 29. Juli 1938', *Internationale Wissenschaftliche Korrespondenz zur Geschichte der deutschen Arbeiterbewegung*, xxvi 1990, pp. 526–39.

Wiener Library London, Zeugenberichte, nos. 192, 459, 886.

Secondary authorities

Ackermann, Anton, 'Ich kam aus der illegalen Arbeit in Berlin', *Beiträge zur Geschichte der deutschen Arbeiterbewegung*, vii 1965, pp. 827–30.

Allen, William Sheridan, 'Die sozialdemokratische Untergrundbewegung: Zur Kontinuität der subkulturellen Werte', in Jürgen Schmädeke and Peter Steinbach (eds), *Der Widerstand gegen den Nationalsozialismus*, Munich, 1985, pp. 849–66.

Anderson, Evelyn, *Hammer or Anvil. The Story of the German Working-class Movement*, London, 1945.

Andreas-Friedrich, Ruth, *Schauplatz Berlin. Ein deutsches Tagebuch*, Munich, 1962.

Anonymous, *Dokumente des Widerstandes. Ein Beitrag zum Verständnis des illegalen Kampfes gegen die Nazidiktatur*. Eine Artikelserie aus der 'Hamburger Volkszeitung', 1947.

Aretin, Karl Otmar Freiherr von, 'Der deutsche Widerstand gegen Hitler', in idem, *Nation, Staat und Demokratie in Deutschland*, Mainz, 1993, pp. 213–46.

Bahne, Siegfried, 'Die Kommunistische Partei Deutschlands' in Erich Matthias and Rudolf Morsey (eds), *Das Ende der Parteien 1933*, Düsseldorf, 1960, pp. 653–739.

Bajohr, Frank, 'In doppelter Isolation – Zum Widerstand der Arbeiterjugendbewegung gegen den Nationalsozialismus', in Wilfried Breyvogel (ed.), *Piraten, Swings und Junge Garde. Jugendwiderstand im Nationalsozialismus*, Bonn, 1991, pp. 17–35.

Beier, Gerhard, *Die illegale Reichsleitung der Gewerkschaften, 1933–1945*, Cologne, 1981.

————'Die illegale Reichsleitung der Gewerkschaften' in Richard Löwenthal and Patrik von zur Mühlen (eds), *Widerstand und Verweigerung in Deutschland, 1933–1945*, Bonn, 1984, pp. 25–50.

Bein, Reinhard, *Widerstand im Nationalsozialismus, Braunschweig 1933–1945*, Braunschweig, 1985.

Bembenek, Lothar, and Schumacher, Fritz, *Nicht alle sind tot, die begraben sind. Widerstand und Verfolgung in Wiesbaden, 1933–1945*, Frankfurt, 1980.

Bennecke, Heinrich, *Hitler und die SA*, Munich, 1962.

Berghahn, V.R., *Modern Germany. Society, Economics and Politics in the 20th Century*, Cambridge, 1982.

Bessel, Richard, *Political Violence and the Rise of Nazism. The Stormtroopers in Eastern Germany, 1925–1934*, New Haven, 1984.

Beuys, Barbara, *Vergesst uns nicht. Menschen im Widerstand 1933–1945*, Reinbek near Hamburg, 1987.

Billstein, Aurel, *Der eine fällt, die andern rücken nach. Dokumente des Widerstands und der Verweigerung in Krefeld, 1933–1945*, Frankfurt, 1973.

Böhnke, Wilfried, *Die NSDAP im Ruhrgebiet, 1920–1933*, Bonn, 1974.

Bracher, Karl Dietrich, *Die deutsche Diktatur. Entstehung, Struktur, Folgen des Nationalsozialismus*, Cologne, 1969.

Brandt, Willy, *Links und Frei. Mein Weg 1930–1950*, Hamburg, 1982.

————*Erinnerungen*, Berlin, 1990.

Bremer, Jörg, *Die Sozialistische Arbeiterpartei Deutschlands (SAP). Untergrund und Exil, 1933–1945*, Frankfurt, 1978.

Bringmann, Fritz, and Diercks, Herbert, *Die Freiheit lebt! Antifaschistischer Widerstand und Naziterror in Elmshorn und Umgebung, 1933–1945*, Frankfurt, 1983.

Broszat, Martin, *Der Staat Hitlers. Grundlegung und Entwicklung seiner inneren Verfassung*, Munich, 1971.

————'Lage der Arbeiterschaft, Arbeiteropposition, Aktivität und Verfolgung der illegalen Arbeiterbewegung, 1933–1945,' in *Bayern in der NS-Zeit*, i, Munich, 1977, pp. 193–325.

Brunn, Gerhard, 'Verfolgung und Widerstand in Köln', in Leo Haupts and Georg Mölich (eds), *Aspekte der nationalsozialistischen Herrschaft in Köln und im Rheinland*, Cologne, 1983, pp. 9–37.

Bry, Gerhard, *Resistance. Recollections from the Nazi Years*, West Orange, N.J., 1979.

Buscher, Paulus, *Das Stigma, 'Edelweiss-Pirat'*, Koblenz, 1988.

————'Aus der Erfahrung des Jugendwiderstandes, 1936–1945', in Hinrich Siefken and Hildegard Vieregg (eds), *Resistance to National Socialism*, Second Nottingham Symposium, Nottingham, 1993, pp. 127–63.

Carsten, F.L., 'Socialist and Working-class Opposition to National Socialism', ibid., pp. 111–26.

Childers, Thomas, *The Nazi Voter. The Social Foundations of Fascism in Germany*, 1919–1933, Chapel Hill, 1983.

———'Who, Indeed, Did Vote for Hitler?' *Central European History*, xvii 1984, pp. 45–53.

Dahlem, Franz, *Am Vorabend des Zweiten Weltkrieges 1938 bis August 1939. Erinnerungen*, 2 vols, Berlin 1977.

Deutschkron, Inge, *Ich trug den Gelben Stern*, Cologne, 1979.

Ditt, Karl, *Sozialdemokraten im Widerstand. Hamburg in der Anfangsphase des Dritten Reiches*, Hamburg, 1984.

Domarus, Wolfgang, *Nationalsozialismus, Krieg und Bevölkerung. Untersuchungen zur Lage, Volksstimmung und Struktur in Augsburg während des Dritten Reiches*, Munich, 1977.

Dorn, Barbara, and Zimmermann, Michael, *Bewährungsprobe – Herne und Wanne-Eickel 1933–1945*, Bochum, 1987.

Duhnke, Horst, *Die KPD von 1933 bis 1945*, Cologne, 1972.

Eiber, Ludwig, *Arbeiter unter der NS-Herrschaft. Textil – und Porzellanarbeiter im nordöstlichen Oberfranken, 1933–1939*, Munich, 1979.

———'Frauen in der Kriegsindustrie. Arbeitsbedingungen, Lebensumstände und Protestverhalten', in *Bayern in der NS-Zeit*, iii, Munich, 1981, pp. 569–644.

Esters, Helmut, and Pelger, Hans, *Gewerkschafter im Widerstand*, Bonn, 1983.

Falter, Jürgen W., 'Warum die deutschen Arbeiter während des "Dritten Reiches" zu Hitler standen', *Geschichte und Gesellschaft*, xiii 1987, pp. 217–31.

———and Hänisch, Dirk, 'Die Anfälligkeit von Arbeitern gegenüber der NSDAP bei den Reichstagswahlen 1928–1933', *Archiv für Sozialgeschichte*, xxvi 1986, pp. 179–216.

Feuchtwanger, Franz, 'Der Militärpolitische Apparat der KPD in den Jahren 1928–1935 *Internationale Wissenschaftliche Korrespondenz zur Geschichte der deutschen Arbeiterbewegung*, xvii 1981, pp. 485–533.

Fischer, Conan, 'The Occupational Background of the SA's Rank and File Membership during the Depression Years, 1929 to mid-1934', in Peter D. Stachura (ed.), *The Shaping of the Nazi State*, London, 1978, pp. 131–59.

———*The German Communists and the Rise of Nazism*, Basingstoke –London, 1991.

Fischer-Defoy, Christine, *Arbeiterwiderstand in der Provinz. Arbeiterbewegung und Faschismus in Kassel und Nordhessen, 1933–1945*, Berlin, 1982.

Foitzik, Jan, *Zwischen den Fronten. Zur Politik, Organisation und Funktion linker politischer Kleinorganisationen im Widerstand, 1933 bis 1939/40*, Bonn, 1986.

Franz, Thomas, and Merk, Jan, 'Jugendwiderstand im Nationalsozialismus', *Internationale Wissenschaftliche Korrespondenz zur Geschichte der deutschen Arbeiterbewegung*, xxviii 1992, pp. 412–20.

Frese, Matthias, *Betriebspolitik im 'Dritten Reich'. Deutsche Arbeitsfront, Unternehmer und Staatsbürokratie in der westdeutschen Grossindustrie 1933–1939*, Paderborn, 1991

Fröhlich, Elke, 'Stimmung und Verhalten der Bevölkerung unter den Bedingungen des Krieges', in *Bayern in der NS–Zeit*, i, Munich, 1977, pp. 571–688.

Garbe, Detlef, *Zwischen Widerstand und Martyrium. Die Zeugen Jehovas im 'Dritten Reich'*, Munich, 1993.

Gellately, Robert, *The Gestapo and German Society. Enforcing Racial Policy, 1933–1945*, Oxford, 1990.

Gillingham, John, 'Die Ruhrbergleute und Hitlers Krieg', in Hans Mommsen and Ulrich Borsdorf (eds), *Glück auf, Kameraden! Die Bergarbeiter und ihre Organisationen in Deutschland*, Cologne, 1979, pp. 325–43.

———*Industry and Politics in the Third Reich. Ruhr Coal, Hitler and Europe*, Wiesbaden, 1985.

Gottfurcht, Hans, 'Als Gewerkschafter im Widerstand', in Löwenthal and zur Mühlen (eds), *Widerstand und Verweigerung in Deutschland*, pp. 51–55.

Gross, Leonhard, *Versteckt. Wie Juden in Berlin die Nazi-Zeit überlebten*, Reinbek near Hamburg, 1983.

Grossmann, Anton, 'Milieubedingen von Verfolgung und Widerstand. Am Beispiel ausgewählter Ortsvereine der SPD', in *Bayern in der NS-Zeit*, v, pp. 433–540.

Hachtmann, Rüdiger, *Industriearbeit im 'Dritten Reich'. Untersuchungen zu den Lohn- und Arbeitsbedingungen in Deutschland 1933–1945*, Göttingen, 1989.

Hauck, Hilde, 'Taktik des trojanischen Pferdes', in Irene Hübner (ed.), *Unser Widerstand. Deutsche Frauen und Männer berichten*, Frankfurt, 1982, pp. 128–34.

Hellfeld, Matthias von, *Edelweisspiraten in Köln. Jugendrebellion gegen das 3. Reich. Das Beispiel Köln-Ehrenfeld*, Cologne, 1981.

———*Bündische Jugend und Hitlerjugend. Zur Geschichte von Anpassung und Widerstand 1930–1935*, Cologne, 1987.

———and Klönne, Arno (eds), *Die betrogene Generation. Jugend in Deutschland unter dem Faschismus*, Cologne, 1985.

Herbert, Ulrich, 'Arbeiterschaft im 'Dritten Reich'. Zwischenbilanz und offene Fragen', *Geschichte und Gesellschaft*, xv 1989, pp. 320–60.

Herlemann, Beatrix, *Auf verlorenem Posten. Kommunistischer Widerstand im Zweiten Weltkrieg. Die Knöchel-Organisation*, Bonn, 1986.

Hetzer, Gerhard, 'Die Industriestadt Augsburg. Eine Sozialgeschichte der Arbeiteropposition', in *Bayern in der NS-Zeit*, iii, pp. 1–233.

Hochmuth, Ursel, and Meyer, Gertrud, *Streiflichter aus dem Hamburger Widerstand, 1933–1945*, Frankfurt, 1980.

Högl, Günther, and Steinmetz, Udo, *Widerstand und Verfolgung in Dortmund, 1933–1945* Dortmund, 1981.

Höhne, Heinz, *Kennwort Direktor. Die Geschichte der Roten Kapelle*, Frankfurt, 1972.

Hüttenberger, Peter, 'Heimtückefälle vor dem Sondergericht München 1933–1939', in *Bayern in der NS-Zeit*, iv, pp. 435–526.

Kardorff, Ursula von, *Berliner Aufzeichnungen. Aus den Jahren 1942–1945*, Munich, 1962.

Karg, Berta Carola, 'Mein Kampf gegen die braune Diktatur', in Löwenthal and zur Mühlen (eds), *Widerstand und Verweigerung in Deutschland*, pp. 102–9.

Kater, Michael H., 'Die Ernsten Bibelforscher im Dritten Reich', *Vierteljahrshefte für Zeitgeschichte*, xvii 1969, pp. 181–218.

———'Zur Soziographie der frühen NSDAP', ibid., xix 1971, pp. 123–59.

———*The Nazi Party. A Social Profile of Members and Leaders, 1919–1945*, Oxford, 1983.

Kele, Max H., *Nazis and Workers. National Socialist Appeals to German Labor*, 1919–1933, Chapel Hill, 1972.

Kenkmann, Alfons, 'Navajos, Kittelbach- und Edelweisspiraten – Jugendliche Dissidenten im 'Dritten Reich', in Wilfried Breyvogel (ed.), *Piraten, Swings und Junge Garde*, Bonn, 1991, pp. 138–58.

Kershaw, Ian, 'Antisemitismus und Volksmeinung. Reaktionen auf die Judenverfolgung in *Bayern in der NS-Zeit*, ii, pp. 281–348.

———'Alltägliches und Ausseralltägliches: ihre Bedeutung für die Volksmeinung, 1933–1939', in Detlev Peukert and Jürgen Reulecke (eds), *Die Reihen fast geschlossen. Beiträge zur Geschichte des Alltags unter dem Nationalsozialismus*, Wuppertal, 1981, pp. 273–92.

———*Popular Opinion and Political Dissent in the Third Reich. Bavaria 1933–1945*, Oxford, 1983.

—— *The Nazi Dictatorship. Problems and Perspectives of Interpretation*, 3rd edition London, 1993.

Keval, Susanna, *Widerstand und Selbstbehauptung in Frankfurt am Main, 1933–1945*, Frankfurt, 1983.

Kleinöder, Evi, 'Verfolgung und Widerstand Katholischer Jugendvereine.

Eine Fallstudie über Eichstätt', *in Bayern in der NS-Zeit*, ii, pp. 175–236.

Klönne, Arno, 'Jugendprotest und Jugendopposition. Von der HJ-Erziehung zum Cliquenwesen der Kriegszeit', ibid., iv, pp. 527–620.

Klotzbach, Kurt, *Gegen den Nationalsozialismus. Widerstand und Verfolgung in Dortmund 1930–1945*, Hanover, 1969.

Köhn, Erich, 'Der Weg zur Gründung des Nationalkomitees "Freies Deutschland" in Leipzig', *Zeitschrift für Geschichtswissenschaft*, xiii 1965, pp. 18–35.

Kratzenberg, Volker, *Arbeiter auf dem Weg zu Hitler? Die nationalsozialistische Betriebszellenorganisation, 1927–1934*, Frankfurt, 1989.

Kuhn, Annette, and Rothe, Valentine, *Frauen im deutschen Faschismus. Frauenarbeit und Frauenwiderstand im NS-Staat*, Düsseldorf, 1982.

Kuropka, Joachim (ed.), *Zur Sache – Das Kreuz! Untersuchungen zur Geschichte des Konflikts um Kreuz und Lutherbild in den Schulen Oldenburgs*, Vechta, 1987.

Küstermeier, Rudolf, *Der Rote Stosstrupp*, Berlin, 1970.

Langkau-Alex, Ursula, *Volksfront für Deutschland? Vorgeschichte und Gründung des 'Ausschusses zur Vorbereitung einer deutschen Volksfront', 1933–1936*, Frankfurt, 1977.

Levine, Herbert S., *Hitler's Free City. A History of the Nazi Party in Danzig, 1925–1939*, Chicago, 1973.

Longerich, Peter, *Die braunen Bataillone. Geschichte der SA*, Munich, 1989.

Löwenthal, Richard, *Die Widerstandsgruppe 'Neu Beginnen'*, Berlin, 1982

Madden, Paul, 'Some Social Characteristics of Early Nazi Party Members 1919–1923', *Central European History*, xv 1982, pp. 34–56.

Mai, Gunther, 'Die Nationalsozialistische Betriebszellenorganisation. Zum Verhältnis von Arbeiterschaft und Nationalsozialismus', *Vierteljahrshefte für Zeitgeschichte*, xxxi 1983, pp. 573–613.

————'Warum steht der deutsche Arbeiter zu Hitler? Zur Rolle der Deutschen Arbeitsfront im Herrschaftssystem des Dritten Reiches', *Geschichte und Gesellschaft*, xii 1986, pp. 212–34.

Mallmann, Klaus-Michael, and Paul, Gerhard, *Herrschaft und Alltag. Ein Industrierevier im Dritten Reich. Widerstand und Verweigerung im Saarland, 1933–1945*, Bonn, 1991.

————'Allwissend, allmächtig, allgegenwärtig? Gestapo, Gesellschaft und Widerstand', *Zeitschrift für Geschichtswissenschaft*, xli November 1993, pp. 984–99.

Mammach, Klaus, 'Zum gemeinsamen Kampf deutscher und polnischer Antifaschisten während des 2. Weltkrieges', *Beiträge zur Geschichte der Arbeiterbewegung*, xii 1970, pp. 118–23.

————*Widerstand 1933–1939. Geschichte der deutschen antifaschistischen Widerstandsbewegung im Inland und in der Emigration*, Cologne, 1984.

Mann, Reinhard, *Protest und Kontrolle im Dritten Reich. Nationalsozialistische Herrschaft im Alltag einer rheinischen Grosstadt*, Frankfurt, 1987.

Manstein, Peter, *Die Mitglieder und Wähler der NSDAP 1919–1933. Untersuchungen zu ihrer schichtmässigen Zusammensetzung*, Frankfurt, 1989.

Marssolek, Inge, and Ott, René, *Bremen im Dritten Reich. Anpassung, Widerstand, Verfolgung*, Bremen, 1986.

Maser, Werner, *Das Regime. Alltag in Deutschland 1933–1945*, Munich, 1983.

Mason, Timothy W., 'Labour in the Third Reich, 1933–1939', *Past and Present, no. 33, April 1966, pp. 112–41.*

————*Sozialpolitik im Dritten Reich. Arbeiterklasse und Volksgemeinschaft*, Opladen, 1972.

————'Arbeiteropposition im nationalsozialistischen Deutschland', in Peukert and Reulecke (eds), *Die Reihen fast geschlossen*, Wuppertal, 1981, pp. 293–311.

Matthias, Erich, *Sozialdemokratie und Nation. Zur Ideengeschichte der sozialdemokratischen Emigration, 1933–1938*, Stuttgart, 1952.

————'Der Untergang der Sozialdemokratie 1933', *Vierteljahrshefte für Zeitgeschichte* iv, 1956, pp. 179–226.

————'Die Sozialdemokratische Partei Deutschlands', in idem and Rudolf Morsey (eds) *Das Ende der Parteien*, Düsseldorf, 1960, pp. 99–278.

————and Weber, Hermann, *Widerstand gegen den Nationalsozialismus in Mannheim*, Mannheim, 1984.

Mehringer, Hartmut, 'Die KPD in Bayern 1919–1945', in *Bayern in der NS-Zeit*, v, pp. 1–286.

————'Die Bayerische Sozialdemokratie bis zum Ende des NS-Regimes', ibid., pp. 287–432.

————*Waldemar von Knoeringen. Eine politische Biographie, Der Weg vom revolutionären Sozialismus zur sozialen Demokratie*, Munich, 1989.

Merkl, Peter H., *The Making of a Stormtrooper*, Princeton, 1980.

Merson, Allan, *Communist Resistance in Nazi Germany*, London, 1985.

Mierendorff, Carl, 'Gesicht und Charakter der nationalsozialistischen Bewegung', *Die Gesellschaft*, 1930, pp. 489–504.

Morsch, Günter, 'Streik im "Dritten Reich" ', *Vierteljahrshefte für Zeitgeschichte*, xxxvi 1988, pp. 649–89.

Mühlberger, Detlef, *The Rise of National Socialism in Westphalia 1920–1933*, unpublished London PhD thesis, 1975.
————'The Sociology of the NSDAP. The Question of Working-class Membership', *Journal of Contemporary History*, xv 1980, pp. 493–511.
————'Germany' in idem (ed.), *The Social Basis of European Fascist Movements*, London, 1987, pp. 40–139.
————*Hitler's Followers. Studies in the Sociology of the Nazi Movement*, London, 1991.
————'*Workers' Party*' or a '*Party without Workers*'? *The Extent and Nature of the Working-class Membership of the NSDAP, 1919–1933*, MS to be published in 1994.
Müller, Roland, *Stuttgart zur Zeit des Nationalsozialismus*, Stuttgart, 1988.
Muth, Heinrich, 'Jugendopposition im Dritten Reich', *Vierteljahrshefte für Zeitgeschichte*, xxx 1982, pp. 369–417.
Noakes, Jeremy, *The Nazi Party in Lower Saxony, 1921–1933*, Oxford, 1971.
————'The Oldenburg Crucifix Struggle 1936: A Case Study of Opposition in the Third Reich', in Stachura (ed.), *The Shaping of the Nazi State*, London, 1978, pp. 210–33.
Overesch, Manfred, *Hermann Brill in Thüringen, 1895–1946. Ein Kämpfer gegen Hitler und Ulbricht*, Bonn, 1992.
Peterson, Edward N., *The Limits of Hitler's Power*, Princeton, 1969.
Peukert, Detlev, *Ruhrarbeiter gegen den Faschismus. Dokumentation über den Widerstand im Ruhrgebiet, 1933–1945*, Frankfurt, 1976.
————*Die KPD im Widerstand. Verfolgung und Untergrundarbeit an Rhein und Ruhr, 1933–1945*, Wuppertal, 1980.
————*Die Edelweisspiraten. Protestbewegungen jugendlicher Arbeiter im Dritten Reich*, Cologne, 1980.
————'Arbeitslager und Jugend-KZ; die Behandlung Gemeinschaftsfremder im Dritten Reich', in idem and Reulecke (eds), *Die Reihen fast geschlossen*, pp. 413–34.
————*Volksgenossen und Gemeinschaftsfremde. Anpassung, Ausmerzung und Aufbegehren unter dem Nationalsozialismus*, Cologne, 1982.
————'Arbeiterwiderstand – Formen und Wirkungsmöglichkeiten', in *Widerstand und Exil der deutschen Arbeiterbewegung, 1933–1945*, Bonn, 1982, pp. 215–364.
————'Der deutsche Arbeiterwiderstand 1933–1945', in Karl Dietrich Bracher, Manfred Funke, Hans-Adolf Jacobsen (eds), *Nationalsozialistische Diktatur*, Düsseldorf, 1983, pp. 633–55.
————'Protest und Widerstand von Jugendlichen im Dritten Reich',

in Löwenthal and zur Mühlen (eds), *Widerstand und Verweigerung in Deutschland*, pp. 177–201.

———and Bajohr, Frank, *Spuren des Widerstands. Die Bergarbeiterbwegung im Dritten Reich und im Exil*, Munich, 1987.

Plato, Alexander von, *'Der Verlierer geht nicht leer aus'. Betriebsräte geben zu Protokoll*, Berlin, 1984.

Pridham, Geoffrey, *Hitler's Rise to Power. The Nazi Movement in Bavaria, 1923–1933*, London, 1973.

Rebentisch, Dieter, and Raab, Angelika, *Neu-Isenburg zwischen Anpassung und Widerstand. Dokumente über Lebensbedingungen und politisches Verhalten, 1933–1945*, Neu-Isenburg, 1978.

Reichhardt, Hans J., 'Möglichkeiten und Grenzen des Widerstandes der Arbeiterbewegung in Walter Schmitthenner and Hans Buchheim (eds), *Der deutsche Widerstand gegen Hitler*, Cologne, 1966, pp. 169–213.

Reutter, Friederike, 'Verfolgung und Widerstand der Arbeiterparteien in Heidelberg' in Jörg Schadt and Michael Caroli (eds), *Heidelberg unter dem Nationalsozialismus*, Heidelberg, 1985, pp. 469–550.

Rossaint, Joseph C., and Zimmermann, Michael, *Widerstand gegen den Nationalsozialismus in Oberhausen*, Frankfurt, 1983.

Ruck, Michael, *Bollwerk gegen Hitler? Arbeiterschaft, Arbeiterbewegung und die Anfänge des Nationalsozialismus*, Cologne, 1988.

Rusinek, Bernd-A., *Gesellschaft in der Katastrophe, Terror, Illegalität, Widerstand – Köln 1944/45*, Essen, 1989.

———'Desintegration und gesteigerter Zwang – Die Chaotisierung der Lebensverhältnisse in den Grosstädten und der Mythos der Ehrenfelder Gruppe', in Breyvogel (ed.), *Piraten, Swings und Junge Garde*, Bonn, 1991, pp. 271–94.

Rüther, Martin, *Arbeiterschaft in Köln, 1928–1945*, Cologne, 1990.

———'Lage und Abstimmungsverhalten der Arbeiterschaft. Die Vertrauensratswahlen in Köln 1934–1935', *Vierteljahrshefte für Zeitgeschichte*, xxxix 1991, pp. 221–64.

Sandvoss, Hans-Reiner, *Widerstand 1933–1945. Berlin-Wedding*, Berlin, 1983.

Sauer, Paul, *Württemberg in der Zeit des Nationalsozialismus*, Ulm, 1975.

Sbosny, Inge, and Schabrod, Karl, *Widerstand in Solingen. Aus dem Leben antifaschistischer Kämpfer*, Frankfurt, 1975.

Schabrod, Karl, *Widerstand gegen Flick und Florian. Düsseldorfer Antifaschisten über ihren Widerstand, 1933–1945*, Frankfurt, 1978.

Schadt, Jörg, 'Verfolgung und Widerstand', in Otto Borst (ed.), *Das Dritte Reich in Baden und Württemberg*, Stuttgart, 1988, pp. 96–120.

Schäfer, Hans Dieter, *Berlin im Zweiten Weltkrieg. Der Untergang der Reichshauptstadt in Augenzeugenberichten*, Munich, 1985.

Schefer, Gitta, 'Wo Unterdrückung ist, da ist auch Widerstand – Frauen gegen Faschismus und Krieg', in Frauengruppe Faschismusforschung, *Mutterkreuz und Arbeitsbuch, Zur Geschichte der Frauen in der Weimarer Republik und im Nationalsozialismus*, Frankfurt, 1981, pp. 273–91.

Schepers, Petra, 'Das Komitee für Proletarische Einheit', in Historisches Museum Hannover, *Widerstand im Abseits*, Hanover, 1992, pp. 47–52.

Schmid, Hans-Dieter, 'Sozialdemokratischer Widerstand', ibid., pp. 15–38.

Schmidt, Ernst, *Lichter in der Finsternis. Widerstand und Verfolgung in Essen, 1933–1945*, Frankfurt, 1980.

Schneider, Ulrich, *Marburg 1933–1945. Arbeiterbewegung und Bekennende Kirche gegen den Faschismus*, Frankfurt, 1980.

Schulz, Klaus-Peter, *Proletarier, Klassenkämpfer, Staatsbürger. 100 Jahre deutsche Arbeiterbewegung*, Munich, 1963.

Schumann, Wolfgang, and Hass, Gerhart, leaders of 'Autorenkollektiv', *Deutschland im zweiten Weltkrieg*, 6 vols, Berlin, 1974–85.

Schüren, Ulrich, 'Rahmenbedingungen für den Widerstand gegen den Nationalsozialismus', in *Widerstand und Exil der deutschen Arbeiterbewegung, 1933–1945*, Bonn, 1982, pp. 125–214.

Seebold, Gustav-Hermann, *Ein Stahlkonzern im Dritten Reich. Der Bochumer Verein 1927–1945*, Wuppertal, 1981.

Stachura, Peter D., 'The Nazis, the Bourgeoisie and the Workers during the Kampfzeit', in idem (ed.), *The Nazi Machtergreifung*, London, 1983, pp. 15–32.

Steinberg, Hans-Josef, 'Die Haltung der Arbeiterschaft zum NS-Regime', in Schmädeke and Steinberg (eds), *Der Widerstand gegen den Nationalsozialismus*, pp. 867–74.

Steinert, Marlis G., *Hitler's War and the Germans. Public Mood and Attitude during the Second World War*, Athens, Ohio, 1977.

Stern, Carola, *In den Netzen der Erinnerung. Lebensgeschichten zweier Menschen*, Reinbek near Hamburg, 1986.

Sywottek, Arnold, *Deutsche Volksdemokratie. Studien zur politischen Konzeption der KPD, 1935–1946*, Düsseldorf, 1971.

Szepansky, Gerda, *Frauen leisten Widerstand, 1933–1945. Lebensgeschichten nach Interviews und Dokumenten*, Frankfurt, 1983.

Tapken, Bernd-Anton, *Die Auseinandersetzung des ISK mit der Politik der KPD und der KPdSU in der Zeit des Exils (1933–1945)*, unpublished MS 1984.

Tausk, Walter, *Breslauer Tagebuch 1933–1940*, Berlin, 1988.

Tenfelde, Klaus, 'Proletarische Provinz. Radikalisierung und Widerstand in Penzberg, Oberbayern, 1900–1945', in *Bayern in der NS-Zeit*, iv, pp. 1–382.

Tröger, Annemarie, 'Die Frau im wesensgemässen Einsatz', in Frauengruppe Faschismusforschung, *Mutterkreuz und Arbeitsbuch*, Frankfurt, 1981, pp. 246–72.

van Dick, Lutz, *Oppositionelles Lehrerverhalten, 1933–1945. Biographische Berichte über den aufrechten Gang von Lehrern und Lehrerinnen*, Weinheim, 1988.

Viebahn, Wilfried, and Kuchta, Walter, 'Widerstand gegen die Nazidiktatur in Köln', in Reinhold Billstein (ed.), *Das andere Köln. Demokratische Tendenzen seit der französischen Revolution*, Cologne, 1979, pp. 283–361.

Voges, Michael, 'Klassenkampf in der Betriebsgemeinschaft. Die "Deutschland-Berichte" der Sopade als Quelle zum Widerstand der Industriearbeiter im Dritten Reich', *Archiv für Sozialgeschichte*, xxi 1983, pp. 329–83.

Wagner, Jonathan F., 'The Hard Lessons of a Political Life: the Career of Socialist Hans Dill (1887–1973)', *Internationale Wissenschaftliche Korrespondenz zur Geschichte der deutschen Arbeiterbewegung*, xxix 1993, pp. 194–207.

Weber, Hermann, 'Die KP in der Illegalität', in Löwenthal and zur Mühlen (eds), *Widerstand und Verweigerung in Deutschland*, pp. 83–101.

Weisenborn, Günther, *Der lautlose Aufstand. Bericht über die Widerstandsbewegung des deutschen Volkes, 1933–1945*, Hamburg, 1953.

Wenke, Bettina, *Interviews mit Überlebenden. Verfolgung und Widerstand in Südwestdeutschland*, Stuttgart, 1980.

Wenzel, Hartmut, 'Widerstandsmythos und Anpassungsrealität: Das Beispiel der Naturfreundejugend', in Breyvogel (ed.), *Piraten, Swings und Junge Garde*, Bonn, 1991, pp. 36–56.

Werner, Wolfgang Franz, *'Bleib übrig'. Deutsche Arbeiter in der nationalsozialistischen Kriegswirtschaft*, Düsseldorf, 1983.

Wickert, Christl, 'Frauenwiderstand? Überlegungen zu einem vernachlässigten Thema am Beispiel Düsseldorfs und Essens', in Anselm Faust (ed.), *Widerstand im Rheinland und in Westfalen, 1933–1945*, Cologne, 1992, pp. 101–12.

Wicht, Wolfgang E., *Glanzstoff. Zur Geschichte der Chemiefaser, eines Unternehmens und seiner Arbeiterschaft*, Neustadt/Aisch, 1992.

Winkler, Dörte, *Frauenarbeit im 'Dritten Reich'*, Hamburg, 1977.

Winkler, Heinrich August, 'Mittelstandsbewegung oder Volkspartei? Zur sozialen Basis der NSDAP', in Wolfgang Schieder (ed.), *Faschismus als soziale Bewegung, Deutschland und Italien im Vergleich*, Hamburg, 1976, pp. 97–118.

——Weimar 1918–1933. Die Geschichte der ersten deutschen Demokratie, Munich, 1993.

Wippermann, Wolfgang, Das Leben in Frankfurt zur NS-Zeit, iv, Frankfurt, 1986.

——Die Berliner Gruppe Baum und der jüdische Widerstand, Berlin, 1981.

Wisotzky, Klaus, Der Ruhrbergbau im Dritten Reich, Studien zur Sozialpolitik im Ruhrbergbau und zum sozialen Verhalten der Bergleute, 1933–1939, Düsseldorf, 1983.

Zimmermann, Michael, 'Ein schwer zu bearbeitendes Pflaster: der Bergarbeiterort Hochlarmark unter dem Nationalsozialismus', in Peukert and Reulecke (eds), Die Reihen fast geschlossen, Wuppertal, 1981, pp. 65–84.

——'Ausbruchshoffnungen: Junge Bergleute in den dreissiger Jahren', in Lutz Niethammer (ed.), 'Die Jahre weiss man nicht, wo man die heute hinsetzen soll', Berlin-Bonn, 1983, pp. 97–132.

Zollitsch, Wolfgang, 'Die Vertrauensratswahlen von 1934 und 1935. Zum Stellenwert der Abstimmungen im "Dritten Reich" am Beispiel Krupp', Geschichte und Gesellschaft, xv 1989, pp. 361–81.

Zorn, Gerda, Widerstand in Hannover. Gegen Reaktion und Faschismus, 1920–1946, Frankfurt, 1977.

zur Mühlen, Patrik von, 'Sozialdemokraten gegen Hitler', in Löwenthal and zur Mühlen (eds), Widerstand und Verweigerung in Deutschland, pp. 57–75.

Index